Rust Programming

Safe, Fast, and Fucking Secure

Herkimer Throckmorton

ISBN: 9781779661715
Imprint: Telephasic Workshop
Copyright © 2024 Herkimer Throckmorton.
All Rights Reserved.

Contents

Getting Started with Rust   13
Understanding Rust Basics   26
Exploring Fucking Rust Syntax   35
Testing, Documentation, and Packages in Rust   51

Advanced Rust Concepts   **67**
Advanced Rust Concepts   67
Advanced Data Structures in Fucking Rust   73
Asynchronous Programming with Fucking Futures   89
Interfacing with Other Languages in Fucking Rust   101
Web Development with Fucking Rust   114
Fucking Concurrency and Parallelism   136

Advanced Topics in Rust   **153**
Advanced Topics in Rust   153
Fucking Memory Safety in Rust   159
Building a Fucking Web Server from Scratch   171
Writing Fucking Safe and Secure Code in Rust   190
Performance Tuning and Optimization in Rust   207
Fucking Rust in Production   224

Index   **241**

Why the Fuck Should You Learn Rust?

Rust is not your average programming language. It's not for the faint of heart or the easily discouraged. No, my friend, Rust is that bad boy you secretly fantasize about, the one with a leather jacket and tattoos, and a mystery too tantalizing to resist. So why the fuck should you learn Rust? Let me break it down for you.

The Power of Fucking Control

First and foremost, Rust gives you unparalleled control over your code. It's like having a personal army of code enforcers ready to knock out bugs and keep your program in tip-top shape. How does it do this, you ask?

Well, Rust combines the best of both worlds: high-level abstractions for productivity and low-level control for performance. With Rust, you can write code that is both safe and fast, without compromising on either. It achieves this through a concept called "ownership."

Ownership in Rust: In the world of Rust, everything has an owner. It's like being the boss of your code. You decide who gets to access or modify your data. This prevents bugs like null pointer dereferences and data races, making your code more reliable and secure. And let's be honest, there's nothing sexier than secure code.

Another cool thing about Rust's ownership system is that it handles memory allocation for you. No more worrying about memory leaks or dangling pointers. Rust ensures that your code only accesses valid memory, saving you from dreaded segmentation faults. It's like having a personal bodyguard for your program's memory.

Empowering Fucking Performance

Now, let's talk performance. Rust is like the Ferrari of programming languages, built for speed and precision. It's perfect for applications that require high performance, such as game engines, web servers, and data-intensive computations.

One of the main reasons why Rust is so damn fast is its zero-cost abstractions. In Rust, you can use high-level programming constructs without sacrificing performance. Thanks to its fearless compiler, Rust optimizes your code to run at blazing speeds, while maintaining memory safety. It's like having a date with the Flash, but without the risk of spontaneously combusting.

But don't just take my word for it. Let's look at a real-world example. Imagine you're developing a web application that needs to handle thousands of requests per second. With Rust, you can leverage its concurrency model and lightweight threads to build highly scalable and performant web services. It's like having a well-oiled machine that can handle any workload thrown at it.

Creating Fucking Secure Applications

In today's age of cyber threats and data breaches, security is paramount. You don't want your code to be the weak link in the chain, exposing sensitive information to attackers. That's where Rust comes in, like a knight in shining armor, protecting your precious data from evil forces.

Rust's approach to security is based on the concept of memory safety. By preventing common programming errors, such as buffer overflows and null pointer exceptions, Rust eliminates entire classes of vulnerabilities. It's like building a fortress with impenetrable walls.

But wait, there's more! Rust also has a built-in package manager called Cargo, which ensures dependencies are secure and up to date. With Cargo, you can rest easy knowing that your code is not relying on vulnerable libraries. It's like having a loyal watchdog, keeping an eye out for any potential threats.

Rust's Fucking Popularity

Why learn a programming language that nobody gives a fuck about? Rust is gaining popularity and for good reason. It's backed by a community of passionate developers who believe in its potential. Companies like Mozilla, Dropbox, and Cloudflare are already using Rust in production, which means there's a growing demand for Rust developers in the job market.

Learning Rust can give you a competitive edge and open up doors to exciting career opportunities. It's like having a golden ticket to the Willy Wonka's Chocolate Factory of software development.

So, my friend, if you're ready to level up your programming skills, embrace the power of control, unleash fucking performance, create secure applications, and join the ranks of Rust enthusiasts, then buckle up and get ready for the ride of your life. Rust is waiting for you, and trust me, it's fucking worth it.

Summary

In this chapter, you've learned why Rust is a language worth giving a fuck about. It offers unparalleled control, empowering performance, enhanced security, and it's gaining popularity in the industry. Now that you know why you should learn Rust, it's time to dive into the nitty-gritty details of getting started with Rust and exploring its fundamentals. So, strap in, grab your favorite beverage, and let's begin our Rust journey together.

Why the Fuck Should You Learn Rust?

Rust is a programming language that has gained significant popularity in recent years. You might be wondering why the fuck you should bother learning yet another programming language, especially when there are so many options available. Well, let me tell you why Rust deserves your attention.

The Power of Fucking Control

One of the biggest reasons to learn Rust is its emphasis on control. Unlike other programming languages that rely on garbage collection or runtime checks, Rust gives you the power to manage your own fucking memory. It uses a system of ownership, borrowing, and lifetimes to ensure memory safety without sacrificing performance.

By learning Rust, you'll gain a deep understanding of how memory management works and how to prevent common bugs like null pointer dereferences, dangling pointers, and data races. This level of control allows you to write fast, efficient code without compromising on safety.

Empowering Fucking Performance

Another reason to learn Rust is its focus on performance. Rust is designed to be a systems programming language, meaning it's optimized for building low-level software that runs close to the hardware. It provides you with the tools and abstractions necessary to write code that can be as fast as C or C++, but with a much stronger fucking type system and memory safety guarantees.

With Rust, you can build high-performance applications, libraries, and even operating systems. Whether you're working on embedded systems, real-time applications, or high-throughput servers, Rust has got you fucking covered.

Creating Fucking Secure Applications

In today's increasingly interconnected world, security is a fucking big concern. Rust takes security seriously and provides a number of features to help you write secure code. Its ownership and borrowing system prevents common vulnerabilities like buffer overflows, null pointer dereferences, and use-after-free bugs. The compiler catches these errors at compile-time, so you don't have to worry about them fucking up your code at runtime.

Additionally, Rust's standard library is designed with security in mind. It includes safe abstractions for handling strings, parsing input, and implementing cryptographic algorithms. When you write code in Rust, you can have more confidence that it won't introduce security vulnerabilities.

Rust's Fucking Popularity

Lastly, Rust's growing popularity is another reason to learn it. Many fucking companies, including Mozilla, Dropbox, and Cloudflare, have adopted Rust for critical systems and infrastructure. It has a vibrant and active community that is constantly developing new libraries, tools, and frameworks. By learning Rust, you'll become part of this fucking awesome community and gain access to a wealth of resources and support.

So, why the fuck should you learn Rust? Because it gives you fine-grained control, empowers you to write high-performance code, helps you create secure applications, and opens up a world of opportunities in the job market.

Now that you understand the value of learning Rust, let's dive into how to get started with this badass language.

Empowering Fucking Performance

In this section, we'll explore how Rust empowers fucking performance and allows you to build high-performance applications. Rust is designed to provide a balance between safety and performance, giving you the best of both worlds. It achieves this through various features and principles that we'll discuss in detail.

Memory Safety and Performance

One of the key factors that contribute to performance in Rust is its memory safety guarantees. Rust's ownership and borrowing system allows for fine-grained control over memory management, eliminating many common performance issues like memory leaks and dangling pointers.

By enforcing strict ownership rules, Rust ensures that memory is managed efficiently and avoid unnecessary memory allocations and deallocations. This not only improves performance but also eliminates potential bugs and security vulnerabilities.

Additionally, Rust encourages the use of stack allocation over heap allocation whenever possible. Stack allocation is much faster than heap allocation since it doesn't involve complex memory management operations. Rust's ownership system helps optimize memory usage by minimizing unnecessary heap allocations, resulting in improved performance.

Zero-Cost Abstractions

Rust provides a concept known as "zero-cost abstractions," which allows you to write high-level code without incurring any performance penalties. This means that you can use abstractions like functions, data structures, and generics without sacrificing performance.

Zero-cost abstractions are achieved through the concept of "monomorphization" and "inlining." When you use generics in Rust, the compiler generates specialized versions of your code for each concrete type you use, eliminating the need for runtime type checks. This process is called monomorphization and ensures that the generated code is as efficient as manually written code.

In addition, the Rust compiler performs inlining, which means it replaces function calls with the actual function code at compile-time. This eliminates the overhead of function calls, resulting in faster execution.

Optimizing Performance with Unsafe Rust

While Rust prioritizes safety, it also provides a mechanism to write performance-critical code using unsafe Rust. Unsafe Rust allows you to bypass certain safety checks and perform low-level operations that are not possible with safe Rust.

By carefully using unsafe Rust, you can write code that is highly optimized and achieves maximum performance. However, it's essential to exercise caution when using unsafe Rust, as it can introduce memory safety issues if not used correctly.

Benchmarking and Profiling

To improve performance, it's crucial to measure and analyze the performance of your code. Rust provides tools and libraries for benchmarking and profiling to help you optimize your code efficiently.

The 'rustc' compiler includes built-in support for benchmarking, allowing you to write microbenchmarks to measure the performance of specific code segments. By benchmarking your code, you can identify bottlenecks and areas that need improvement.

Rust also provides profiling tools like 'perf' and 'valgrind' to analyze the runtime behavior of your application. Profiling can help you identify performance hotspots, memory leaks, and inefficient resource usage, allowing you to optimize your code for better performance.

Concurrency and Parallelism

Rust's powerful concurrency model enables you to write high-performance applications that take advantage of modern multi-core processors. The concept of "ownership" eliminates data races, a common issue in concurrent programming, by enforcing strict rules for mutable memory access.

Rust provides abstractions like threads, locks, and channels for concurrent programming. The 'std::thread' module allows you to create lightweight threads, and the 'std::sync' module provides synchronization primitives like mutexes and condition variables.

Parallelism is achieved through the use of libraries like 'rayon', which provides high-level parallel primitives. With 'rayon', you can write parallel algorithms that automatically leverage the available CPU cores, maximizing performance.

Real-World Example: High-Performance Web Servers

To illustrate the performance capabilities of Rust, let's consider the example of building high-performance web servers. Rust is well-suited for this task due to its low-level control, zero-cost abstractions, and memory-safety guarantees.

Rust web frameworks like Rocket and Actix-Web provide high-performance foundations for building scalable and efficient web servers. These frameworks leverage Rust's performance-oriented features and provide abstractions that don't sacrifice performance.

In addition, Rust's support for asynchronous programming with 'futures' and 'async/await' allows you to build web servers that can handle high levels of concurrent requests without blocking and wasting resources.

By leveraging the performance capabilities of Rust, you can develop web servers with blazing-fast response times, efficient resource utilization, and high scalability.

Summary

In this section, we explored how Rust empowers fucking performance by leveraging its memory safety guarantees, zero-cost abstractions, support for unsafe Rust, benchmarking, profiling, concurrency, and parallelism capabilities.

Rust's focus on performance makes it an excellent choice for developing high-performance applications, ranging from systems programming to web development. By combining safety and performance, Rust helps you build robust, fast, and fucking secure software.

Creating Fucking Secure Applications

In this section, we will explore the importance of creating secure applications in Rust. We will discuss various concepts and techniques that can help you build robust and resilient software, protecting it from malicious attacks, vulnerabilities, and potential threats.

Understanding Fucking Security Threats

Before diving into the process of creating secure applications, it is important to understand the threats that your software might face. In today's digital landscape, there are numerous potential risks that can compromise the security of your application. These include:

- **Injection Attacks:** This occurs when an attacker manipulates user-supplied input to execute unauthorized commands or gain access to sensitive data. Common examples include SQL injection and cross-site scripting (XSS) attacks.

- **Buffer Overflows:** A buffer overflow happens when a program tries to write more data into a buffer than it can handle, potentially leading to a crash or allowing an attacker to inject and execute malicious code.

- **Information Leakage:** This refers to the unintended disclosure of sensitive information, such as passwords, encryption keys, or personal data. It can occur through insecure network connections, misconfigured servers, or vulnerable code implementation.

- **Denial of Service (DoS) Attacks:** In a DoS attack, an attacker overwhelms a system with excessive requests or malicious traffic, causing it to become unavailable for legitimate users.

- **Privilege Escalation:** This type of attack involves an attacker gaining elevated access privileges, allowing them to perform unauthorized actions or access restricted resources within a system.

- **Social Engineering:** Social engineering attacks exploit human psychology to manipulate individuals into revealing sensitive information or performing actions that compromise security.

By understanding these threats, you can take the necessary steps to mitigate the risks and ensure the security of your applications.

Implementing Fucking Secure Coding Practices

To create secure applications in Rust, it is crucial to follow secure coding practices. Here are some key principles to keep in mind:

- **Validate and Sanitize Input:** Always validate and sanitize user input to prevent injection attacks and potential code vulnerabilities. Perform proper data validation, implement input filtering, and use parameterized queries for database interactions.

- **Use Strong Authentication and Encryption:** Implement strong authentication mechanisms, including secure password hashing algorithms and robust session management. Utilize industry-standard encryption protocols, such as HTTPS/TLS, to protect data in transit.

- **Enforce Least Privilege:** Follow the principle of least privilege, granting users and processes only the necessary access rights and permissions. This reduces the potential damage that can be caused by compromised accounts or malicious software.

- **Keep Dependencies Updated:** Regularly update and patch your application's dependencies to address any security vulnerabilities that might arise. Stay informed about security advisories and follow best practices for dependency management.

- **Input Validation and Output Encoding:** Implement strong input validation to prevent data integrity issues and buffer overflows. Apply proper output encoding techniques to safeguard against cross-site scripting (XSS) attacks.

- **Secure Configuration Management:** Follow secure configuration guidelines for your application, database, and server setup. This includes hardening the system, disabling unnecessary services, and enabling appropriate security features.

By incorporating these secure coding practices into your software development process, you can significantly enhance the security of your Rust applications.

Utilizing Fucking Safe Rust Features

Rust offers a set of features and constructs that promote secure programming practices. Leveraging these features can help mitigate vulnerabilities and reduce the risks of common security issues. Here are some essential safe Rust features:

- **Ownership and Borrowing:** Rust's ownership and borrowing system ensures memory safety by preventing data races and null pointer dereferences. By adhering to the ownership model, you can eliminate common security bugs like use-after-free and double-free vulnerabilities.

- **Safe Abstractions:** Rust provides safe abstractions for common tasks, such as string manipulation, file I/O, and networking. Utilize these abstractions instead of implementing low-level operations yourself, as they are designed with security in mind.

- **Error Handling:** Proper error handling is critical for security. Rust's Result and Option types encourage developers to handle errors explicitly, reducing the likelihood of unchecked exceptions and unexpected program states.

- **Functional Programming Paradigms:** Functional programming concepts like immutability, pure functions, and referential transparency can lead to more secure code. These paradigms help minimize side effects and make code easier to reason about, improving overall security.

- **Concurrency and Thread Safety:** Rust's lightweight concurrency model and built-in thread safety support allow you to write secure and scalable concurrent applications. Using Rust's synchronization primitives, such as mutexes and channels, can help prevent data races and other concurrency-related vulnerabilities.

Auditing and Testing Fucking Security

Auditing and testing your Rust applications for security vulnerabilities is crucial in ensuring their robustness. Here are some methods and tools you can use:

- **Code Reviews:** Conduct thorough code reviews to identify potential security issues. An extra pair of eyes can often spot vulnerabilities that might go unnoticed during development.

- **Static Analysis Tools:** Utilize static analysis tools like Clippy, RustSec, and Cargo audit to identify common security weaknesses and vulnerabilities in your code and dependencies.

- **Fuzz Testing:** Fuzz testing involves feeding a program with a large amount of input, often generated randomly or using specific patterns, to uncover unexpected behavior or vulnerabilities. Tools like cargo-fuzz can assist with automated fuzz testing in Rust.

- **Penetration Testing:** Conduct penetration testing on your application, either through manual or automated means, to simulate real-world attacks and identify potential security flaws.

- **Security Libraries and Tools:** Utilize established security libraries and tools specific to Rust, such as sodiumoxide for cryptography and r2d2 for connection pooling, to enhance the security of your applications.

By incorporating these auditing and testing practices into your development workflow, you can proactively identify and address security vulnerabilities in your Rust applications.

Wrap Up

Creating secure applications in Rust is essential in today's digital landscape. By understanding security threats, implementing secure coding practices, utilizing safe Rust features, and conducting thorough auditing and testing, you can build robust and resilient software that is protected against potential attacks.

Remember, security is an ongoing process. Stay up to date with the latest security trends and best practices, and continuously monitor and update your applications to ensure they remain secure in the face of evolving threats.

Now that we have covered the importance of creating secure applications, let's move on to exploring more advanced topics in Rust.

Rust's Fucking Popularity

Rust has gained significant fucking popularity in recent years, emerging as a powerful programming language that offers a unique combination of fucking safety, performance, and security. This section will explore the reasons behind Rust's rise to fame and why you should give a damn about learning it.

The Need for Fucking Safer Code

One of the primary reasons for Rust's popularity is the growing need for safer code in modern software development. As applications become increasingly complex, the risk of fucking memory leaks, null pointer dereferences, and data races becomes more significant. Traditional languages like C and C++ provide flexibility but often at the cost of code safety.

Rust takes a different fucking approach. It provides compiler-enforced memory safety guarantees without the need for manual memory management or garbage collection. By leveraging the concept of ownership and borrowing, Rust ensures that only one piece of code can have exclusive access to a resource at any given time. This eliminates common bugs like fucking use-after-free and data races.

With Rust, you can fucking sleep easy knowing that your code is less susceptible to crashes, security vulnerabilities, and hard-to-debug issues caused by memory mismanagement. This level of safety brings peace of mind and boosts the overall quality of software applications.

Unleashing Fucking Performance

While safety is crucial, Rust doesn't fucking compromise on performance. Rust is designed to give you low-level control over system resources without sacrificing speed. The absence of runtime overhead, coupled with efficient memory management, makes Rust programs fucking fast. In fact, Rust code can often rival the performance of C and C++.

The key to Rust's performance lies in its ownership model and strict compile-time checks. By eliminating runtime checks for memory safety, Rust code can be optimized for fucking speed. The compiler ensures that your code adheres to certain safety rules at compilation time, allowing it to unleash the full power of modern hardware.

Whether you're building high-performance applications, system utilities, or even game engines, Rust offers the speed and efficiency you fucking need.

Building Fucking Secure Applications

In an increasingly interconnected world, security is more critical than ever. Rust's focus on memory safety and thread safety inherently makes it a great fucking choice for building secure applications. The ownership system in Rust prevents common security vulnerabilities like buffer overflows, code injection, and data races.

Furthermore, Rust's type system allows you to express complex invariants and constraints at compile time. This helps catch bugs and security vulnerabilities early in the development process. With Rust, you can fucking mitigate security risks and build software that guards against potential threats.

The fucking security benefits of Rust have not gone unnoticed. The language has been adopted by major tech companies, security-conscious organizations, and developers worldwide who want to ensure the robustness and security of their software applications.

Fucking into the Future

Rust's popularity is not just a passing trend; it's here to fucking stay. The language has gained a vibrant and active community that contributes to its growth and development. This means that Rust is constantly evolving, with new features and improvements being discussed, tested, and implemented.

Moreover, Rust's versatility extends beyond systems programming. It has gained traction in web development, networking, embedded systems, and even blockchain development. Rust provides powerful abstractions and frameworks that make it easy to tackle a wide range of fucking projects.

By learning Rust, you're not only equipping yourself with a robust and reliable language but also joining a fucking community of passionate developers who are reshaping the future of software development.

Summary

In this section, we explored the reasons behind Rust's fucking popularity. We highlighted its focus on safety, performance, and security, which make it an attractive choice for modern software development. Rust's emphasis on memory safety, coupled with its low-level control over system resources, offers developers the best of both worlds – a language that is safe and fucking fast. Additionally, Rust's ability to build secure applications sets it apart from many other programming languages. Finally, we saw that Rust's growing community and versatility ensure its relevance in a wide variety of fucking domains. So, why the fuck should you learn Rust? Because it gives you the tools to write safe, fast, and secure code that will remain fucking relevant for years to come.

Getting Started with Rust

Installing Rust Compiler and Tools

Before you dive into the world of Rust programming, you need to get your hands dirty and set up your development environment. In this section, we will walk you through the process of installing the Rust compiler and the necessary tools to get started.

Why the Fuck Do You Need to Install Rust?

Well, how the fuck are you supposed to write code in Rust if you don't have the Rust compiler installed? It's like trying to bake a fucking cake without an oven. So, to embrace the awesomeness of Rust, let's get this shit installed!

Step 1: Installing Rustup

The first step in installing Rust is to get *rustup*, which is a Rust toolchain installer. Rustup makes it easy to manage your Rust installation and keep it up to date.

To get *rustup*, follow these steps:

1. Open your favorite fucking web browser and go to the official Rust website (*https://www.rust-lang.org/*).

2. Look for the "Get Rust" or "Install" button, click that shit!

3. You will be redirected to the *rustup* installation page. There, you will find different installation methods for various operating systems. Select the appropriate method for your operating system. Yeah, you got this!

4. Once you have downloaded the *rustup* installer, run it like you would any other fucking program. Just follow the instructions, you know the drill!

Step 2: Setting Up Your Fucking Development Environment

Now that you have *rustup* installed, it's time to set up your development environment. This step includes configuring the Rust toolchain, updating the necessary components, and selecting the default toolchain.

To set up your development environment, follow these steps:

1. Open up your favorite fucking terminal or command prompt. Yeah, the one where you feel like a fucking hacker!

2. Type the following command and hit that Enter key:

   `rustup update`

   This command will update your Rust toolchain to the latest version. You wouldn't want to miss out on any fucking cool features, would you?

3. After the update is complete, you can set the default toolchain by running the following command:

   `rustup default stable`

   This will set the default toolchain to the latest stable version of Rust. If you want to use a specific version, you can specify it in the command.

4. Finally, add the Rust binaries to your system's PATH variable by running the following command:

   `rustup show`

   This fucker will display some information about your Rust installation, including the location of the Rust binaries. Add that location to your PATH variable, and you're good to go! If you don't know how to do that, well, Google fucking knows everything!

5. To verify that Rust is installed correctly, run the following command:

   `rustc --version`

   If everything is set up properly, you should see the version of Rust installed on your machine. Pat yourself on the back, buddy! You're ready to kick some Rusty ass!

Step 3: Writing Your First Fucking Rust Program

Now that you have Rust installed and your development environment is all set up, let's write your first Rust program. We'll keep it simple, just to get you started.

```
fn main() {
    println!("Hello, world!");
}
```

Copy and paste the code into a new file, give it the extension ".rs" (for example, "hello.rs"), and save that shit.

Step 4: Compiling and Running Rust Code

In order to run your Rust code, you need to compile it first. But don't worry, it's as easy as breathing.

To compile and run your Rust code, follow these steps:

1. Open up your fucking terminal or command prompt (if you closed it).

2. Navigate to the directory where you saved your Rust code using the `cd` command. For example:

   ```
   cd path/to/your/code
   ```

   You can use the `ls` command to list the files in the current directory and make sure you're in the right place.

3. Once you're in the right directory, run the following command to compile your Rust code:

   ```
   rustc hello.rs
   ```

   This will generate an executable file with the same name as your source file (in this case, "hello") that you can run.

4. Finally, run your Rust program by typing the following command:

   ```
   ./hello
   ```

   If everything went smoothly, you should see the glorious message "Hello, world!" printed to the screen. Congratulations, you've just written and run your first Rust program! Now go out there and conquer the fucking world with your Rust skills!

Summary

In this section, we covered the installation process for the Rust compiler and the necessary tools to get started. We walked you through the steps of installing *rustup* and setting up your development environment. We also showed you how to write your first Rust program and compile it. Now you have the foundation to delve deeper into Rust programming.

Remember, learning Rust is fucking awesome, and with the right tools in your belt, you can create safe, fast, and fucking secure applications. So keep exploring, experimenting, and pushing the boundaries of what you can do with Rust! And always, always, keep that curiosity and passion for code burning. Happy programming, you badass Rustacean!

Setting Up Your Fucking Development Environment

Before you can start coding like a fucking rockstar in Rust, you need to set up your development environment. This section will guide you through the process of installing the Rust compiler and tools, configuring your editor, and getting everything ready for some serious coding action.

Installing Rust Compiler and Tools

To write Rust code, you need the Rust compiler and associated tools installed on your machine. Luckily, Rust has excellent documentation and provides a simple way to install everything you need.

The first step is to visit the official Rust website at https://www.rust-lang.org and navigate to the "Install" page. Here, you will find various ways to install Rust depending on your operating system. They support all the major platforms, including Windows, macOS, and Linux.

For Windows users, you can download the Rust installer and run it, following the on-screen instructions. On macOS, you can use the Homebrew package manager by executing the following command in the terminal:

```
\$ brew install rust
```

For Linux users, the Rust website provides detailed instructions for different distributions like Ubuntu, Fedora, and Arch Linux. Choose the one that matches your setup and follow the instructions provided.

After the installation process finishes, open a terminal or command prompt and type the following command to verify that Rust is properly installed:

```
\$ rustc --version
```

If everything is set up correctly, you should see the version of the Rust compiler printed on the screen. Congrats, you're one step closer to becoming a fucking Rust ninja!

Configuring Your Fucking Editor

Now that you have Rust installed, it's time to set up your editor for optimal Rust coding experience. The choice of editor is highly subjective, but some popular ones among Rust developers are Visual Studio Code, IntelliJ IDEA, and Sublime Text.

If you're using Visual Studio Code, there are a couple of essential extensions you should install to enhance your productivity. First, search for the "Rust"

GETTING STARTED WITH RUST   17

extension by Rust-lang in the Visual Studio Code marketplace and install it. This extension provides syntax highlighting, code formatting, and other convenient features specifically tailored for Rust development.

Next, install the "CodeLLDB" extension by Vadim Chugunov if you want to debug your Rust code directly from Visual Studio Code. This extension integrates LLDB, a powerful debugger, into the editor, allowing you to set breakpoints, inspect variables, and step through your code with ease.

For IntelliJ IDEA users, JetBrains provides a dedicated Rust plugin that you can install from the plugin settings. This plugin offers a rich set of features, including code completion, refactoring tools, and integration with the Cargo package manager.

Sublime Text users can install the "Rust Enhanced" package using the built-in package manager. This package provides syntax highlighting, code completion, and build system integration for Rust projects.

Of course, these are just a few examples, and you can use any editor that supports Rust. The Rust community prides itself on providing excellent tooling support for a wide range of editors, so feel free to use your favorite one.

Writing Your First Fucking Rust Program

Now comes the fun part – writing your first Rust program! Open your editor, create a new file, and save it with a ".rs" extension, which is the convention for Rust source code files.

Let's start with a classic "Hello, World!" program. Type the following code into your file:

```rust
fn main() {
    println!("Hello, World!");
}
```

This code defines a function named `main` that simply prints out the string "Hello, World!" to the console using the `println!` macro. Macros are a powerful feature in Rust that allow for code generation and metaprogramming.

To run your program, open a terminal or command prompt, navigate to the directory where you saved your Rust file, and enter the following command:

```
\$ rustc filename.rs
```

Replace `filename` with the actual name of your Rust file. This command compiles your Rust code into an executable binary. If there are no errors, you can run the program by typing:

```
\$ ./filename
```

Voila! You should see the message "Hello, World!" printed to the console.

Compiling and Running Rust Code

Compiling and running a single Rust file is all well and good, but what if you have a project consisting of multiple files and dependencies? Fear not, for Rust has a powerful build system called Cargo that takes care of all the complicated stuff for you.

Cargo is like the Swiss Army knife of Rust development. It handles dependency management, builds your project, runs tests, and even generates documentation. It's incredibly convenient and saves you a ton of time and effort.

To create a new Rust project with Cargo, open a terminal or command prompt, navigate to the directory where you want your project to reside, and enter the following command:

```
\$ cargo new project-name
```

Replace `project-name` with the desired name of your project. Cargo will generate a basic project structure for you, including a `src` directory for your source code and a `Cargo.toml` file that contains the project metadata and dependencies.

In the `src` directory, you'll find a file named `main.rs`. This file is where your project begins, and it already contains a "Hello, World!" program to get you started.

To compile and run your project, use the following command:

```
\$ cargo run
```

Cargo will take care of all the compilation and execute your code. If everything goes well, you should see the familiar "Hello, World!" message printed to the console.

Cargo also has other useful commands. For example, you can run tests using `cargo test` or build an optimized release version of your project using `cargo build --release`. These additional commands make it easy to develop, test, and distribute your Rust applications.

Summary

In this section, you learned how to set up your development environment for Rust programming. You installed the Rust compiler and tools, configured your editor, and wrote your first Rust program. We also introduced Cargo, Rust's build system, and showed you how to create and run a Rust project using Cargo.

Now that you have your development environment set up, it's time to dive deeper into the language and explore the powerful features of Rust. In the next section, we'll cover the basics of variables, data types, functions, and control flow in Rust. Get ready to level up your coding game!

Writing Your First Fucking Rust Program

Congratulations, you badass motherfucker! You've made it to the exciting part: writing your first fucking Rust program. Prepare yourself for an exhilarating journey into the world of safe, fast, and secure programming.

But before we dive in, let's take a moment to understand why the fuck Rust is worth learning.

Why the Fuck Should You Learn Rust?

Rust is the new badass on the block, and it's gaining popularity faster than a viral TikTok video. Here are a few reasons why learning Rust will give you an edge:

- **The Power of Fucking Control:** Rust empowers you to have fine-grained control over your code, letting you catch bugs at compile-time, rather than letting them lurk around during runtime. Say goodbye to those pesky null pointer exceptions and memory leaks.

- **Empowering Fucking Performance:** Rust's zero-cost abstractions allow you to write high-level code without sacrificing performance. With Rust, you can build blazing-fast applications that will leave legacy languages in the dust.

- **Creating Fucking Secure Applications:** Rust's ownership model and strict borrow checker guarantee memory safety and thread safety, leaving no room for nasty security vulnerabilities. Say goodbye to buffer overflows and data races!

- **Rust's Fucking Popularity:** Rust is becoming the go-to language for systems programming, network services, game engines, and countless other projects that demand reliability and performance. By learning Rust, you'll position yourself as a fucking programming rockstar in the job market.

Alright, now that you're convinced that learning Rust is fucking worth it, let's roll up our sleeves and write your first fucking Rust program!

Installing Rust Compiler and Tools

Before we can start writing some badass Rust code, we need to get our hands dirty and install the Rust compiler and tools. Follow these steps to get your Rust environment up and running:

1. Head over to the official Rust website at `https://www.rust-lang.org`.

2. Click on the "Get Started" button.

3. Choose the appropriate installation method for your operating system and follow the step-by-step instructions. Don't worry, they have clear and concise fucking instructions for all major operating systems.

Once you're done with the installation, open up your terminal and type `rustc --version`. If you see a version number, congratulations! You're ready to kick some serious Rust ass.

Setting Up Your Fucking Development Environment

Now that we have Rust installed, let's set up your fucking development environment. While you can technically write Rust code in Notepad like some kind of animal, we'll use a proper text editor or integrated development environment (IDE) to make our lives easier.

Here are a few popular choices for your Rust development environment:

- **Visual Studio Code (VS Code):** A lightweight and powerful text editor with excellent Rust support.

- **IntelliJ IDEA with Rust Plugin:** If you're an IntelliJ fan, you can use this plugin for Rust development.

- **Atom with Rust Language Server:** Atom is a hackable text editor, and the Rust Language Server plugin provides solid Rust support.

Choose the one that tickles your fancy, install the necessary plugins if required, and fire up your development environment. You're now ready to unleash the full power of Rust.

Writing Your First Fucking Rust Program

It's time to get down and dirty with some handcoded Rust, my friend. In your favorite text editor or IDE, create a new file with the extension ".rs" (e.g., `hello_world.rs`). This file will contain your first Rust program.

Type the following code into your file:

```rust
fn main() {
    println!("Hello, you badass motherfucker!");
}
```

Let's break down this code to understand what's going on:

- **fn main()**: This is the entry point of every Rust program. It's where the magic begins.
- **println!()**: This is a macro that prints the specified text to the console. In our case, it will print "Hello, you badass motherfucker!".

Save your file and open up your terminal again. Navigate to the directory where you saved the file and run the following command:

```
\$ rustc hello\_world.rs
```

If everything went smoothly, you should see a new file called "hello_world" in the same directory. This is the compiled binary of your Rust program. To run it, simply type:

```
\$ ./hello\_world
```

You should see the following output:

```
Hello, you badass motherfucker\index{motherfucker}!
```

There you have it, your first fucking Rust program is up and running! Bask in the glory of your achievement.

Compiling and Running Rust Code

Now that you've written your first Rust program, let's take a closer look at the compilation process. Rust's compiler, `rustc`, performs a series of steps to transform your code into a binary that the computer can execute.

Here's a high-level overview of the compilation process:

1. **Lexing and Parsing:** The compiler reads your Rust source code and breaks it down into a stream of tokens.
2. **Abstract Syntax Tree (AST) Generation:** The tokens are then used to construct an AST, which represents the structure of your program.
3. **Name Resolution:** The compiler resolves the names of modules, functions, variables, and other entities in your code.

GETTING STARTED WITH RUST

4. **Type Checking:** Rust is a strongly typed language, so the compiler checks that your code follows the rules of the language and has no type errors.

5. **Borrow Checking:** This is where Rust's unique ownership and borrowing system kicks in. The compiler ensures that your code follows the rules of memory safety and data race prevention.

6. **Code Generation:** Once all checks pass, the compiler generates machine code optimized for the target architecture.

7. **Linking:** Finally, the compiler links the generated machine code with any external libraries or dependencies, producing the final binary.

Phew, that's a lot of fucking work! But don't worry, you don't need to understand all the nitty-gritty details just yet. As you continue your journey with Rust, you'll gradually gain a deeper understanding of these concepts.

Summary

In this section, we took our first steps into the badass world of Rust. We discussed the reasons why learning Rust is fucking worth it, and we set up our development environment by installing the Rust compiler and choosing a text editor or IDE.

Then, we wrote our first fucking Rust program and explored the compilation process that transforms our code into an executable binary.

Now that you know the basics, get ready to dive deeper into the rabbit hole of Rust. In the next section, we'll explore the fundamentals of variables and data types in fucking Rust. Brace yourself, it's about to get even more exciting!

Compiling and Running Rust Code

In this section, we will delve into the process of compiling and running Rust code. As you may already know, Rust is a compiled language, which means that the code you write needs to be translated into machine-readable instructions before it can be executed. This compilation process ensures that your code runs efficiently and takes advantage of Rust's low-level control and safety features.

The Rust Compiler and Tools

Before we can begin compiling and running our Rust code, we need to have the Rust compiler and tools installed on our system. If you haven't done so already, head over to the official Rust website (https://www.rust-lang.org/) and follow the installation instructions for your operating system.

Once the installation process is complete, you can verify that everything has been set up correctly by opening a terminal or command prompt and typing the following command:

```
\$ rustc --version
```

If you see the version number of the Rust compiler printed on your screen, congratulations! You have successfully installed Rust on your system.

Setting Up Your Development Environment

Now that we have Rust installed, let's set up our development environment. While you can use any text editor or integrated development environment (IDE) to write Rust code, many developers prefer using the powerful and lightweight code editor, Visual Studio Code (VS Code).

To get started with VS Code, head over to the VS Code website (https://code.visualstudio.com/) and download and install the appropriate version for your operating system. Once installed, open VS Code and install the "Rust" extension by following these steps:

1. Click on the Extensions icon in the activity bar on the side of the VS Code window.

2. Search for "Rust" in the Extensions Marketplace.

3. Click on the "Rust" extension by the Rust Programming Language developers.

4. Click on the "Install" button to install the extension.

With the "Rust" extension installed, you now have access to powerful code analysis and debugging features specifically designed for Rust development.

Writing Your First Rust Program

Now that our development environment is set up, let's dive right into writing our first Rust program. Open your favorite text editor or VS Code and create a new file called hello.rs. In this file, we will write a simple program that prints the text "Hello, World!" to the console.

```rust
fn main() {
    println!("Hello, World!");
}
```

In the code above, we have defined a function called `main` with no arguments. The `println!` macro is used to print the text "Hello, World!" to the console. Macros in Rust are similar to functions but have a slightly different syntax.

Compiling and Running Rust Code

Now that we have our program ready, it's time to compile and run it. Open a terminal or command prompt, navigate to the directory where you saved the `hello.rs` file, and enter the following command:

```
\$ rustc hello.rs
```

The Rust compiler will read the `hello.rs` file, compile it into a binary executable, and generate an output file called `hello`. Note that the output file doesn't have an extension because it's a binary executable.

To run our program, simply enter the following command:

```
\$ ./hello
```

You should see the "Hello, World!" message printed to the console. Congratulations! You have successfully compiled and run your first Rust program.

A Note on Rust's Compilation Speed

Rust is known for its fast and efficient performance, but its compilation speed can sometimes be a bottleneck during development. The Rust compiler performs extensive static analysis and type checking, which can take some time, especially for larger codebases.

To mitigate this issue, Rust provides a tool called `cargo`, which is a package manager and build system for Rust. We will explore `cargo` in more detail in Chapter 1.6, but for now, it's important to know that `cargo` can significantly speed up the compilation process by caching dependencies and performing incremental builds.

In conclusion, compiling and running Rust code involves installing the Rust compiler and tools, setting up your development environment (such as using VS Code), writing your code, and using the `rustc` command to compile and the generated executable to run the program. Remember, Rust's compilation speed can be improved with the use of `cargo` and its build optimizations.

Summary

In this section, we covered the process of compiling and running Rust code. We learned how to install the Rust compiler and tools, set up our development environment using VS Code, write a simple "Hello, World!" program, and compile and run it using the `rustc` command. We also discussed the importance of `cargo` for improving compilation speed. In the next section, we will dive deeper into the basics of Rust, including variables, data types, functions, and control flow. Stay fucking tuned!

Understanding Rust Basics

Variables and Data Types in Fucking Rust

In this section, we will dive into the world of variables and data types in Fucking Rust. Understanding how to declare and use variables, as well as the different data types available, is crucial in any programming language. So, buckle up and let's get started!

Declaring Variables in Fucking Rust

In Fucking Rust, you declare variables using the `let` keyword. Here's a basic example:

```
let age = 25;
\end{lstlstiing}

In this example, we declare a variable \texttt{age} and

Rust is a statically typed language\index{language}, whi

\subsubsection{Primitive Data Types in Fucking Rust}

Fucking Rust provides several primitive\index{primitive}

\begin{itemize}
    \item \textbf{Integer Types}: Fucking Rust offers se
```

```latex
    \item \textbf{Floating-Point Types}: Fucking Rust supp
    \item \textbf{Boolean Type}: The boolean data type in
    \item \textbf{Character Type}: The \texttt{char} data
\end{itemize}

\subsubsection{Type Inference in Fucking Rust}

Fucking Rust is smart enough to infer the type of a variab

\begin{lstlisting}[language=Rust]
let name = ``John"; // type inferred as \&str
let count = 42; // type inferred as i32
```

In this example, Fucking Rust automatically deduces the data types of the variables name and count based on their initial values.

Constants in Fucking Rust

In addition to variables, Fucking Rust allows you to define constants using the const keyword. Constants are values that cannot be changed throughout the execution of a program. Here's an example:

```
const PI: f64 = 3.14159;
```

In this example, we define a constant PI with the value 3.14159. The data type of the constant is explicitly specified as f64, a 64-bit floating-point number.

Naming Conventions in Fucking Rust

When naming variables or constants in Fucking Rust, there are a few conventions to keep in fucking mind:

- Use snake_case: Variable and constant names should be written in lowercase letters, with words separated by underscores. For example: my_variable.

- Be descriptive: Choose variable names that are meaningful and describe the purpose of the value they hold. This makes your code more readable and easier to understand.

- Avoid starting with an underscore: Starting a variable name with an underscore indicates that the variable is unused or ignored. However, this can be used to suppress compiler warnings.

Summary

In this section, we covered the basics of variables and data types in Fucking Rust. We learned how to declare variables using the `let` keyword, explored various primitive data types, discussed type inference, and touched on constants and naming conventions.

Now, it's time to put your new knowledge into practice. Below are a few exercises to test your understanding. Have fun!

Exercises

1. Declare a variable `temperature` and assign it a value of 76.5. Choose an appropriate data type for the variable.

2. Create a constant `MAX_ATTEMPTS` with a value of 3. This constant will be used to limit the number of login attempts in a program.

3. Write a program that calculates the area of a rectangle. Take input from the user for the length and width of the rectangle, and output the calculated area.

Additional Resources

There is so much more to learn about variables and data types in Fucking Rust. Here are some additional resources to further expand your fucking knowledge:

- Official Fucking Rust documentation: `https://www.rust-lang.org/learn`

- "The Rust Programming Language" book by Steve Klabnik and Carol Nichols

- "Rust by Example" hands-on tutorial: `https://doc.rust-lang.org/stable/rust-by-example/`

Remember, mastering variables and data types is just the first step on your journey to becoming a Fucking Rust ninja. Keep exploring and experimenting, and soon you'll be writing secure and performant code like a pro!

Functions and Control Flow in Rust

In Rust, functions are the building blocks of code organization and reusability. They allow you to encapsulate a piece of code and call it whenever needed. In this section, we will explore functions in Rust, including their syntax, parameters, return values, and control flow statements.

Function Syntax

The syntax of a function in Rust is as follows:

```
fn function_name(parameter1: Type1, parameter2: Type2) ->
    // Function body
}
```

Let's break down the parts of this syntax:

- `fn`: This keyword is used to declare a function.

- `function_name`: This is the name of the function, and you should choose a descriptive name that reflects its purpose.

- `parameter1: Type1, parameter2: Type2`: These are the input parameters of the function. You can have zero or more parameters, each separated by a comma. Each parameter is defined with its name followed by a colon and its type.

- `-> ReturnType`: This specifies the return type of the function. If the function doesn't return anything, you can use `()` to indicate the unit type.

- `// Function body`: Here, you write the actual code that will be executed when the function is called.

Now let's dive deeper into each aspect of the function syntax.

Parameters

Functions can have zero or more parameters. Parameters allow you to pass values to the function for it to work with. Let's take a look at some examples:

```
fn greet(name: \&str) {
    println!("Hello, {}!", name);
}
```

```rust
fn add_numbers(a: u32, b: u32) -> u32 {
    a + b
}
```

In the first example, the `greet` function takes a single parameter name of type `&str`. The `&str` type represents a string slice, which is a borrowed view of a string.

In the second example, the `add_numbers` function takes two parameters a and b, both of type u32. The function adds the two numbers and returns their sum, which is of type u32.

Note that Rust uses a concept called borrowing, which allows you to pass values to functions without transferring ownership. This helps prevent unnecessary data copying and allows for efficient memory usage.

Return Values

Functions in Rust can return values using the `return` keyword. However, in Rust, the last expression in a function is automatically returned, so the `return` keyword is rarely used. Let's see an example:

```rust
fn square(x: u32) -> u32 {
    x * x
}
```

The `square` function takes an input x of type u32, multiplies it by itself, and returns the result. The return type is specified as u32.

Control Flow Statements

Rust provides several control flow statements that allow you to alter the flow of execution in your code. These include `if`, `else`, `match`, `loop`, `while`, and `for`. Let's explore each of them with examples.

- The `if` statement allows you to conditionally execute a block of code based on a boolean condition. Here's an example:

```rust
fn is\_even(number: u32) -> bool {
    if number % 2 == 0 {
        true
    } else {
        false
```

```rust
        }
}
```

In this example, the function `is_even` takes a number as input and checks if it is even using the modulus operator (%). If the number is even, the `if` block returns `true`, otherwise the `else` block returns `false`.

- The `match` statement allows you to match the value of an expression against a set of patterns and execute the corresponding code block. Here's an example:

```rust
fn get_day_of_week(day: u32) -> &str {
    match day {
        1 => "Monday",
        2 => "Tuesday",
        3 => "Wednesday",
        4 => "Thursday",
        5 => "Friday",
        6 => "Saturday",
        7 => "Sunday",
        _ => "Invalid day",
    }
}
```

In this example, the function `get_day_of_week` takes a day number as input and uses the `match` statement to return the corresponding day of the week as a string slice.

- The `loop` statement allows you to create an infinite loop that can be exited using the `break` keyword when a specific condition is met. Here's an example:

```rust
fn countdown(n: u32) {
    let mut count = n;
    loop {
        println!("{}", count);
        count -= 1;
        if count == 0 {
            break;
        }
    }
}
```

In this example, the function `countdown` takes an input n and prints a countdown starting from n.

- The `while` statement allows you to repeatedly execute a block of code as long as a certain condition holds true. Here's an example:

```rust
fn factorial(n: u32) -> u32 {
    let mut result = 1;
    let mut i = 1;
    while i <= n {
        result *= i;
        i += 1;
    }
    result
}
```

In this example, the function `factorial` calculates the factorial of a number n using a `while` loop.

- The `for` statement allows you to iterate over a collection or a range of values. Here's an example:

```rust
fn print\_numbers() {
    for i in 1..=5 {
        println!("{}", i);
    }
}
```

In this example, the function `print_numbers` prints the numbers from 1 to 5 using a `for` loop and the range operator (..=).

Summary

In this section, we covered the basics of functions in Rust. We discussed their syntax, parameters, return values, and control flow statements. Understanding these concepts is crucial for writing modular and reusable code in Rust.

Now that you have a good grasp of functions and control flow in Rust, it's time to dive deeper into other advanced topics. In the next chapter, we will explore advanced data structures in Rust, including vectors, arrays, slices, and hash maps. Get ready for some hardcore data manipulation with fucking performance!

Mutable vs. Immutable Variables

In Rust, variables can be declared as either mutable or immutable. This concept is fundamental to Rust's ownership system, which ensures memory safety and prevents data races. Understanding the difference between mutable and immutable variables is crucial for writing safe and efficient Rust code.

Immutable Variables

Immutable variables are declared using the `let` keyword. Once assigned a value, the value cannot be changed. This means that you cannot modify the data stored in an immutable variable after it has been assigned.

Using immutable variables has several benefits. First, it promotes a functional programming style where data is not modified but transformed. This makes it easier to reason about the code and prevents unexpected side effects. Second, it allows for better compiler optimizations since the compiler can assume that the value of an immutable variable does not change.

Here's an example that demonstrates the use of immutable variables:

```rust
fn main() {
    let name = "Alice";
    println!("Hello, {}!", name);
}
```

In this example, the variable name is immutable and is assigned the value "Alice". We are then able to use the value of name in the `println!` macro. If we try to modify the value of name elsewhere in the code, the compiler will raise an error.

Mutable Variables

Mutable variables, on the other hand, are declared using the `let mut` syntax. These variables can be modified and updated after they are assigned a value. This flexibility comes at a cost, as mutating variables introduces the potential for bugs and makes code harder to reason about.

Here's an example that demonstrates the use of mutable variables:

```rust
fn main() {
    let mut count = 0;
    count += 1;
    println!("Count: {}", count);
}
```

In this example, the variable count is mutable and is initially assigned the value 0. We then increment its value by 1 using the += operator and print the updated value. Mutable variables are particularly useful in scenarios where we need to modify state or update variables inside loops or functions.

However, it's important to note that Rust encourages minimizing mutable state as much as possible. By default, variables are immutable, and you should only use mutable variables when necessary. This promotes safer code and reduces the risk of bugs caused by unexpected changes in mutable state.

Rust's Borrowing and Mutable Borrowing

In Rust, the ownership system ensures that each piece of data has a single owner at any given time. This prevents data races and guarantees memory safety. When working with mutable and immutable variables, Rust enforces strict rules called borrowing and mutable borrowing to prevent data races.

Borrowing is the act of lending a reference to a value. Immutable variables are borrowed by default when passed to a function or assigned to another variable. This allows multiple parts of the code to read the value without making any modifications.

Mutable borrowing, on the other hand, allows for temporary mutability. Only one mutable reference to a value can exist in a particular scope. This prevents multiple parts of the code from simultaneously modifying the same data, ensuring that no data races occur.

Here's an example that demonstrates borrowing and mutable borrowing:

```rust
fn main() {
    let mut num = 5;
    let immutable\_borrow = \&num;
    let mutable\_borrow = \&mut num;

    // Error: Cannot modify num while it's borrowed as in
    // num += 1;

    *mutable\_borrow += 1;
    println!("num: {}", num);
}
```

In this example, we create an immutable borrow of num by assigning it to the variable immutable_borrow. We then try to modify num by incrementing it, which causes a compilation error. This shows that an immutable borrow prevents changes to the borrowed value.

Next, we create a mutable borrow of `num` by assigning it to the variable `mutable_borrow`. We can modify `num` through the mutable borrow by dereferencing it using the * operator. This demonstrates that mutable borrowing allows changes to the borrowed value.

Summary

In this section, we've explored the difference between mutable and immutable variables in Rust. Immutable variables promote a functional programming style and allow for better compiler optimizations. Mutable variables provide flexibility but should be used sparingly to minimize mutable state and reduce the risk of bugs.

Rust's ownership system enforces strict rules for borrowing and mutable borrowing to prevent data races. Borrowing allows multiple parts of the code to read a value, while mutable borrowing allows temporary mutability but only one mutable reference at a time.

Understanding the concept of mutable vs. immutable variables and Rust's ownership system is essential for writing safe and efficient Rust code. By using immutable variables by default and minimizing mutable state, you can build robust and predictable programs in Rust.

Now that you understand the basics of variables in Rust, it's time to delve deeper into the language and explore more advanced concepts. In the next sections, we will explore Rust's syntax, error handling, and memory management, among other topics. So buckle up and get ready for a wild ride with Rust—where safety, speed, and fucking security are the name of the game!

Additional Resources:

- The Rust Programming Language Book: `https://doc.rust-lang.org/book/`

- Rust by Example: `https://doc.rust-lang.org/stable/rust-by-example/`

- Rust Playground: `https://play.rust-lang.org/`

Exploring Fucking Rust Syntax

Structures, Enums, and Pattern Matching

In Rust, structures, enums, and pattern matching are powerful features that allow you to define custom data types and work with them effectively. These concepts form the building blocks of complex data structures and control flow in Rust. In this section, we will explore the fundamentals of structures, enums, and pattern matching and learn how to use them in your Rust programs.

Structures: Defining Custom Data Types

A structure, often referred to as a struct, is a way to define a custom data type that can hold multiple values of different types. It is similar to a class in object-oriented programming languages. Structs are commonly used to represent real-world entities or complex data structures.

To define a struct, you use the 'struct' keyword followed by the name of the struct and a block of code that specifies its fields. Each field consists of a name and a type separated by a colon. Let's take a look at an example:

```
struct Person {
    name\index{name}: String,
    age: u32,
    is\_employed: bool,
}
```

In this example, we define a struct called 'Person' with three fields: 'name' of type 'String', 'age' of type 'u32' (an unsigned 32-bit integer), and 'is_employed' of type 'bool'.

To create an instance of a struct, you can use the following syntax:

```
let person = Person {
    name: String::from("John Doe"),
    age: 25,
    is\_employed: true,
};
```

Here, we create a new 'person' object with the specified field values. Note that we use the 'String::from' function to create a 'String' object for the 'name' field. Once you have an instance of a struct, you can access its fields using dot notation. For example, to get the name of a person:

```
println!("Name: {}", person.name);
```

Structs can also have methods associated with them, allowing you to define behavior specific to the struct. We will cover this in more detail in later sections.

EXPLORING FUCKING RUST SYNTAX

Enums: Defining Variants

Enums, short for enumerations, enable the definition of a type by enumerating its possible values. Enums are useful in situations where a value can take on one of several distinct forms.

To define an enum, you use the 'enum' keyword followed by the name of the enum and a block of code that specifies its variants. Each variant can have additional data associated with it. Let's look at an example:

```rust
enum Language {
    Rust,
    Python,
    Java,
    JavaScript,
    Other(String),
}
```

In this example, we define an enum called 'Language' with five variants: 'Rust', 'Python', 'Java', 'JavaScript', and 'Other'. The 'Other' variant takes a 'String' as its associated data.

To create an instance of an enum variant, you simply use its name:

```rust
let favorite\_language = Language::Rust;
let other\_language = Language::Other(String::from("Go"));
```

Here, we create two instances of the 'Language' enum: 'favorite_language' with the 'Rust' variant and 'other_language' with the 'Other' variant and a 'String' as its associated data.

Enums are often used in combination with pattern matching, which we will explore next.

Pattern Matching: Control Flow with Style

Pattern matching is a powerful feature in Rust that allows you to match the structure of data against a set of patterns and execute code based on the match. It provides concise and expressive control flow.

The 'match' keyword is used to perform pattern matching in Rust. Let's see an example of how to use it with a struct:

```rust
struct Point {
    x: u32,
    y: u32,
```

```rust
}

fn main() {
    let p = Point { x: 0, y: 0 };

    match p {
        Point { x: 0, y: 0 } => println!("Origin"),
        Point { x: 0, y } => println!("On y-axis at y = "),
        Point { x, y: 0 } => println!("On x-axis at x = "),
        Point { x, y } => println!("On the plane at x = "),
    }
}
```

In this example, we define a struct called 'Point' with 'x' and 'y' coordinates. In the 'match' expression, we match against the different patterns defined for 'Point'. Depending on the values of 'x' and 'y', specific code blocks will be executed. This allows us to handle different cases in a concise and readable way.

Pattern matching is not limited to structs. It can also be used with enums to match against different variants and associated data. Let's see an example:

```rust
enum Coin {
    Penny,
    Nickel,
    Dime,
    Quarter(usize),
}

fn value\_in_cents(coin: Coin) -> usize {
    match coin {
        Coin::Penny => 1,
        Coin::Nickel => 5,
        Coin::Dime => 10,
        Coin::Quarter(diameter) => {
            println!("Quarter with diameter: {} mm", dia
            25
        },
    }
}
```

EXPLORING FUCKING RUST SYNTAX 39

In this example, we define an enum called 'Coin' with different variants. The 'Quarter' variant also includes the diameter of the quarter. In the 'value_in_cents' function, we match against the different variants and perform specific actions for each case.

Pattern matching in Rust is exhaustive, meaning that you need to handle all possible cases. This ensures that you don't accidentally miss any scenarios, making your code more reliable and less prone to bugs.

Summary

In this section, we explored the concepts of structures, enums, and pattern matching in Rust. Structures allow us to define custom data types with multiple fields, while enums enable the definition of types with distinct variants. Pattern matching provides a concise and powerful way to handle different cases based on the structure of data. Understanding these concepts is crucial for building complex data structures and implementing control flow in Rust programs.

To solidify your understanding, try implementing a graph data structure using structs and enums. Use pattern matching to traverse the graph and perform different operations based on the current node. This exercise will help you practice the concepts covered in this section and apply them to a real-world scenario.

Remember, mastering these foundational concepts is essential for becoming proficient in Rust programming. So keep practicing, experimenting, and pushing the boundaries of what you can do with Rust!

Error Handling with Fucking Result and Option Types

In Rust, error handling is a fucking crucial aspect of writing reliable and robust code. The language provides two main types for error handling: Result and Option. These types allow you to handle both expected and unexpected errors in a fucking elegant and concise manner.

Handling Errors with Fucking Result Type

The Result type in Rust is designed to handle functions that may return either a value or an error. It is an enum with two variants: Ok and Err. The Ok variant represents a successful operation and contains the result value, while the Err variant represents an error and contains an error value or message.

To handle a function that returns a Result, you can use the match expression to pattern match the result and handle both the success and error cases. Let's take a fucking example of a function that reads a file and returns a Result:

```rust
use\index{use} std\index{std}::fs::File;

fn read_file(path: \&str) -> Result<String, std::io::Erro
    let file = File::open(path)?;
    let mut contents = String::new();
    file.read_to\_string(\&mut contents)?;
    Ok(contents)
}

fn main() {
    let result = read_file("example.txt");

    match result {
        Ok(contents) => println!("File contents: {}", co
        Err(error) => println!("Error: {}", error),
    }
}
```

In the above fucking code, the read_file function returns a Result<String, std::io::Error>. Inside the match expression, we handle the Ok variant by printing the file contents, and the Err variant by printing the error message. Additionally, Rust provides syntactic sugar in the form of the question mark operator (?). This operator can be used to streamline error handling by automatically propagating errors from functions that return a Result. It is especially useful when you have multiple functions in a fucking row that can return errors. The question mark operator will return the error immediately if it encounters one, without the need to manually handle every fucking error.

Unwrapping Optionals with Fucking Option Type

The Option type in Rust is used when a value can be either present or absent. It also uses an enum with two variants: Some and None. The Some variant contains the actual value, while the None variant represents the absence of a value. Option types are typically used in situations where a value may or may not exist, such as when searching for an element in a collection. Let's see a fucking example:

```rust
fn find_element(array: \&[i32], target: i32) -> Option<u
    for (i, \&value) in array.iter().enumerate() {
        if value == target {
```

```rust
            return Some(i);
        }
    }
    None
}

fn main() {
    let array = [1, 2, 3, 4, 5];

    match find_element(&array, 3) {
        Some(index) => println!("Element found at index: {
        None => println!("Element not found"),
    }
}
```

In this example, the find_element function searches for a target value in an array and returns the index of the element if found, or None if not found. The match expression is used to handle both cases and print the appropriate fucking message. Similar to the question mark operator for Result types, Rust provides the unwrap and expect methods for Option types. These methods allow you to directly access the value if it exists, but they will panic if the value is None. It is important to use these methods with caution and fucking handle the panic in a proper way.

Combining Fucking Result and Option Types

In real-world applications, it is common to use both Result and Option types in combination to handle a wide range of scenarios. For example, a function may return a Result<Option<T>, E>, where T is the value that may or may not exist, and E is the fucking error type.

Using a combination of Result and Option types allows you to handle errors, absence of values, or both at the same time with fucking grace. Here's an example that demonstrates this:

```rust
fn find_user_by_id(id: u32) -> Result<Option<String>, St
    let users = get_all_users();

    match users {
        Ok(users) => {
            let user = users.iter().find(|&user| user.id
```

```
            match user {
                Some(user) => Ok(Some(user.name.clone())),
                None => Ok(None),
            }
        }
        Err(error) => Err(format!("Error getting users: 
    }
}

fn main() {
    let result = find_user\_by\_id(42);

    match result {
        Ok(Some(name)) => println!("User found: {}", nam
        Ok(None) => println!("User not found"),
        Err(error) => println!("Error: {}", error),
    }
}
```

In this example, the find_user_by_id function returns a Result<Option<String>, String>. Inside the match expressions, we handle the fucking cases where the result is Ok(Some(name)), Ok(None), or Err(error) and print the appropriate messages.

By fucking combining Result and Option types, you can express complex error handling and absence of value scenarios in a fucking concise and readable manner.

Conclusion

In this section, we fucking explored how to handle errors and absence of values in Rust using the Result and Option types. We learned how to use pattern matching, the question mark operator, and the unwrap and expect methods to handle fucking error and optional values. Additionally, we saw how Result and Option types can be combined to handle complex scenarios. With this knowledge, you are well-equipped to write code that handles errors and absence of values like a fucking pro in Rust.

Remember, error handling is a fucking vital aspect of programming, and Rust provides you with the tools to handle it with fucking elegance and security. So embrace the power of Result and Option types and write code that is not only safe and fast but also fucking reliable. Happy coding, you Rustacean badass!

Traits and Generics in Fucking Rust

In Rust, traits and generics are essential features that enable code reusability and flexibility. They allow you to write generic code that can work with different types and define behavior that can be shared across multiple types. So, let's dive into the fucking world of traits and generics in Rust!

Traits: Defining Fucking Behaviors

Traits in Rust are similar to interfaces in other programming languages. They define a set of methods that a type must implement in order to be considered as implementing that trait. You can think of traits as a contract that guarantees certain behavior. Here's an example:

```rust
trait Printable {
    fn print(\&self);
}

struct Book {
    title\index{title}: String,
    author\index{author}: String,
}

impl Printable for Book {
    fn print(\&self) {
        println!("Title: {}", self.title);
        println!("Author: {}", self.author);
    }
}
```

In this example, we define a trait called `Printable` with a single method `print()`. Then, we implement this trait for the `Book` struct. Now, any instance of `Book` can be printed using the `print()` method.

Traits can also have associated types and default implementations. Associated types allow a trait to define a type that will be specified by the implementor, while default implementations provide a default behavior that can be overridden. This makes traits even more fucking powerful!

Generics: Writing Fucking Reusable Code

Generics in Rust allow you to write code that can work with different types without sacrificing safety. They provide a way to define functions, structs, and enums that use placeholder types, which are then instantiated with specific types at compile time. Let's see how it works with an example:

```rust
fn get_first<T>(list: &[T]) -> Option<&T> {
    list.first()
}

fn main() {
    let numbers = vec![1, 2, 3, 4, 5];
    let first_number = get_first(&numbers);
    match first_number {
        Some(n) => println!("The first number is: {}", n),
        None => println!("The list is empty."),
    }
}
```

In this example, we define a generic function called `get_first()` that takes a slice of any type T and returns an optional reference to that type. We then call this function with a vector of integers and print the first number.

Generics can also be used with structs and enums. This allows you to write data structures and algorithms that can handle different types without duplicating code. It's fucking awesome!

Implementing Traits on Generics: Super Fucking Powers

One of the most powerful features in Rust is the ability to implement traits on generic types. This allows you to define behavior for a whole range of types without having to write separate implementations for each type.

For example, let's say we have a trait called Add that defines an addition operation. We can implement this trait for all types that support addition:

```rust
trait Add<RHS=Self> {
    type Output;
    fn add(self, rhs: RHS) -> Self::Output;
}

impl<T, U> Add<U> for T
```

```rust
where
    T: std::ops::Add<U>,
{
    type Output = T::Output;
    fn add(self, rhs: U) -> Self::Output {
        self + rhs
    }
}
```

In this example, we define the Add trait with an associated type Output, and a method add() that takes the right-hand side of the addition. We then implement this trait for any type T that supports addition with a type U. With this implementation, we can use the addition operator + on any types that implement the Add trait. Rust will figure out the appropriate implementation at compile time. So fucking powerful!

Advanced Fucking Tricks

Now that you understand the basics of traits and generics, let's explore some advanced tricks that can take your code to the next fucking level!

- **Higher-Order Traits:** Traits can also be used as generic type parameters. This allows you to write code that operates on any type that implements a specific trait. For example, you can write a function that accepts any type that can be printed using the Printable trait.

- **Trait Bounds:** You can specify trait bounds on generic types to restrict which types can be used as type arguments. This allows you to enforce certain behavior or properties for the generic type. For example, you can specify that a generic type must implement both the Printable and Clone traits.

- **Associated Consts and Functions:** Traits can also have associated constants and functions. Associated constants provide a way to define constants specific to a trait, while associated functions allow you to define functions that can be called on the trait itself, without an instance.

- **Operator Overloading:** Rust allows you to overload operators for your custom types using traits. This means you can define how your types behave with operators such as +, -, and *, among others. It's fucking cool!

- **Dynamic Dispatch:** Rust's traits also support dynamic dispatch, which allows you to write code that works with different types at runtime. This can be useful when you have a collection of different types that implement the same trait and you want to call trait methods on them without knowing their concrete types. It's a powerful technique that adds some fucking flexibility!

Fucking Exercises

Now, it's time for you to practice your skills with some fucking exercises! Don't worry; they're not as fucking difficult as they might sound. Just try your best and have fun while learning Rust!

1. Implement a trait called `Shape` with a method `area()` that calculates the area of the shape. Then, create structs for different shapes (e.g., `Circle`, `Rectangle`) that implement this trait and calculate their areas.
2. Write a generic function called `reverse_list()` that takes a mutable slice of any type and reverses the elements in place.
3. Create a trait called `Encrypt` with a method `encrypt()` that encrypts a given string. Then, implement this trait for the type `String` by converting the string to uppercase.
4. Write a generic function called `find_max()` that takes a slice of any type that implements the `PartialOrd` trait and returns the maximum element in the slice.

Remember, the fucking sky is the limit when it comes to what you can do with traits and generics in Rust. So, keep exploring, experimenting, and pushing the boundaries of what's possible!

Additional Resources

If you're hungry for more fucking knowledge about traits and generics in Rust, here are some additional resources that you might find helpful:

- **The Rust Programming Language:** This is the official book about Rust that covers all aspects of the language, including traits and generics. It's a fucking great resource for both beginners and experienced Rustaceans.

- **Rust by Example:** This online resource provides hands-on examples of various Rust concepts, including traits and generics. It's a fucking great way to learn by doing!

- **The Rustnomicon:** This is a more advanced book that explores the dark arts of Rust. It goes into deep detail about traits, generics, and other language features. If you're feeling adventurous and want to dive into the depths of Rust, this is the fucking guide for you.

- **The Rust Standard Library Documentation:** This is the official documentation for the Rust standard library. It provides detailed information about all the traits and generics available in Rust, along with many examples.

- **Official Rust Website:** The official Rust website is filled with resources, tutorials, and guides to help you on your journey to becoming a Rustacean. Check out the "Learn" section for more fucking goodies!

So, grab your favorite fucking resource, keep practicing, and enjoy the journey of mastering traits and generics in Rust! They are powerful tools in your arsenal that will make your code more reusable, flexible, and fucking awesome. Happy coding!

Lifetimes and Memory Management in Rust

In Rust programming, memory management is a critical aspect of creating safe and efficient code. Rust's approach to memory management is unique, using a mechanism called lifetimes to ensure that references to data remain valid for the duration of their usage. This section will delve into the concept of lifetimes and how they are utilized in Rust's memory management system.

Understanding Lifetimes

In Rust, lifetimes serve as a way to track and enforce the lifespan of references to data. They ensure that references are always valid and prevent the use of dangling pointers or accessing memory that has been deallocated. Lifetimes are a static analysis feature of the Rust compiler that guarantees memory safety without the need for garbage collection.

A lifetime represents the span during which a reference is valid and refers to a specific location in memory. It is denoted by an apostrophe symbol ('), followed by a lowercase letter or an underscore. For example, the lifetime 'a can be used to represent a reference that is valid for a certain duration within a function.

Relations between Lifetimes and Borrowing

Lifetimes are tightly connected to Rust's borrowing and ownership system. When a reference is borrowed from a variable, the lifetime of that reference must not exceed the lifetime of the borrowed variable itself. This ensures that references do not outlive the data they point to, preventing any invalid memory access. The Rust compiler analyzes the relationships between lifetimes and borrows to determine their validity. It enforces strict rules to eliminate potential dangling or conflicting references. If the compiler detects any potential violations, it will fail to compile the code and provide helpful error messages to guide the developer in resolving these issues.

Annotations and Lifetime Syntax

To specify lifetimes in Rust, you can use lifetime annotations. These annotations explicitly define the relationship between the lifetimes of references in your code. They are typically used when working with functions that accept multiple references or when returning references from functions.

Lifetime annotations are placed after the ampersand symbol (&) in function signatures and can be named anything you want. However, it is recommended to use descriptive names to improve code readability. For example, in the function signature `fn foo<'a>(x: &'a i32, y: &'a i32) -> &'a i32`, both x and y have the same lifetime 'a, indicating that the returned reference will have the same lifetime as the input references.

Lifetimes and Structs

Lifetimes are also crucial when dealing with structs that contain references as fields. Rust ensures that the lifetimes of the references are properly managed to avoid dangling references or memory leaks.

When defining a struct that contains references, you need to explicitly annotate the lifetimes of the references. This ensures that the struct does not outlive the data it references. For example, consider a struct that holds a reference to a string slice:

```
struct StringHolder<'a> {
    data: \&'a str,
}
```

In this example, the lifetime annotation 'a indicates that the reference held by `data` cannot outlive the struct itself. The lifetime of the reference is tied to the lifetime of the struct.

EXPLORING FUCKING RUST SYNTAX

Lifetime Elision

Rust's lifetime elision rules allow the omission of explicit lifetime annotations in certain cases, making code more concise and readable. These rules are based on common patterns and can automatically infer the correct lifetimes in many situations.

The lifetime elision rules are relatively complex, but the basic idea is that the Rust compiler will analyze the code and make assumptions about the lifetimes based on predefined patterns. It can determine the lifetimes of references based on their usage and the surrounding scope.

Although lifetime elision can simplify code, it is essential to understand the rules behind it and the situations where explicit lifetime annotations are still required. This understanding will help you write clearer and safer code in Rust.

Memory Management and Drop Trait

In addition to managing lifetimes, Rust's memory management also involves deallocating memory when it is no longer needed. For this purpose, Rust provides the `Drop` trait. This trait allows you to define custom behavior for freeing resources when a value goes out of scope.

By implementing the `Drop` trait for a struct, you can specify what actions need to be performed when the struct is no longer used. This is particularly useful when working with resources like file handles or network connections. Rust will automatically call the `drop` method for any value that implements the `Drop` trait when it goes out of scope.

It's worth noting that Rust's ownership system and the `Drop` trait work together to provide deterministic memory management. Resources are deallocated as soon as they are no longer referenced, ensuring efficient memory usage and avoiding memory leaks.

Lifetimes in Action

To better understand how lifetimes work in practice, let's consider an example scenario. Imagine you're developing a function that finds the longest common prefix among a given list of strings. Here's what the function implementation might look like:

```rust
fn longest_common_prefix<'a>(strings: &[&'a str]) -> &'a str {
    if strings.is_empty() {
        return "";
```

```
    }

    let first = strings[0];

    for (i, _) in first.char_indices() {
        for string in &strings[1..] {
            if !string.starts_with(&first[..i+1]) {
                return &first[..i];
            }
        }
    }

    first
}
```

In this example, we use the lifetime annotation `'a'` to indicate that the returned reference from `longest_common_prefix` has the same lifespan as the input references. This ensures that the returned reference remains valid and points to a valid memory location within the input strings.

The function starts by handling the edge case of an empty input list, returning an empty string in this case. Then, it uses the first string as a reference point and iterates through its characters. For each character, it checks if the character sequence forms a prefix for all the other strings. If not, it returns the longest prefix found so far.

This example demonstrates how lifetimes help prevent dangling references and ensure that the returned reference remains valid within the given lifetimes.

Further Resources

To deepen your understanding of lifetimes and memory management in Rust, here are some additional resources:

- "The Rust Programming Language" book by Steve Klabnik and Carol Nichols provides a comprehensive guide to Rust, covering lifetimes and memory management in detail.

- The official Rust documentation has a section dedicated to explaining lifetimes (https://doc.rust-lang.org/book/ch10-03-lifetime-syntax.html).

- The Rust Playground (https://play.rust-lang.org/) is a useful tool for experimenting and testing code related to lifetimes.

Summary

In this section, we explored the concept of lifetimes in Rust programming. Lifetimes are essential for ensuring memory safety, preventing dangling references, and enabling efficient memory management. We learned about lifetime annotations, their relation to borrowing, and how they are used in structs. We also discussed lifetime elision, the `Drop` trait, and witnessed lifetimes in action through an example function. By mastering lifetimes and understanding Rust's memory management principles, you'll be able to create safe and performant applications in Rust.

Testing, Documentation, and Packages in Rust

Writing Fucking Unit Tests

Unit tests are a crucial part of the development process. They help ensure that your code functions as expected, identify and fix bugs early on, and provide a safety net when making changes or refactoring. In this section, we will explore how to write fucking unit tests in Rust, using the built-in testing framework.

An Overview of Fucking Unit Testing in Rust

In Rust, unit tests are defined within the same module as the code they are testing. They are annotated with the '`#[cfg(test)]`' attribute, which tells the compiler to include them only when running tests. This ensures that the tests do not affect the performance of the final production code.
To create a unit test, you define a new function with the '`#[test]`' attribute. This attribute indicates that the function is a test, and the Rust testing framework will execute it accordingly. Let's start by writing a simple test for a function that adds two integers together:

```
#[cfg(test)]
mod tests {
    #[test]
    fn test_addition() {
        assert_eq!(add(2, 3), 5);
    }
```

```
fn add(a: i32, b: i32) -> i32 {
    a + b
}
}
```

In this example, we have a test function called 'test_addition()' that calls the 'add()' function and checks if the result is equal to 5 using the 'assert_eq!()' macro. The 'assert_eq!()' macro compares two values and panics if they are not equal. If all assertions pass, the test is considered successful.

Testing Fucking Error Conditions

While testing successful code paths is important, it is equally crucial to test error conditions and edge cases. Thankfully, Rust provides a convenient way to check for expected errors using the 'assert_panic!()' macro. Consider the following example:

```
\#[cfg(test)]
mod tests {
    \#[test]
    \#[should_panic(expected = ``index out of bounds'')]
    fn test\_index\_out\_of_bounds() {
        let vec = vec![1, 2, 3];
        vec[3];
    }
}
```

Here, we have a test function called 'test_index_out_of_bounds()' that attempts to access an element at index 3 in a vector with only 3 elements. We expect this operation to panic with the message "index out of bounds". The 'should_panic' attribute specifies that the test should pass if a panic with the expected message occurs.

Testing Fucking Asynchronous Code

Asynchronous programming is becoming increasingly common in modern software development. Rust's testing framework provides support for testing asynchronous code using the 'tokio-test' crate. Let's look at an example of testing an asynchronous function:

TESTING, DOCUMENTATION, AND PACKAGES IN RUST

```
\#[cfg(test)]
mod tests {
    use\index{use} tokio\index{tokio}::runtime\index{runti
    use tokio\_test::block_on;

    \#[test]
    fn test\_async_function() {
        let mut rt = Runtime::new().unwrap();
        let result = block_on(async_function());
        assert!(result.is\_ok());
    }

    async fn async_function() -> Result<(), ()> {
        // Perform asynchronous operations here
        Ok(())
    }
}
```

In this example, we use the 'tokio-test' crate to create a runtime and execute the asynchronous function 'async_function()'. The 'block_on()' function ensures that the asynchronous code is awaited until completion before making any assertions.

Organizing Fucking Unit Tests

As your project grows, you'll likely have multiple tests across different modules and files. To organize your tests effectively, Rust provides the ability to group tests into test modules. This allows you to structure your tests in a logical and maintainable manner.

To create a test module, you use the '#[cfg(test)]' attribute on a sub-module and define test functions within it. Let's consider an example of organizing unit tests for a simple calculator module:

```
\#[cfg(test)]
mod tests {
    mod addition_tests {
        \#[test]
        fn test\_positive\_addition() {
            // Test positive number addition
```

```
            }

            \#[test]
            fn test\_negative\_addition() {
                // Test negative number addition
            }
        }

        mod subtraction_tests {
            \#[test]
            fn test\_positive\_subtraction() {
                // Test positive number subtraction
            }

            \#[test]
            fn test\_negative\_subtraction() {
                // Test negative number subtraction
            }
        }
}
```

In this example, we have created two test modules: 'addition_tests' and 'subtraction_tests'. Within each module, we define test functions specific to addition and subtraction operations, respectively. This modular approach helps maintain code organization and improves code readability.

Running Fucking Unit Tests

Now that we have written our unit tests, it's time to run them. Rust provides a simple command-line interface to execute tests. To run all the tests in your project, use the following command:

```
cargo test
```

By default, the testing framework runs tests in parallel to speed up the testing process. If you prefer to run tests sequentially, you can use the '--jobs 1' flag:

```
cargo\index{cargo} test\index{test} --jobs 1
```

You can also run specific tests or filter tests by name using the 'cargo test <test_name>' command:

TESTING, DOCUMENTATION, AND PACKAGES IN RUST

```
cargo test test\_addition
```

Additionally, Rust's testing framework provides many other options for customizing test execution. You can control the test output, ignore specific tests, run tests based on attributes, and more. For a complete list of options, refer to the official Rust documentation.

Summary

Unit tests in Rust are straightforward to write and provide a robust way to validate the correctness of your code. By following the principles covered in this section, you can write effective unit tests that ensure your code functions as expected, handles errors correctly, and supports asynchronous operations. Remember to organize your tests logically, run them regularly, and leverage the testing framework's flexibility to customize your testing process.

Now that you have a solid understanding of writing fucking unit tests in Rust, let's move on to exploring documentation, package management, and publishing in Rust.

Documenting Your Fucking Code

Documenting your code is an essential part of being a responsible and considerate programmer. It not only helps others understand your work but also serves as a valuable reference for yourself in the future. In this section, we will explore the importance of documentation and discuss some best practices for documenting your fucking Rust code.

Why the Fuck Should You Document Your Code?

Documentation plays a crucial role in software development. Here are a few reasons why you should give a fuck about documenting your code:

- **Communication:** Documentation allows you to convey the purpose, functionality, and usage of your code to other developers. It helps them understand how to use your code correctly, saving them time and frustration.

- **Maintainability:** Well-documented code is easier to maintain. When you revisit your code after a while, you might not remember the intricate details.

Having good documentation will jog your memory and help you make changes without introducing bugs.

- **Collaboration:** In a team environment, proper documentation fosters collaboration. It enables team members to work together effectively and ensures that everyone is on the same fucking page.

- **Open Source Contributions:** If you plan to contribute to open source projects or share your code with the world, documentation is a must. It allows others to understand your intentions, encourages collaboration, and increases the likelihood of your code being accepted.

Now that you understand the importance of documentation, let's dive into some best practices for documenting your fucking Rust code.

Use Fucking Comments

Comments are a simple yet effective way to document your code. In Rust, you can add comments using the double-slash (`//`) for single-line comments or use the forward slash and asterisk (`/* */`) for multi-line comments. Here's an example:

```rust
// This function adds two numbers and returns the result
fn add_numbers(a: i32, b: i32) -> i32 {
    a + b
}
```

When writing comments, strive for clarity and conciseness. Clearly explain the purpose, inputs, outputs, and any peculiarities of your code. Don't be afraid to sprinkle in a little humor or personality. After all, coding should be fucking fun!

Generate Fucking API Documentation

In addition to inline comments, Rust provides a powerful tool called `rustdoc` that generates beautiful API documentation directly from your code. By using well-formatted comments and doc comments, you can easily generate comprehensive documentation for your project.

To generate documentation, you need to write doc comments above the items you want to document. Doc comments start with `///` and support Markdown formatting. Here's an example:

TESTING, DOCUMENTATION, AND PACKAGES IN RUST

```
/// This struct represents a fucking person.
///
/// A person has a name and an age.
pub struct Person {
    name\index{name}: String,
    age: u32,
}
```

Once you have your doc comments in place, you can run the following command to generate the documentation:

```
\$ cargo doc --open
```

This command will build your code and open the generated documentation in your browser. It's like having your own personal fucking documentation website!

Follow Fucking Documentation Conventions

To ensure consistency across the Rust ecosystem, it's important to follow some conventions when documenting your code. The Rust community has established a set of guidelines known as the Rustdoc conventions. Here are some key points to keep in mind:

- Begin each doc comment with a summary that provides an overview of the item being documented.

- Use Markdown formatting to add emphasis, code samples, lists, and links within your doc comments.

- Document all public items, including functions, structs, traits, and methods.

- Use descriptive names for your items and document their purpose, inputs, outputs, and usage examples.

- Make sure your code examples are valid and runnable. A fucking example that doesn't compile is about as useful as a broken condom.

- Include a "Returns" section if your function returns a value, and specify the type and any possible errors.

Following these conventions will make your code more accessible and contribute to the overall improvement of the Rust fucking ecosystem.

Document Improve, Repeat

Documentation is not a one-time thing. It's an ongoing process that evolves with your code. Whenever you make significant changes or add new features, take the fucking time to update the documentation accordingly.
Additionally, if you receive feedback from users or colleagues, use it to improve your documentation. Keeping the documentation up to date will save everyone a lot of time and frustration in the long run.

Do Not Be a Documentation Nazi

While documentation is essential, don't become a fucking documentation Nazi. Striking a balance between documentation and code is crucial. Sometimes, code can be self-explanatory, and adding excessive comments can clutter the codebase. Use your common fucking sense when deciding what needs to be documented and how much. Focus on delivering clear, concise, and meaningful information without overwhelming readers with unnecessary documentation.

Additional Fucking Resources

If you want to become a master of fucking documentation, here are some additional resources to check out:

- **The Rustdoc Book:** The official documentation for `rustdoc` can be found in the Rust documentation itself. Go to https://doc.rust-lang.org/rustdoc to explore its complete fucking glory.

- **The Rust Programming Language Book:** Chapter 14 of the `rustdoc` book covers documentation conventions in depth. Read it at https://doc.rust-lang.org/book/ch14-00-more-about-cargo.html.

- **Exemplify Rust Documentation:** This fucking awesome GitHub repository contains examples of well-documented Rust projects. Check it out at https://github.com/boringcactus/exemplify to see how the pros do it.

Summary

Documenting your fucking code should be a habit, not an afterthought. Good documentation makes your code more understandable, maintainable, and enjoyable to work with. By using comments, generating API documentation, following conventions, and continuous improvement, you will become a documentation god in no fucking time.

In the next section, we will explore managing dependencies with `Cargo`, Rust's package manager. So buckle up, motherfuckers!

Managing Dependencies with Fucking Cargo

In this section, we will explore how to manage dependencies in Rust using the powerful tool called *Cargo*. Cargo is the official package manager and build system for Rust that simplifies the management of dependencies, compilation, documentation, and testing of Rust projects. It is designed to make your life as a Rust developer easier and more efficient.

What the Fuck is Cargo?

Before we dive into the details, let's take a moment to appreciate the beauty of Cargo. Just like a trustworthy delivery driver, Cargo takes care of all the heavy shit, so you don't have to. It handles downloading, building, and managing dependencies for your Rust projects, so you can focus on writing kick-ass code. With Cargo, you don't need to worry about manually tracking down libraries, dealing with version conflicts, or setting up complex build configurations. It's like having a personal assistant that takes care of your project's logistics.

Creating a New Fucking Rust Project

To get started with Cargo, you need to create a new Rust project. Open up your terminal, navigate to the directory where you want to create your project, and run the following command:

```
cargo new my\_project
```

This command creates a new directory named *my_project* with the basic structure for a Rust project. It includes a *Cargo.toml* file, which is used to define your project's dependencies.

Managing Dependencies with Fucking Cargo.toml

The *Cargo.toml* file is where you declare your project's dependencies and provide other configuration information. It uses a simple syntax known as *TOML* (Tom's Obvious, Minimal Language) to specify the package name, version, and the dependencies required by your project. Let's take a look at an example *Cargo.toml* file:

```toml
[package]
name = "my_project"
version = "0.1.0"
edition = "2018"

[dependencies]
tokio = "1.0.0"
reqwest = { version = "0.11", features = ["json"] }
```

In this example, we have a package section that specifies the name, version, and edition of our project. The dependencies section is where we define the external crates we need. In this case, we have two dependencies: *tokio* and *reqwest*. We specify the version numbers for each crate, and in the case of *reqwest*, we also enable a feature called *json*.

Fetching and Building Dependencies

Once you have defined your dependencies in the *Cargo.toml* file, it's time to fetch and build them. Run the following command:

```
cargo build
```

This command tells Cargo to fetch the specified dependencies and build them based on the information in your *Cargo.toml* file. Cargo will automatically download the required crates and their dependencies from the central package registry, compile them, and generate the necessary build artifacts. It's like having a magical genie that grants all your dependency wishes.

Updating Dependencies

Dependencies are living creatures that evolve over time. New versions are released, bugs are fixed, and features are added. To keep your project up to date and benefit from the latest improvements, you need to periodically update your dependencies. Cargo makes this process fucking simple. Run the following command:

```
cargo update
```

This command tells Cargo to check for any updates to your project's dependencies and fetch the latest versions. Cargo is not shy about updating your dependencies,

Testing Your Fucking Rust Code

Cargo provides built-in support for testing your Rust code. Tests are an essential part of any software project to ensure that your code behaves as expected. To run tests using Cargo, simply run the following command:

```
cargo test
```

Cargo will search your project for all test functions, execute them, and report the results. It's like having a loyal army of automated testers that save you from embarrassing bugs. The output will tell you which tests passed, which ones failed, and any other relevant information or errors.

Publishing Your Fucking Rust Crate

Once you are satisfied with your code and ready to share it with the world, you can publish your Rust crate to the central package registry called *crates.io*. This allows other developers to use your crate as a dependency in their projects. To publish your crate, you need to create an account on *crates.io* and run the following command:

```
cargo\index{cargo} publish
```

Cargo will package your crate, upload it to *crates.io*, and make it available for anyone to use. It's like becoming a rock star and sharing your music with the world. Just remember to put on your best performance, as the whole world will be watching (well, maybe not the whole world, but you get the point).

Conclusion

Managing dependencies is a crucial aspect of software development, and Cargo does it in a way that makes you want to give it a big fucking hug. With Cargo, you can easily declare and manage your project's dependencies, build and test your code, and even publish your crates to the Rust package registry. It's a powerful tool that saves you time, reduces headaches, and helps you focus on what you do best: writing awesome Rust code.
So, embrace the power of Fucking Cargo and enjoy the smooth sailing through the Rust package ecosystem. Happy coding, my fellow Rustaceans!

Publishing Your Fucking Rust Package

Publishing your Rust package is a crucial step in sharing your fucking awesome work with the world. By making your code available to others, you contribute to the open-source community and enable collaboration and improvement. So let's dive into the process of publishing your fucking Rust package!

Preparing Your Package for Publication

Before you can publish your package, you need to make sure that it's ready for the fucking world to see. Here are some important steps to take:

- **Clean up your code:** Go through your codebase and tidy things the fuck up. Remove any commented-out code, unused dependencies, or redundant files. Make sure your code is easy to understand and well-documented. Nobody wants to work with a messy codebase, so put some fucking effort into it!

- **Write comprehensive documentation:** Documentation is key, my friend. Take the time to explain the purpose of your package, how it should be used, and any potential gotchas or limitations. Provide examples and tutorials to guide users in the right fucking direction. Documentation shows that you give a damn about the user experience and want to make their lives easier.

- **Include tests:** Tests are your best fucking friends when it comes to ensuring the stability and reliability of your package. Write unit tests to cover various scenarios and use cases. This will help users gain confidence in your package and make them more likely to use it.

- **Versioning:** Decide on a versioning scheme for your package. Use semantic versioning (X.Y.Z) to convey the impact of changes. This helps users understand if an update will introduce breaking changes or not. Be consistent and transparent with your versioning to avoid causing unnecessary headaches for your users.

- **Choose a fucking license:** Decide on the license you want to release your package under. There are various open-source licenses available, such as the MIT License or the Apache License. Consider the needs of your users and the goals of your project when choosing a license. And for fuck's sake, make sure you understand the implications of the license you choose!

TESTING, DOCUMENTATION, AND PACKAGES IN RUST 63

Once you've tackled these steps, your package will be in a much better shape for publication. Trust me, people will appreciate your professionalism and attention to detail.

Publishing with Fucking Cargo

Now that your package is ready, it's time to publish that shit! In Rust, we have a fantastic tool called Cargo that makes the process a breeze. Here's how you can use Cargo to publish your fucking Rust package:

1. **Create a fucking Cargo account:** First things first, you need to create an account on crates.io, the official package registry for Rust. Go to `https://crates.io` and sign up for an account. This will allow you to publish and manage your packages.

2. **Log in with Cargo:** Once you've created your account, you need to log in through Cargo. Open your terminal or command prompt and use the following command:

    ```
    cargo login
    ```

    Cargo will prompt you for your crates.io API token, which you can find in your account settings on the website. Paste that fucker in, and you're good to go.

3. **Prepare your package metadata:** In your package's root directory, you need to create a `Cargo.toml` file if you haven't already. This is where you define metadata like your package's name, version, authors, dependencies, and more. Refer to the official Cargo documentation for the details of this fucking file structure.

4. **Build your package:** Before you can publish, you need to build your package to ensure it's in a working state. Run the following command:

    ```
    cargo\index{cargo} build\index{build} --release\index
    ```

    The `--release` flag tells Cargo to build an optimized release version of your package. Don't forget to run your tests as well to catch any bugs or fuck-ups.

5. **Publish that fucking package**: Finally, it's time to publish your package to crates.io. Run the following command:

```
cargo\index{cargo} publish
```

Cargo will upload your package to the registry and make it available for others to use. If all goes well, you'll receive a confirmation message of your successful publication. Pat yourself on the back, my friend. You did it!

Promoting Your Fucking Rust Package

Publishing your package is just the first fucking step. Now you need to get the word out and let people know how amazing your package is. Here are some strategies to promote your fucking Rust package:

- **Write a kickass README**: The README file is the first fucking thing potential users see when they visit your package's repository. Make it compelling and informative. Explain what your package does, how it solves a problem, and provide usage examples. Include badges for build status, code coverage, and version number. Show off a bit, but stay fucking humble.

- **Contribute to the community**: Engage with the Rust community by answering questions on forums, participating in discussions, and contributing to open-source projects. By being an active member, you'll gain visibility and credibility, making people more likely to check out your package.

- **Write a blog post or tutorial**: Create content that showcases your package's capabilities. Write a blog post or tutorial explaining a problem your package solves and how to use it. Be fucking thorough and provide step-by-step instructions. This not only educates people but also attracts them to your package.

- **Leverage social media**: Tweet about your package, share it on LinkedIn, or post in relevant subreddits or Rust-related communities. Use engaging visuals and captivating messages to pique people's curiosity. Don't just spam links; provide value and encourage discussions.

TESTING, DOCUMENTATION, AND PACKAGES IN RUST

- **Join conferences and meetups:** Attend Rust conferences or local meetups to showcase your package. Give talks, demos, or lightning talks to show people what your package can do. Networking is key in building a strong community around your package.

- **Maintain and update your package:** Don't just publish your package and forget about it. Continue to improve, fix bugs, add features, and release updates. Show that you're dedicated to maintaining a high-quality package and that users can rely on you.

By following these promotion strategies, you'll increase the visibility and adoption of your fucking Rust package. Remember, you've built something awesome, so don't shy away from letting the world know about it!

Closing Thoughts

Publishing your fucking Rust package is an exciting milestone in your journey as a software developer. It allows you to share your knowledge, contribute to the community, and make an impact. But remember, publishing is just the beginning. Continuously improve, engage with users, and be open to feedback. Your package has the potential to change the fucking world, so don't take it lightly. Now go forth, my friend, and release that orgasmically beautiful Rust package into the wild. The world is waiting for your fucking genius.

Advanced Rust Concepts

Advanced Rust Concepts

Advanced Rust Concepts

In this chapter, we will dive deeper into advanced concepts in Rust, building upon the foundations laid in the previous chapter. We will explore more sophisticated data structures, asynchronous programming, interfacing with other languages, web development with Rust, concurrency and parallelism, and other advanced topics. Get ready to level up your Rust skills and tackle more complex projects!

Understanding Advanced Rust Concepts

As you progress in your journey to master Rust, it's important to delve into more advanced concepts. This section will serve as a guide to help you expand your knowledge and become a proficient Rust programmer.

Ownership and Borrowing

One of the key features of Rust is its ownership system, which ensures memory safety without relying on garbage collection. We have already touched upon ownership and borrowing in the previous chapter, but here we will explore the topic in more depth.

Ownership allows Rust to guarantee at compile-time that memory is managed properly, preventing common issues such as null pointer dereferences, use-after-free bugs, and data races. However, it can be a challenging concept to grasp fully. To recap, every value in Rust has a unique owner, and there can only be one owner at a time. When a value goes out of scope, Rust automatically deallocates its memory. This system ensures that memory leaks and dangling references are impossible in safe Rust code.

Borrowing, on the other hand, allows temporary access to a value without taking ownership. This is crucial for writing efficient and safe Rust code. There are two types of borrows: immutable borrows (references) and mutable borrows (mutable references). The borrow checker enforces strict rules to prevent data races and ensure memory safety.

Let's consider an example to better understand ownership and borrowing:

```rust
fn main() {
    let mut x = 5;
    let y = \&mut x;
    *y += 1;
    println!("The value of x is: {}", x);
}
```

In this code snippet, we create a mutable variable 'x' and a mutable reference 'y' to 'x'. We then modify the value of 'x' through the reference 'y'. Finally, we print the updated value of 'x'. The code compiles and runs successfully, demonstrating the principles of ownership and borrowing.

However, misuse of ownership and borrowing can lead to compilation errors. The borrow checker will reject code that violates Rust's borrowing rules. For example, attempting to use both mutable and immutable references to the same data at the same time will result in a compile-time error. This prevents data races, a common source of bugs in concurrent programming.

To overcome ownership and borrowing challenges, Rust provides various techniques, such as borrowing scopes and reference lifetimes. These advanced concepts allow you to optimize your code without compromising safety.

Smart Pointers and Interior Mutability

In addition to regular references, Rust provides smart pointers that offer additional capabilities beyond borrowing. Smart pointers are data structures that act like pointers but have additional metadata and capabilities.

One common smart pointer is 'Box<T>', which allows you to store values on the heap rather than the stack. This is useful when you need to control the size of a type at runtime or when dealing with large data structures.

Another powerful smart pointer is 'Rc<T>', which stands for Reference Counted. 'Rc<T>' allows you to have multiple ownership of the same data, tracking the number of references to determine when to deallocate memory. This is particularly useful in scenarios where you need to share data across multiple parts of your program.

ADVANCED RUST CONCEPTS

Smart pointers can also provide interior mutability, allowing you to mutate data even when there are immutable references to it. This is achieved through types such as 'Cell<T>' and 'RefCell<T>'. Interior mutability can be handy in situations where you need to modify data within a data structure while still borrowing it immutably.

Understanding smart pointers and interior mutability opens up a wide range of possibilities for designing flexible and efficient Rust code. However, it's important to use them judiciously, as misuse can lead to runtime errors or performance issues.

Advanced Error Handling

The 'Result' and 'Option' types are fundamental to error handling in Rust. In this section, we will explore advanced techniques for error handling using these types. Rust encourages the use of 'Result' and 'Option' to handle possible failures explicitly, providing a concise and idiomatic way to deal with errors. However, working with nested 'Result' and 'Option' types can become cumbersome. To tackle this issue, Rust provides combinators and methods such as 'and_then', 'map', and 'unwrap_or_else' to compose and transform results and options. These functional programming-inspired techniques allow you to handle errors and optional values in an elegant and concise way.

Beyond combinators, Rust also offers the '?' operator, known as the "try" operator, to simplify error propagation. The '?' operator automatically unwraps and returns the value from a 'Result' or 'Option' if it is 'Ok' or 'Some', respectively. If the value is 'Err' or 'None', the operator will propagate the error or return early from the enclosing function, saving you from writing verbose error handling code.

Let's consider an example to illustrate these advanced error handling techniques:

```rust
fn get\_username() -> Result<String, Box<dyn Error>> {
    let path = ``username.txt";
    let username = std::fs::read_to\_string(path)?;
    Ok(username.trim().to\_string())
}

fn process\_username() -> Result<(), Box<dyn Error>> {
    let username = get\_username()?;
    println!("Welcome, {}!", username);
    Ok(())
}

fn main() {
```

```
14      if let Err(err) = process\_username() {
15          eprintln!("Error: {}", err);
16          std::process::exit(1);
17      }
18  }
```

In this code snippet, we have three functions: 'get_username', which reads a username from a file and returns it as a 'Result'; 'process_username', which processes the username and outputs a welcome message; and 'main', which orchestrates the execution.

By utilizing the '¿ operator, we can propagate errors from the inner functions to the outer function, where they are handled appropriately. This allows us to write concise and readable code while maintaining robust error handling.

These advanced error handling techniques empower you to write reliable and robust Rust code, gracefully handling different failure scenarios.

Concurrency and Parallelism

Rust's fearless concurrency and parallelism capabilities set it apart from many other programming languages. In this section, we will explore Rust's concurrency primitives, such as threads and synchronization mechanisms, and learn how to leverage them effectively.

Concurrency is the ability of a program to execute multiple tasks simultaneously, while parallelism refers to actually making use of multiple physical cores to execute tasks in parallel. Rust provides powerful abstractions for both scenarios.

The Rust standard library offers a module called 'std::thread', which provides facilities to create and manage threads. You can spawn threads and join them to synchronize their execution. The 'std::sync' module provides synchronization primitives like 'Mutex', 'RwLock', and 'Barrier', which ensure exclusive access to shared data and allow coordination between threads.

Additionally, Rust's ownership system and borrowing rules ensure safe sharing of data between threads without data races. The borrow checker helps prevent common synchronization issues, making concurrent programming in Rust more robust and less error-prone.

For parallelism, Rust provides the 'rayon' crate, which offers high-level abstractions for writing parallel algorithms. The 'rayon' crate utilizes task parallelism, automatically distributing computations across available cores, resulting in efficient parallel execution.

ADVANCED RUST CONCEPTS

Let's consider a simple example to illustrate concurrent and parallel programming in Rust:

```rust
use std::sync::{Arc, Mutex};
use\index{use} std\index{std}::thread\index{thread};

fn main() {
    let counter = Arc::new(Mutex::new(0));
    let mut handles = vec![];

    for _ in 0..10 {
        let counter = Arc::clone(\&counter);
        let handle = thread::spawn(move || {
            let mut num = counter.lock().unwrap();
            *num += 1;
        });
        handles.push(handle);
    }

    for handle in handles {
        handle.join().unwrap();
    }

    println!("Counter: {:?}", *counter.lock().unwrap());
}
```

In this code snippet, we create a shared counter using the 'Arc' (Atomic Reference Counting) type from the 'std::sync' module. We spawn ten threads, each incrementing the counter. By using a 'Mutex' to guard access to the counter, we ensure safe concurrent access.

After joining all the threads, we print the final value of the counter. The output may vary due to the unpredictable order in which the threads execute, but you can be confident that there are no data races or synchronization issues.

Rust's concurrency and parallelism capabilities allow you to harness the full power of modern, multi-core processors while keeping your code safe and efficient. Understanding these concepts and utilizing them effectively will enable you to build high-performance Rust applications.

Advanced Trait and Generics Usage

Traits and generics are powerful features in Rust that enable code reuse and abstraction. In this section, we will explore advanced techniques for trait implementation and usage, as well as leveraging generics effectively.

Rust's trait system allows you to define shared behavior across different types. By implementing traits, you can define a common interface for various types, enabling code to be written in a generic and modular way.

When it comes to advanced trait usage, associated types and trait bounds offer additional flexibility. Associated types allow you to define types within a trait, abstracting over concrete types. This can be useful when working with generic algorithms that require specific types.

Trait bounds allow you to restrict trait implementations to specific types or sets of types. You can use trait bounds to express complex relationships between types, ensuring that only appropriate types can be used with certain traits. This increases the safety and clarity of your code.

Generics complement traits by enabling you to write code that can operate on different types without sacrificing type safety. Rust's generic system allows you to write concise and reusable code that can be applied to a wide range of scenarios. Let's take a look at an example that demonstrates advanced trait and generics usage:

```
trait MathOperation {
    type Output;

    fn compute(\&self, a: Self::Output, b: Self::Output)
}

struct\index{struct} Calculator;

impl MathOperation for Calculator {
    type Output = f64;

    fn compute(\&self, a: Self::Output, b: Self::Output)
        a + b
    }
}

fn main() {
    let calculator = Calculator;
    let result = calculator.compute(3.14, 2.67);
```

```
    println!("Result: {}", result);
}
```

In this code snippet, we define a trait called 'MathOperation', which represents a generic mathematical operation. The trait has an associated type, 'Output', which allows us to parameterize the trait over different output types.

We then implement the 'MathOperation' trait for the 'Calculator' struct, setting the associated type 'Output' to 'f64' and defining the 'compute' method accordingly.

In the 'main' function, we create an instance of 'Calculator' and use the 'compute' method to perform a sum operation. The 'Result' is then printed to the console.

By using traits and generics in this way, we can write code that is flexible and reusable. With associated types and trait bounds, we can express even more complex relationships between types, further enhancing our code's expressiveness and safety.

Summary

In this section, we have explored advanced concepts in Rust, including ownership and borrowing, smart pointers and interior mutability, advanced error handling, concurrency and parallelism, and advanced trait and generics usage. Understanding and mastering these concepts will empower you to write more sophisticated Rust code and tackle complex projects.

Continue to the next section to learn about even more advanced topics in Rust, including memory safety, building a web server from scratch, secure coding practices, performance tuning and optimization, and deploying Rust applications in production.

Advanced Data Structures in Fucking Rust

Vectors, Arrays, and Slices in Rust

In this section, we will explore some of the fundamental data structures in Rust, namely vectors, arrays, and slices. These structures play a crucial role in storing and manipulating collections of elements in a variety of scenarios. Understanding how to use them effectively is essential for writing high-performance and secure Rust code.

Vectors

A vector, also known as a dynamic array, is a resizable collection of elements of the same type. Vectors are allocated on the heap and provide flexible and efficient access to their elements. Let's take a closer look at how to create and use vectors in Rust.

To create a vector, we use the `vec!` macro followed by the elements enclosed in square brackets. Here's an example:

```rust
let mut numbers: Vec<i32> = vec![1, 2, 3, 4, 5];
```

In this example, we create a vector of integers (`i32`) named `numbers` and initialize it with the values 1, 2, 3, 4, and 5.

We can access individual elements of a vector using square brackets and the index of the element. Keep in mind that indexing starts from zero. For example, to access the third element of `numbers`, we can use the following code:

```rust
let third_number = numbers[2];
```

In addition to accessing elements, we can modify them as well. Let's assume we want to change the value of the second element in `numbers` to 10. We can do this using the following code:

```rust
numbers[1] = 10;
```

To add elements to a vector, we can use the `push` method. This method appends an element to the end of the vector. For example, let's add the value 6 to `numbers`:

```rust
numbers.push(6);
```

To remove elements from a vector, we can use the pop method. This method removes the last element from the vector and returns it. Here's an example:

```rust
let last\_number = numbers.pop();
```

It's important to note that vectors can only hold elements of the same type. If you try to add elements of different types, the Rust compiler will throw an error.

Arrays

Unlike vectors, arrays in Rust have a fixed size determined at compile time. Arrays are allocated on the stack and are often used when the number of elements is known in advance and does not need to change dynamically. Let's see how arrays work in Rust.

ADVANCED DATA STRUCTURES IN FUCKING RUST

To create an array, we declare its type, followed by square brackets containing the number of elements and the initial values enclosed in curly braces. Here's an example:

```
let weekdays: [String; 7] = [
    String::from("Monday"),
    String::from("Tuesday"),
    String::from("Wednesday"),
    String::from("Thursday"),
    String::from("Friday"),
    String::from("Saturday"),
    String::from("Sunday"),
];
```

In this example, we create an array named `weekdays` that can hold 7 elements of type `String`. Each element is initialized with the corresponding day of the week. We can access individual elements of an array using square brackets and the index, just like with vectors. For example, to retrieve the third element of `weekdays`, we can use the following code:

```
let third_day = weekdays[2].clone();
```

Note that we use `.clone()` here because arrays do not have ownership. In Rust, ownership is a key concept for memory safety, and by default, ownership is not transferred when accessing array elements.

Array elements cannot be added or removed like in vectors, as their size is fixed. If you need a collection with a dynamic size, you should use vectors instead.

Slices

Slices in Rust provide a way to reference a contiguous portion of a vector or an array. Slices are useful when you want to work with a subset of the elements without copying them. Let's take a look at how slices can be used in practice.

To create a slice, we use the range syntax with the starting and ending indices separated by two dots (..). The starting index is inclusive, while the ending index is exclusive. Here's an example that creates a slice from the first three elements of a vector:

```
let numbers\_slice = \&numbers[0..3];
```

In this example, `numbers_slice` references the first three elements of the `numbers` vector. Changes made to the slice will be reflected in the original vector, and vice versa.

Slices can also be used as function parameters to work with a subset of a vector or an array. For example, consider a function that calculates the sum of a subset of integers:

```
fn sum_subset(numbers: &[i32]) -> i32 {
    let mut sum = 0;
    for &num in numbers {
        sum += num;
    }
    sum
}

let numbers_sum = sum_subset(&numbers[2..5]);
```

In this example, we define a function `sum_subset` that takes a slice of `i32` elements as a parameter. We iterate over the slice and calculate the sum of all the numbers. We then call this function with a slice of the `numbers` vector from the third to the fifth element.

Slices provide a powerful way to manipulate and pass around subsets of collections without incurring the cost of copying the elements.

Summary

In this section, we explored vectors, arrays, and slices in Rust. Vectors allow us to dynamically resize collections of elements, while arrays provide fixed-size collections. Slices provide a way to reference portions of vectors and arrays without copying the elements.

Understanding these data structures is critical for writing efficient and secure Rust code. By using vectors, arrays, and slices appropriately, you can build powerful and performant applications in Rust. So go ahead and unleash the full potential of Rust by harnessing the versatility of these data structures.

Now that we have a solid understanding of vectors, arrays, and slices, let's dive deeper into some advanced concepts in Rust in the next chapter. We will explore advanced data structures, asynchronous programming, interfacing with other languages, web development, and concurrency in the context of Rust. Get ready for some exciting and mind-bending Rust concepts ahead!

ADVANCED DATA STRUCTURES IN FUCKING RUST

Hash Maps and HashMaps Motherfucker

In this section, we're going to explore one of the most powerful data structures in Rust: the fucking HashMap. A HashMap is a collection of key-value pairs, where each key is associated with a value. It provides efficient insertion, deletion, and retrieval of elements based on their keys.

Why the Fuck Should You Use Hash Maps?

Hash maps are incredibly useful in a wide variety of applications. They are particularly valuable when you need to quickly find and retrieve data based on a specific key. For example, suppose you're building a fucking social media app and you want to store user information. You can use a hash map to map each user's unique ID to their corresponding data, such as their username, email, and profile picture. This allows you to efficiently retrieve user data based on their ID, without having to search through every fucking user in your database.

How the Fuck Do Hash Maps Work?

A hash map in Rust is implemented as an array of linked lists. The array is divided into buckets, and each bucket contains a linked list of key-value pairs. When you insert a new key-value pair into the hash map, Rust uses a hash function to determine the fucking bucket where the pair should be stored. This hash function calculates a numeric hash value based on the key. The hash value is then used as an index to find the appropriate bucket in the array.

Resolving Hash Collisions

Sometimes, two different keys may produce the same hash value. This is known as a hash collision. Rust handles hash collisions by using separate chaining. In separate chaining, each bucket contains a linked list of key-value pairs. When a collision occurs, the new key-value pair is added to the linked list in the appropriate bucket.

Retrieving Values from a Hash Map

To retrieve a value from a hash map, you provide the fucking key and the hash map returns the associated value, if it exists. Rust uses the hash function to calculate the hash value of the key and then looks for the key in the appropriate bucket's linked list. If the key is found, the corresponding value is returned; otherwise, an error is returned.

Example Usage of Hash Maps

Let's consider a real-world example to understand how the fuck hash maps can be used. Imagine you are developing a bookstore application, and you want to keep track of the number of copies of each book in stock. You can use a hash map to store the book titles as keys and the corresponding quantity as values. Here's a simple fucking example:

```rust
use\index{use} std\index{std}::collections::HashMap;

fn main() {
    let mut book_stock: HashMap<String, u32> = HashMap::new();

    // Adding books to the hash map
    book_stock.insert(String::from("The Catcher in the Rye"), 5);
    book_stock.insert(String::from("To Kill a Mockingbird"), 8);
    book_stock.insert(String::from("1984"), 3);

    // Retrieving the stock of a specific book
    if let Some(stock) = book_stock.get("The Catcher in the Rye") {
        println!("{} copies in stock.", stock);
    } else {
        println!("Book not found.");
    }
}
```

In this example, we create a new hash map called `book_stock`, where the keys are of type `String` and the values are of type `u32`. We insert three book titles as keys and their corresponding quantities as values. Then, we retrieve the stock for a specific book using the `get` method. If the book is found, we print the stock; otherwise, we print an error message.

Fucking Caveats and Limitations

While hash maps are extremely useful, there are a few caveats and limitations to be aware of:

- Hash maps do not guarantee any specific order of key-value pairs. If you need to maintain a specific order, you may need to use a different data structure.

ADVANCED DATA STRUCTURES IN FUCKING RUST

- If the hash map is resized, all existing keys and values will be rehashed and copied to new buckets. This can have a performance impact, especially if the hash map contains a large number of elements.

- Hash maps require keys that implement the Eq and Hash traits. If you want to use a custom type as a key, you need to implement these traits for that type.

- Hash maps have a fixed load factor of 0.75, which means that once the hash map is 75% full, it will automatically resize itself to accommodate more elements. This resizing process can be fucking expensive, so keep an eye on the performance if you're dealing with a large number of elements.

Further Resources and Exercises

To solidify your understanding of hash maps in Rust, I fucking encourage you to explore the Rust documentation on HashMap and experiment with different fucking scenarios. Try implementing your own hash map data structure using separate chaining or open addressing.

If you want to dive deeper into the world of hashing and data structures, I recommend the book "Algorithms, Part I" by Robert Sedgewick and Kevin Wayne. It covers essential topics in computer science, including hash tables and hashing algorithms, in a clear and concise manner.

In addition, here are some exercises for you to tackle:

1. Write a function that takes a string as input and returns the frequency of each character using a hash map.

2. Implement a hash map data structure that supports resizing and handles collisions using open addressing.

3. Create a command-line spell checker that suggests corrections for misspelled words using a hash map containing a dictionary of words.

4. Design a hash map-based cache system for a web application that stores recently accessed data to improve performance.

Remember, practice is fucking key to mastering Rust and becoming an exceptional programmer. So get your hands dirty and have fun exploring the wonderful world of hash maps!

Custom Data Structures for Fucking Performance

In this section, we will explore how to create custom data structures in Rust that are optimized for fucking performance. While Rust provides a rich set of built-in data structures, there might be scenarios where you need specialized data structures to improve the performance of your code. By creating custom data structures, you can tailor them to the specific requirements of your application and squeeze out every bit of performance.

Understanding the Need for Custom Data Structures

Before diving into creating custom data structures, it's essential to understand when and why you might need them. Here are a few scenarios where custom data structures can be valuable:

- **Domain-specific optimization:** In some domains, such as game development or scientific simulations, you may need data structures that are optimized for specific operations or constraints. Creating custom data structures can help you achieve better performance in these scenarios.

- **Memory efficiency:** Rust provides high-level data structures, but sometimes they might not be memory-efficient enough for your use case. By designing custom data structures, you can minimize memory overhead and improve overall performance.

- **Algorithmic requirements:** Certain algorithms require specialized data structures to achieve optimal performance. By creating custom data structures tailored to these algorithms, you can ensure efficient execution.

Now that we understand the need for custom data structures, let's explore how to create them in Rust.

Designing and Implementing Custom Data Structures

Designing and implementing custom data structures require careful consideration of the underlying requirements and expected usage patterns. Here are the steps involved in creating custom data structures for fucking performance.

Step 1: Define the API

Start by defining the API of your custom data structure. Think about what operations you want to support and how you want to interact with the data. Consider what performance characteristics you want to achieve and the trade-offs you are willing to make. Document the API using Rust's documentation syntax so that others can understand how to use your data structure effectively.

Step 2: Decide on Internal Representation

Next, decide on the internal representation of your data structure. This decision heavily depends on the requirements of your specific use case. Consider factors such as memory efficiency, cache-awareness, and the operations you need to perform. Rust provides various data structures for different use cases, like vectors, arrays, and linked lists. Choose the appropriate Rust data types or create your own custom types, if needed.

Step 3: Implement Operations

Implement the operations defined in the API for your custom data structure. Take into account the desired performance characteristics and ensure correctness by writing comprehensive test cases. Rust's testing framework provides excellent support for writing tests and ensuring the functionality of your data structure.

Step 4: Optimize for Performance

Once you have a working implementation, you can start optimizing your custom data structure for performance. Consider techniques such as algorithmic improvements, reducing memory allocation, minimizing branching, and improving cache locality. Benchmark your data structure against real-world scenarios to validate the performance improvements.

Example: Custom Trie Data Structure

To illustrate the process of creating custom data structures in Rust, let's design and implement a custom trie data structure optimized for string search operations. A trie, also known as a prefix tree, is an efficient data structure for storing and searching strings. The trie organizes characters of different strings in a tree-like structure, allowing for fast lookup and search operations.

Here's an example implementation of a custom trie data structure in Rust:

```rust
// Define TrieNode struct
struct TrieNode {
    children: [Option<Box<TrieNode>>; 26], // 26 possible
    is\_word: bool,
}

// Define the Trie structure
pub struct Trie {
    root: Option<Box<TrieNode>>,
}
```

```rust
impl Trie {
    // Constructor for Trie
    pub fn new() -> Self {
        Trie {
            root: Some(Box::new(TrieNode {
                children: [None; 26],
                is_word: false,
            })),
        }
    }

    // Insert a word into the Trie
    pub fn insert(&mut self, word: String) {
        let mut current = self.root.as_mut().unwrap();

        for ch in word.chars() {
            let index = ch as usize - 'a' as usize;
            current = current.children[index].get_or_in
                children: [None; 26],
                is_word: false,
            }));
        }

        current.is_word = true;
    }

    // Search for a word in the Trie
    pub fn search(&self, word: String) -> bool {
        let mut current = self.root.as_ref();

        for ch in word.chars() {
            let index = ch as usize - 'a' as usize;
            if let Some(node) = current.and_then(|node|
                current = Some(&node);
            } else {
                return false;
            }
        }
```

```
50          current.map_or(false, |node| node.is\_word)
51      }
52  }
```

In this example, we define a `TrieNode` struct to represent each node in the trie, and a `Trie` struct to represent the trie itself. We implement the `new`, `insert`, and `search` methods on the `Trie` struct. The `search` method searches for a word in the trie, and the `insert` method inserts a word into the trie.

With this custom trie data structure, you can efficiently store a large number of strings and perform fast search operations. It demonstrates the process of designing and implementing a custom data structure in Rust for fucking performance.

Resources and Further Reading

Creating custom data structures requires a solid understanding of Rust's memory model, lifetimes, and ownership. Here are some resources and references to deepen your knowledge:

- **The Rust Programming Language:** The official book on Rust provides a comprehensive introduction to the language, ownership, and data structures.

- **Rust by Example:** An online resource that offers hands-on examples of Rust concepts, including data structures and algorithms.

- **The Rustonomicon:** This unofficial guide dives deep into the unsafe aspects of Rust, which can be useful for optimizing custom data structures.

- **Rustlings:** This interactive tutorial provides exercises to strengthen your Rust skills, including data structures.

- **GitHub Rust projects:** Exploring open-source Rust projects on GitHub can give you insights into how others have designed and implemented custom data structures.

By mastering the art of designing and implementing custom data structures in Rust, you can elevate your programming skills and build high-performance applications.

Exercises

1. Implement a custom stack data structure using Rust's Vec as the underlying storage. The stack should support the following operations: push, pop, and is_empty.

2. Create a custom data structure that efficiently stores a collection of words and allows you to find all anagrams of a given word. The data structure should support the following methods: insert, find_anagrams, and remove.

3. Design and implement a custom priority queue data structure that supports the following operations: insert, extract_min, and is_empty. Ensure that the priority queue is implemented with efficient time complexity for all operations.

These exercises will test your understanding of data structures and their implementation in Rust. Solving them will deepen your knowledge and improve your skills in creating custom data structures for fucking performance.

Exploring Fucking Unsafe Rust

In this section, we will dive deep into the world of fucking unsafe Rust. Brace yourselves, because shit is about to get real! Unsafe Rust allows you to bypass some of the language's built-in safety features, giving you ultimate control and power over your code. However, with great fucking power comes great fucking responsibility, as Uncle Ben (not the one from Rust mascot Ferris) once said.

Understanding Fucking Unsafe Rust

Unsafe Rust is a way to write code that sidesteps some of the language's safety checks. It allows you to write code that is more low-level and closer to the underlying hardware, giving you the flexibility and efficiency you need in certain situations. However, it also means that you need to take up the role of a responsible programmer, because you are now responsible for ensuring memory safety and other low-level details.

When should you use fucking unsafe Rust? Well, ideally, you should only use it when absolutely necessary. Unsafe Rust is most commonly used in the following scenarios:

- Interfacing with unsafe code: When you need to interact with code written in another language (like C or C++), which might not have Rust's safety guarantees, you can use unsafe Rust to bridge the gap and ensure compatibility.

- Performance optimizations: In certain cases, the strict checks and abstractions of safe Rust might hinder performance. In such situations, you can leverage unsafe Rust to write more efficient code with less overhead.
- Implementing abstractions: Sometimes, in order to provide high-level abstractions, you might need to drop down to the lower level with unsafe Rust. This allows you to build custom data structures or libraries that would be impractical or impossible with safe Rust alone.

Working with Fucking Raw Pointers

One of the core concepts in unsafe Rust is fucking raw pointers. A raw pointer is simply a memory address, without any safety guarantees or restrictions. It can be dereferenced to access the data it points to, but you need to ensure that the memory is valid and properly aligned.

To create a raw pointer, you can use the fucking dereference operator (*) on a reference, like this:

```
let x = 42;
let raw_ptr = \&x as *const i32;
```

In this example, we create a raw pointer `raw_ptr` that points to the memory address of variable x. Note that we use the as keyword to explicitly cast the reference to a raw pointer type *const i32.

To safely dereference a raw pointer, you can use the unsafe keyword and wrap your code inside an unsafe block:

```
let x = 42;
let raw_ptr = \&x as *const i32;

unsafe {
    let value = *raw_ptr;
    println!("Value at {} is: {}", raw_ptr, value);
}
```

Inside the unsafe block, we can dereference the raw pointer `raw_ptr` by using the fucking dereference operator (*), just like we would with a regular reference. However, make sure you double-check that the pointer is valid and the memory it points to is still valid, otherwise you risk causing undefined behavior.

Living on the Fucking Edge with Unsafe Functions

In addition to raw pointers, unsafe Rust also allows you to define unsafe functions. These are functions that can perform operations that are not checked by the compiler for safety. You should only use unsafe functions when absolutely necessary and ensure that you uphold the responsibility of making sure the code is safe.

To define an unsafe function, simply use the `unsafe` keyword before the function definition:

```rust
unsafe fn dangerous_function() {
    // Unsafe code...
}
```

Inside an unsafe function, you have the power to do crazy shit, like dereferencing multiple raw pointers at once or even modifying mutable static variables. But remember, with great power comes great responsibility! You need to uphold the safety invariants that Rust normally enforces.

Writing Fucking Unsafe Blocks

Unsafe blocks are another way to contain unsafe code inside an otherwise safe Rust program. This allows you to isolate the unsafe code, making it clear where the unsafe operations are happening and restricting the scope of potential fuck-ups. To create an unsafe block, use the `unsafe` keyword followed by a pair of curly braces:

```rust
let x = 42;
let raw_ptr = &x as *const i32;

unsafe {
    // Unsafe code...
}
```

Inside the unsafe block, feel free to unleash your wildest programming fantasies, but also make sure you follow the fucking rules. Remember, you're responsible for ensuring the safety of the code within the block.

Fucking Unsafe Rust and Multithreading

Unsafe Rust plays a crucial role when it comes to multithreading. Rust's safe concurrency is built on top of unsafe abstractions that manage memory

ADVANCED DATA STRUCTURES IN FUCKING RUST

synchronization and thread safety. By using atomic operations and mutexes, you can achieve safe concurrent patterns.

One important concept in unsafe multithreading is the `Sync` trait. It guarantees that a type can be safely shared across threads. However, implementing the `Sync` trait requires unsafe Rust, as you need to ensure that the type is actually safe to be shared.

For example, let's say we have a struct `Counter` that we want to use concurrently:

```rust
use std::sync::atomic::{AtomicUsize, Ordering};

struct Counter {
    count: AtomicUsize,
}

unsafe impl Sync for Counter {}

impl Counter {
    fn increment(&self) {
        self.count.fetch_add(1, Ordering::SeqCst);
    }

    fn decrement(&self) {
        self.count.fetch_sub(1, Ordering::SeqCst);
    }

    fn get_count(&self) -> usize {
        self.count.load(Ordering::SeqCst)
    }
}
```

In this example, we use the `AtomicUsize` type from the `std::sync::atomic` module to safely manage the count. We implement the `Sync` trait for `Counter` by using the `unsafe` keyword. This tells Rust that we have manually ensured the safety for concurrent access to `Counter`.

Unsafe Code and the Fucking FFI

Another area where unsafe Rust shines is when you need to interface with code written in other languages, such as C or C++. The Foreign Function Interface (FFI) allows you to call functions and work with data from these languages in Rust.

To work with the FFI, you'll need to use unsafe Rust, as there are no guarantees about the safety of the external code.

Here is an example of using unsafe Rust for FFI:

```rust
extern "C" {
    fn some\_c_function(arg: i32) -> i32;
}

unsafe {
    let result = some\_c_function(42);
    println!("Result from C function: {}", result);
}
```

In this example, we use the `extern` keyword to declare a foreign function `some_c_function`. We then wrap the call to the foreign function inside an `unsafe` block, acknowledging that we're dealing with unsafe code.

Fucking Building Blocks: Unsafe Rust Libraries

Unsafe Rust is also essential for building lower-level libraries that provide more control and flexibility to the users. These libraries expose safe APIs while relying on unsafe Rust internally to implement the low-level functionality. This separation of concerns allows users to enjoy the safety of safe Rust code while providing power and performance through unsafe Rust.

When designing an unsafe Rust library, it's crucial to carefully document the unsafe parts and provide the necessary guidance to prevent misuse. Clear examples, explanations, and warnings about potential pitfalls should be provided to help users understand the inherent risks and responsibilities associated with using the library.

Conclusion

Unsafe Rust is a powerful tool that gives you the freedom to write low-level code with ultimate control and efficiency. However, it comes with significant risks and responsibilities. When using unsafe Rust, remember to be fucking cautious, be fucking responsible, and always double-check that your code upholds the safety guarantees that Rust normally enforces.

In the next chapter, we will explore asynchronous programming with fucking futures, allowing you to build concurrent and responsive applications in Rust. Get ready to take your fucking Rust skills to the next level!

Asynchronous Programming with Fucking Futures

Understanding Fucking Async/Await

In this section, we will delve into the concept of fucking async/await in Rust and understand how it enables asynchronous programming. We will explore the benefits of using fucking futures and see how they simplify writing concurrent operations. Finally, we will build fucking async applications and leverage the power of async/await in Rust.

Introduction to Fucking Async/Await

Asynchronous programming allows you to write code that doesn't block the execution of other code. It enables you to perform multiple tasks simultaneously without waiting for each task to complete before moving on to the next one. Fucking async/await is a powerful feature introduced in Rust that makes writing asynchronous code more readable and manageable.

With fucking async/await, you can write asynchronous code in a way that looks like synchronous code. It allows you to write functions that can pause their execution while waiting for an asynchronous operation to complete. This makes your code easier to read and reason about, without the complexity of explicit callbacks or custom async abstractions.

Fundamentals of Fucking Futures

Before we dive deeper into fucking async/await, let's understand the concept of fucking futures. A fucking future represents a value that may not be available immediately, but will be available in the future. It is a fundamental abstraction in Rust for representing asynchronous computations.

A fucking future can be thought of as a promise for a value. It represents the result of an asynchronous operation, such as reading from a file, making a network request, or performing a database query. When the operation completes, the fucking future resolves to a value or an error.

Fucking futures provide a unified API for working with asynchronous operations. They enable you to compose, transform, and combine asynchronous operations using combinators and operators. This allows you to build complex asynchronous workflows in a concise and expressive manner.

Syntax and Usage of Fucking Async/Await

In Rust, you can define asynchronous functions using the 'async' keyword. An asynchronous function can contain one or more 'await' expressions, which pause the execution of the function until the result of an asynchronous operation is available. The 'await' keyword can only be used within an asynchronous context, such as an asynchronous function or an asynchronous block.

Let's take a look at an example to understand the syntax and usage of fucking async/await:

```rust
async fn fetch\_data(url: \&str) -> Result<String, reqwes
    let response = reqwest::get(url).await?;
    response.text().await
}
```

In the above example, we define an asynchronous function 'fetch_data' that fetches data from a given URL using the 'reqwest' crate. The 'await' keyword is used to pause the execution of the function until the response is available.

To call an asynchronous function, you also need to be in an asynchronous context. This means that the calling function or block needs to be marked as 'async' as well. Here's an example of how to call the 'fetch_data' function:

```rust
\#[tokio::main]
async fn main() {
    match fetch\_data("https://example.com").await {
        Ok(data) => println!("Data: {}", data),
        Err(error) => println!("Error: {}", error),
    }
}
```

In the above example, we define the 'main' function as an asynchronous function using the 'async' keyword. We use the 'tokio' crate's 'main' macro to run the asynchronous code. We call the 'fetch_data' function using the 'await' keyword and handle the result accordingly.

Error Handling and Propagation

Fucking async/await also simplifies error handling and propagation in asynchronous code. When an asynchronous function returns a fucking future that resolves to a result, you can use the '¿' operator just like in synchronous code to propagate errors.

ASYNCHRONOUS PROGRAMMING WITH FUCKING FUTURES

If an error occurs during the execution of an asynchronous operation, the fucking future returned by the operation will resolve to an 'Err' variant. You can use the '?' operator to handle the error in a concise manner and propagate it up the call stack. Here's an updated version of the 'fetch_data' function that demonstrates error handling and propagation using fucking async/await:

```
async fn fetch\_data(url: \&str) -> Result<String, reqwest
    let response = reqwest::get(url).await?;
    response.text().await.map_err(Into::into)
}
```

In the above example, we use the '?' operator to handle the potential error returned by 'reqwest::get(url).await'. If an error occurs, the function will immediately return the 'Err' variant, propagating the error to the caller.

Building Fucking Async Applications

Now that we have a good understanding of fucking async/await, let's explore how we can build asynchronous applications using Rust. Asynchronous programming is particularly useful in scenarios where you have to perform I/O-bound or CPU-bound operations that can benefit from concurrent execution. Rust provides several libraries and crates that make it easier to build asynchronous applications. Some popular libraries and crates include:

- **Tokio:** A runtime for asynchronous programming in Rust that provides a powerful set of tools and abstractions.

- **Actix:** A powerful actor framework for building asynchronous, event-driven applications.

- **async-std:** A lightweight async runtime that provides similar functionality to Tokio.

- **Futures:** A library that provides asynchronous programming tools and abstractions, including fucking futures.

When building asynchronous applications, it's important to keep in mind that fucking async/await is not a silver bullet. It's important to understand the underlying principles and trade-offs of asynchronous programming. Always consider the performance implications and choose the appropriate abstractions and libraries for your specific use cases.

Conclusion

In this section, we explored the concept of fucking async/await in Rust and how it enables asynchronous programming. We learned about the fundamentals of fucking futures and how they represent asynchronous computations. We also delved into the syntax and usage of fucking async/await, including error handling and propagation. Finally, we discussed building fucking async applications and explored some popular libraries and crates for asynchronous programming in Rust. Fucking async/await is a powerful feature that makes writing asynchronous code more readable and manageable. It allows you to write code that looks synchronous but executes asynchronously, enabling you to build high-performance and concurrent applications in Rust. So embrace the power of fucking async/await and take your Rust programming to the next fucking level!

Using Fucking Futures for Concurrent Operations

Concurrency is a fucking powerful concept in programming that allows you to perform multiple tasks simultaneously. In Rust, one of the most effective ways to handle concurrency is by using fucking futures.

A future is a Rust type that represents an asynchronous operation. It is like a promise that something will happen in the future. Futures allow you to write asynchronous code that is more efficient and responsive compared to traditional synchronous code.

Why Fucking Use Futures?

There are several reasons why you should consider using futures for concurrent operations in Rust:

1. **Efficiency:** Futures enable you to effectively utilize CPU resources by executing multiple tasks concurrently. This can dramatically improve the performance and responsiveness of your application.

2. **Scalability:** With futures, you can easily scale your application to handle a large number of concurrent operations. It provides a flexible and powerful foundation for building highly scalable systems.

3. **Composability:** Futures can be chained, combined, and composed to create complex workflows without blocking the execution. This composability allows you to build asynchronous pipelines that are easy to reason about and maintain.

4. **Error Handling:** Futures provide a robust error handling mechanism. You can propagate and handle errors in a structured and ergonomic way, making your code more reliable and less prone to bugs.

Fucking Creating Futures

In Rust, there are multiple ways to create futures. The most common method is to use the `futures` crate, which provides a rich set of combinators and utilities for working with futures.

To create a future, you can use the `async` keyword along with the `async_block` macro, which allows you to define an asynchronous block of code. Here's an example:

```rust
use\index{use} futures::future\index{future}::ready;

async fn fetch\_data(url: String) -> Result<String, Box<dy
    // ... code to fetch data from the URL ...
}

fn main() {
    let future = async {
        let data = fetch\_data("https://example.com".to\_s
        println!("Fetched data: {}", data);
        Ok(())
    };

    // Execute the future
    tokio::runtime::Runtime::new()
        .unwrap()
        .block_on(future);
}
```

In this example, the `fetch_data` function returns a `Result<String, Box<dyn std::error::Error>>` future. The `future` variable represents the composed future that fetches data and prints it. Finally, the `block_on` method from the `tokio` crate is used to execute the future.

Fucking Composing Futures

One of the powerful features of futures is the ability to combine and compose them into more complex workflows. This allows you to create sophisticated concurrent operations without blocking the execution. The `futures` crate provides a variety of combinators to compose futures. Some commonly used ones include:

- `and_then`: Chains multiple futures together, running them sequentially.
- `map`: Applies a function to the output of a future.
- `map_err`: Applies a function to the error of a future.
- `join`: Runs multiple futures concurrently and collects all their results.
- `select`: Runs multiple futures concurrently and returns the result of the first completed future.

Let's see an example that demonstrates the composition of futures:

```rust
use futures::future::{ready, join};

async fn fetch_data1() -> u32 {
    // ... code to fetch data from source 1 ...
}

async fn fetch_data2() -> String {
    // ... code to fetch data from source 2 ...
}

async fn process_data(data1: u32, data2: String) -> Res
    // ... process the fetched data ...
}

fn main() {
    let future = async {
        let data1 = fetch_data1().await;
        let data2 = fetch_data2().await;
        process_data(data1, data2).await?;
        Ok(())
```

```rust
    };

    // Execute the future
    tokio::runtime::Runtime::new()
        .unwrap()
        .block_on(future);
}
```

In this example, the fetch_data1 and fetch_data2 functions return futures that fetch data from different sources. The process_data function takes the fetched data and processes it. Finally, all the futures are composed together in the future variable.

Fucking Error Handling with Futures

Error handling in concurrent operations is crucial to ensure the reliability and stability of your application. Fortunately, Rust provides a robust error handling mechanism for futures.

When working with futures, you can use the Result type to handle errors. If a future returns an error, it can be propagated to the calling future or handled using combinators like map_err.

Here's an example that demonstrates error handling with futures:

```rust
use futures::future::{ready, ok};

async fn fetch_data() -> Result<String, String> {
    Err("Failed to fetch data".to_string())
}

async fn process_data(data: Result<String, String>) -> Re
    let data = data?;
    println!("Fetched data: {}", data);
    Ok(())
}

fn main() {
    let future = async {
        let data = fetch_data().await?;
        process_data(Ok(data)).await?;
        Ok(())
```

```rust
    };

    // Execute the future
    tokio::runtime::Runtime::new()
        .unwrap()
        .block_on(future);
}
```

In this example, the `fetch_data` function returns a `Result<String, String>` future that intentionally fails. The `process_data` function takes the result of the previous future and processes it. The `?` operator is used to propagate the error or unwrap the value.

Fucking Implementing Concurrency with Tokio

In Rust, the `tokio` crate is widely used for implementing asynchronous and concurrent operations based on futures. It provides a powerful runtime that manages the execution of concurrent tasks.

To use `tokio`, you need to add it as a dependency in your `Cargo.toml` file:

```toml
[dependencies]
tokio = { version = "1", features = ["macros"] }
```

Here's an example that demonstrates concurrent operations using `tokio`:

```rust
use std::time::Duration;
use tokio::time::delay_for;

async fn task1() {
    println!("Task 1 started");
    delay_for(Duration::from_secs(1)).await;
    println!("Task 1 completed");
}

async fn task2() {
    println!("Task 2 started");
    delay_for(Duration::from_secs(2)).await;
    println!("Task 2 completed");
}

fn main() {
```

```rust
    let future = async {
        let t1 = tokio::spawn(task1());
        let t2 = tokio::spawn(task2());
        tokio::try\_join!(t1, t2).unwrap();
    };

    // Execute the future
    tokio::runtime::Runtime::new()
        .unwrap()
        .block_on(future);
}
```

In this example, the `task1` and `task2` functions represent two concurrent tasks. The `tokio::spawn` method is used to spawn these tasks, and the `try_join!` macro is used to combine the tasks and wait for their completion.

Fucking Conclusion

Using futures for concurrent operations in Rust allows you to write efficient, scalable, and composable asynchronous code. It provides a robust error handling mechanism and enables you to build high-performance applications. In this section, we introduced the concept of futures, demonstrated how to create and compose them, and explained error handling with futures. We also explored the `tokio` crate, which is widely used for implementing concurrency in Rust. Now that you understand the basics of using fucking futures for concurrent operations, it's time to dive deeper into other advanced Rust concepts. Keep fucking learning and exploring, and remember, Rust is all about safe, fast, and fucking secure programming!

Building Fucking Async Applications

Now that you have a solid understanding of asynchronous programming and futures in Rust, it's time to put that knowledge to use and start building some fucking async applications. In this section, we will explore various techniques and tools for building robust and efficient async applications in Rust.

Using Fucking Async/Await

Asynchronous programming in Rust has become much simpler and more intuitive with the introduction of the 'async' and 'await' keywords. The 'async' keyword is used to define an asynchronous function, while the 'await' keyword is used to suspend the execution of the function until a future completes. To demonstrate the power of async/await in Rust, let's consider a common real-world example: fetching data from a remote API. We can use the 'reqwest' crate, which provides a convenient API for making HTTP requests.

```rust
use\index{use} reqwest\index{reqwest}::Error;

async fn fetch\_data(url: \&str) -> Result<String, Error:
    let response = reqwest::get(url).await?;
    response.text().await
}


\#[tokio::main]
async fn main() -> Result<(), Error> {
    let url = ``https://api.example.com/data";
    let data = fetch\_data(url).await?;
    println!("{}", data);
    Ok(())
}
```

In this example, the 'fetch_data' function is defined as an asynchronous function that uses the 'reqwest::get' function to fetch data from a given URL. We use the 'await' keyword to await the completion of the HTTP request and obtain the response. Finally, the response body is extracted using the 'text' method. The 'tokio::main' attribute is used to define the entry point of the application and runs the async main function. It is provided by the Tokio runtime, which is a widely used async runtime for Rust.

Using Fucking Futures for Concurrent Operations

Async/await makes it easy to write asynchronous code, but sometimes you need to perform multiple concurrent operations and wait for all of them to complete. Rust provides a powerful abstraction called 'Futures' to handle such scenarios.

The 'Futures' crate provides combinators that allow you to compose multiple futures into a single future that completes when all the inner futures complete. One such combinator is 'join_all', which takes a collection of futures and returns a future that completes when all the inner futures complete.

Let's consider an example where we need to fetch data from multiple APIs concurrently:

ASYNCHRONOUS PROGRAMMING WITH FUCKING FUTURES

```rust
use futures::executor::block_on;
use reqwest::Error;

async fn fetch_data(url: &str) -> Result<String, Error> {
    let response = reqwest::get(url).await?;
    response.text().await
}

async fn fetch_all_data(urls: Vec<&str>) -> Vec<Result<S
    let fetch_futures = urls.iter().map(|url| fetch_data
    futures::future::join_all(fetch_futures).await
}

fn main() {
    let urls = vec![
        "https://api1.example.com/data",
        "https://api2.example.com/data",
        "https://api3.example.com/data",
    ];
    let results = block_on(fetch_all_data(urls));

    for result in results {
        match result {
            Ok(data) => println!("{}", data),
            Err(error) => eprintln!("Error: {}", error),
        }
    }
}
```

In this example, the 'fetch_all_data' function takes a vector of URLs and uses the 'fetch_data' function to create a collection of futures. The 'join_all' combinator is then used to wait for all the futures to complete. The function returns a vector of results that can be processed individually.

The 'main' function uses the 'block_on' function from the 'futures' crate to block the current thread until the async code is complete. This is necessary because the 'main' function cannot be marked as 'async'. Finally, the results are printed to the console.

Building Fucking Async Applications

Building asynchronous applications often requires more than just fetching data from APIs. In many cases, you'll need to handle events, perform I/O operations, or wait for timers to fire. Rust provides libraries and frameworks that can help you build powerful async applications.

One such framework is 'actix', a high-performance actor framework for Rust. Actix allows you to build concurrent, asynchronous, and fault-tolerant applications with ease. It provides abstractions for handling HTTP requests, managing state, and distributing workloads across multiple threads.

Let's take a look at a simple example of building a web server using the Actix framework:

```rust
use actix_web::{get, web, App, HttpResponse, HttpServer,

\#[get("/")]
async fn index() -> impl Responder {
    HttpResponse::Ok().body("Hello, world!")
}

\#[actix_web::main]
async fn main() -> std::io::Result<()> {
    HttpServer::new(|| {
        App::new()
            .service(index)
    })
    .bind("127.0.0.1:8080")?
    .run()
    .await
}
```

In this example, we define a 'get' handler function called 'index' that returns a static response. We use the 'actix_web' crate to define the HTTP routes and run the server. The 'main' function sets up an Actix HTTP server on 'localhost:8080' and runs it asynchronously.

Actix allows you to scale your applications easily by handling thousands of concurrent connections efficiently. It also provides powerful features such as request routing, middleware, and WebSocket support.

Fucking Async Applications: Real-World Examples

To give you a taste of what you can build with async applications in Rust, let's explore a few real-world examples:

1. **Chat Application:** Build a chat application using Actix and WebSocket communication. Allow users to send and receive messages in real-time.

2. **Web Scraping:** Use async libraries like 'reqwest' and 'scraper' to scrape data from websites. Perform multiple concurrent requests and extract information asynchronously.

3. **Real-Time Analytics:** Build a real-time analytics dashboard using Actix and a database like PostgreSQL. Track and visualize data in real-time as it arrives from various sources.

These examples demonstrate the power and versatility of async applications in Rust. With the right tools and libraries, you can build high-performance, scalable, and fault-tolerant systems.

Summary

In this section, we explored the process of building async applications in Rust. We learned how to use async/await to write asynchronous code, work with futures for concurrent operations, and build async applications using frameworks like Actix. We also discussed real-world examples of async applications to inspire you to explore further.

Asynchronous programming in Rust allows you to build efficient, scalable, and responsive applications. By embracing async/await and utilizing the powerful tools and libraries available, you can take full advantage of Rust's strengths in building modern software. So go ahead, embrace the fucking async world of Rust and build some amazing applications!

Interfacing with Other Languages in Fucking Rust

Writing Fucking Foreign Function Interfaces (FFIs)

In this section, we will dive into the fascinating world of writing Fucking Foreign Function Interfaces (FFIs) in Rust. FFIs allow us to seamlessly integrate Rust code with code written in other programming languages, enabling us to take full advantage of the language's safety and performance benefits in a wider ecosystem. Whether you want to integrate with C/C++ libraries or even call JavaScript code from Rust, FFIs are the way to fucking go!

Understanding FFIs

Before we get started, let's quickly go over what the fuck an FFI is. In simple terms, an FFI is a set of rules and tools that enable different programming languages to call each other's functions and share data. It's like a universal fucking translator for programming languages.

When it comes to Rust, FFIs provide a way to interact with code written in other languages while maintaining Rust's key features, such as memory safety and zero-cost abstractions. This means we can use Rust as a powerful glue language that brings safety and performance to the table while integrating seamlessly with existing codebases.

The Basics of FFI in Rust

To write an FFI in Rust, we need to follow a set of conventions and annotations. Let's walk through the key steps involved in writing an FFI.

1. Define an External Function The first step is to define a function in Rust that will be accessible from other languages. We do this by using the `extern` keyword and specifying the C calling convention. Here's an example:

```rust
#[no_mangle]
pub extern "C" fn add(a: i32, b: i32) -> i32 {
    a + b
}
```

In this example, the `add` function takes two `i32` arguments and returns their sum as an `i32`. The `#[no_mangle]` attribute disables the Rust compiler's name mangling, ensuring that the function name remains unchanged in the generated binary.

2. Linking with Other Languages To make our Rust code callable from other languages, we need to generate a dynamic or static library that can be linked with the target language. We can do this by adding the following lines to our `Cargo.toml` file:

INTERFACING WITH OTHER LANGUAGES IN FUCKING RUST

```
[lib]
crate-type = ["cdylib"]
```

This configuration tells Cargo to build a dynamic library (.dll, .dylib, or .so) that can be linked with other languages.

3. Writing Language Bindings Language bindings act as a bridge between Rust and other programming languages. They provide an interface that allows calling Rust functions from the target language.

For example, when integrating with C code, we need to write a C header file (.h) that declares the Rust functions we want to call. Here's an example of the C header file for our add function:

```c
#ifndef ADD_H
#define ADD_H

extern int add(int a, int b);

#endif
```

With this header file, other programming languages can include it to call the add function as if it were a native C function.

4. Calling Rust Functions from Other Languages Once we have our Rust code and language bindings set up, we can call our Rust functions from other programming languages.

For example, in C, we can include the generated header file and call the add function like this:

```c
#include "add.h"
#include <stdio.h>

int main() {
    int result = add(2, 3);
    printf("Result: %d\n", result);
    return 0;
}
```

By making use of FFIs in Rust, we can integrate with other languages seamlessly, opening up a world of possibilities to leverage existing libraries, frameworks, and APIs.

Tips and Tricks for Writing FFIs

Writing FFIs can be a complex task, but there are a few tips and tricks that can make your life easier:

1. Handle Data Types and Conversions Different programming languages have different data types. When writing an FFI, it's crucial to handle data type conversions correctly. Rust provides convenient functions and types, such as From and Into, to help with these conversions. Make sure to understand how data types are represented in both Rust and the target language to avoid unexpected behavior.

2. Consider Memory Management When working with FFIs, it's essential to consider memory management. Rust's ownership model doesn't directly translate to all programming languages. For example, if you're calling Rust functions from C, you need to be mindful of allocating and deallocating memory correctly.

3. Test with Different Programming Languages To ensure the correctness and compatibility of your FFI implementation, it's crucial to create tests that cover various use cases. Test your FFI code with different programming languages and scenarios to catch any potential issues or bugs.

4. Leverage Existing Tools and Libraries The Rust ecosystem provides various tools and libraries that can simplify the process of writing FFIs. For example, the libc crate provides Rust bindings to the C standard library. Utilize these resources to save time and effort.

Conclusion

In this section, we explored the exciting world of Fucking Foreign Function Interfaces (FFIs) in Rust. We learned how FFIs allow us to seamlessly integrate Rust code with other programming languages, enabling us to leverage Rust's safety and performance benefits in a wider ecosystem.

We covered the basics of writing an FFI in Rust, including defining external functions, linking with other languages, writing language bindings, and calling

INTERFACING WITH OTHER LANGUAGES IN FUCKING RUST   105

Rust functions from other languages. We also shared some tips and tricks to make your FFI implementation smoother and more robust.
Now that you understand the fundamentals of FFIs in Rust, you can confidently incorporate Rust into projects that require interoperability with other programming languages. So go forth and unleash the fucking power of Rust in the multilingual world of software development!

Integrating with C/C++ Libraries

One of the greatest strengths of Rust is its ability to seamlessly integrate with existing C and C++ libraries. This allows Rust developers to leverage the vast ecosystem of well-established and battle-tested libraries, while still benefiting from Rust's safety and performance guarantees. In this section, we will explore the principles and techniques involved in integrating Rust with C and C++ libraries.

The Foreign Function Interface (FFI)

The Foreign Function Interface (FFI) is a mechanism that allows different programming languages to call each other's functions and share data. It defines a set of rules and conventions for passing arguments, returning values, and handling memory allocation between different languages. Rust's FFI enables seamless interoperability with C and C++ code, making it possible to call C/C++ functions from Rust and vice versa.

To integrate with a C or C++ library in Rust, you typically need to perform the following steps:

1. **Declare function prototypes:** Rust needs to know the function signatures of the C/C++ functions you want to use. You can declare these function prototypes using the `extern` keyword in a Rust module.

2. **Link against the library:** Rust provides a `libc` crate that allows you to link against C libraries. You can specify the C/C++ library you want to link with in your `Cargo.toml` file, and Rust's build system (`cargo`) will take care of the details.

3. **Call C/C++ functions from Rust:** Once you have declared the function prototypes and linked against the library, you can call the C/C++ functions as if they were regular Rust functions. Rust will handle the translation of data types and memory management behind the scenes.

4. **Pass data between Rust and C/C++:** When passing data between Rust and C/C++, it is crucial to ensure memory safety. Rust provides types like `CStr` and `CString` to safely handle C-style strings, while Rust's `repr` attribute allows you to control the memory layout of Rust structs to match C/C++ data structures.

5. **Handle error conditions:** C and C++ libraries often use error codes and exceptions to handle error conditions. Rust's `Result` and `panic` mechanisms allow you to handle C/C++ errors in a safe and idiomatic way.

Example: Integrating with a C Library

Let's walk through an example of integrating Rust with a C library called `libexample`. This library provides a function called `calculate_sum` that takes an array of integers and returns their sum.

First, we need to declare the function prototype. In Rust, we can do this using the `extern` keyword:

```
extern ``C'' {
    fn calculate\_sum(numbers: *const i32, count: usize) -> i32;
}
```

Next, we need to link against the `libexample` library in our `Cargo.toml` file:

```
[dependencies]
libc = ``0.2"
```

Now, we can call the `calculate_sum` function from Rust:

```
use libc::{c_int, c_void};

fn main() {
    let numbers = vec![1, 2, 3, 4, 5];
    let sum = unsafe { calculate\_sum(numbers.as\_ptr(), numbers
    println!("Sum: {}", sum);
}

extern ``C'' {
    fn calculate\_sum(numbers: *const c_int, count: usize) -> c_:
}
```

INTERFACING WITH OTHER LANGUAGES IN FUCKING RUST

In this example, we use the `libc` crate to define the C-compatible types `c_int` and `c_void`. We mark the `calculate_sum` function as `unsafe` because it calls into a C function that is not guaranteed to be memory-safe. With this integration, we can seamlessly call the C function `calculate_sum` from Rust and handle the result in an idiomatic way.

Caveats and Considerations

While integrating Rust with C/C++ libraries opens up new possibilities, there are some caveats and considerations to keep in mind:

- **Memory Safety**: Rust's safety guarantees only apply within the Rust code. When calling C/C++ code, you need to ensure that the code is memory-safe and does not violate Rust's borrowing and ownership rules.

- **Name Mangling**: C++ compilers often perform name mangling, which changes the names of C++ functions to include additional information about their types and parameters. When integrating with C++ libraries, you may need to take this into account and use the mangled names in your Rust code.

- **ABI Compatibility**: The Application Binary Interface (ABI) defines how functions and data are represented and accessed at a low level. It is essential to ensure that the Rust code and the C/C++ library use compatible ABIs to avoid runtime errors or crashes.

- **Error Handling**: C and C++ libraries often use error codes or exceptions for error handling. When integrating with Rust, it is important to handle these errors in a safe and idiomatic way, using Rust's `Result` type or panics.

Resources and Further Reading

Integration with C/C++ libraries is a vast topic, and there is much more to explore. Here are some resources and further reading to deepen your understanding:

- *The Rust FFI Omnibus* - A collection of examples and explanations of common FFI patterns and techniques in Rust. Available at `https://jakegoulding.com/rust-ffi-omnibus/`.

- *Rust Unofficial Book: Foreign Function Interface* - An in-depth guide on how to interface Rust with C and C++ libraries. Available at `https://doc.rust-lang.org/unstable-book/ffi.html`.

- *Rust Reference: Interoperability with C* - Official Rust documentation on how to interface with C code. Available at https://doc.rust-lang.org/reference/items/external-blocks.html.

- *The Rustonomicon: Sharing with C* - The Rustonomicon is a collection of documentation on advanced topics in Rust. This chapter specifically covers sharing and interoperating with C code. Available at https://doc.rust-lang.org/nomicon/ffi.html.

- *The C++ ABI: A Summary* - A detailed guide on C++ ABIs and their implications for interoperability with other languages. Available at https://itanium-cxx-abi.github.io/cxx-abi/.

Conclusion

Integrating Rust with C/C++ libraries opens up a whole world of possibilities, allowing you to leverage existing code and benefit from Rust's safety and performance. By understanding the principles of the Foreign Function Interface (FFI) and following the proper techniques, you can seamlessly call C/C++ functions from Rust and vice versa. As you dive deeper into Rust development, mastering FFI integration will become an invaluable tool in your arsenal. Remember, integrating with C/C++ libraries requires careful consideration of memory safety, name mangling, ABI compatibility, and error handling. With the right approach and understanding, you can successfully bridge the gap between Rust and the rich ecosystem of C and C++ libraries. So go forth, integrate fearlessly, and build amazing applications!

Fucking Rust and Web Assembly (WASM)

In this section, we will explore the exciting combination of Rust and Web Assembly (WASM). Web Assembly is a binary instruction format that allows high-performance code to run in web browsers. It provides a way to write efficient, low-level code that can be executed on various platforms, including the web. By compiling Rust code to Web Assembly, we can leverage the power and safety of Rust while running it in the browser environment.

How Rust and Web Assembly Work Fucking Together

To understand how Rust and Web Assembly work together, let's start with a brief overview of Web Assembly. Web Assembly is designed to be a low-level target for

INTERFACING WITH OTHER LANGUAGES IN FUCKING RUST

programming languages, enabling them to run at near-native speeds. It defines a compact binary format that is executed by a virtual machine in the browser. Rust, with its focus on safety and performance, is an ideal language for generating Web Assembly. The Rust compiler can produce compact and optimized Web Assembly code that runs efficiently in the browser. Additionally, Rust's strict memory management and strong typing system ensure that the generated Web Assembly code is safe and secure.

When compiling Rust code to Web Assembly, the Rust compiler translates the code into a low-level representation called LLVM Intermediate Representation (IR). This IR is then passed through the Emscripten toolchain, which converts the IR into Web Assembly bytecode. Finally, the resulting bytecode can be executed in the browser using a Web Assembly virtual machine.

Benefits of Fucking Rust and Web Assembly

Utilizing Rust and Web Assembly offers several advantages for web development. Firstly, Rust's focus on memory safety and zero-cost abstractions prevents common bugs like null pointer dereferences and buffer overflows, making the resulting Web Assembly code more secure and less prone to vulnerabilities.

Secondly, Rust's performance characteristics make it an excellent choice for resource-intensive applications. By compiling Rust code to Web Assembly, we can leverage the performance benefits of Rust in the browser, providing a smooth and responsive user experience.

Additionally, Rust's cargo package manager and the Web Assembly ecosystem has matured significantly in recent years. This means that you can easily integrate existing Rust libraries and frameworks into your Web Assembly projects. You can leverage the growing ecosystem and community support to build powerful and feature-rich web applications.

Getting Fucking Started with Rust and Web Assembly

Before diving into Rust and Web Assembly, you need to set up your development environment. Ensure that you have Rust and the necessary Web Assembly tools installed. You may also need to install additional dependencies, like Emscripten, if you're planning to use it in your workflow.

Once you have the development environment set up, you can start writing Rust code that targets Web Assembly. The syntax and semantics of Rust code targeting Web Assembly are the same as regular Rust code with a few additional annotations for interfacing with JavaScript APIs.

To compile your Rust code to Web Assembly, you can use the 'wasm-pack' tool. This tool simplifies the process of building, testing, and publishing your Web Assembly code. It creates a package that can be easily consumed by JavaScript applications.

Integrating Fucking JavaScript and Rust

While Web Assembly allows you to run Rust code in the browser, you will often need to interact with JavaScript to access browser APIs, manipulate the DOM, or handle user interactions. Rust provides excellent support for integrating with JavaScript through Web Assembly.

To interact with JavaScript, Rust provides a Foreign Function Interface (FFI) that allows you to call JavaScript functions from Rust and vice versa. You can define an interface between Rust and JavaScript using the 'wasm-bindgen' library. This library generates the necessary glue code to handle the type conversions and function calls between the two languages.

With the 'wasm-bindgen' library, you can seamlessly pass data between Rust and JavaScript, allowing you to leverage the strengths of both languages. For example, you can write the performance-critical parts of your application in Rust, while handling the user interface and other high-level functionality in JavaScript.

Real-World Examples of Fucking Rust and Web Assembly

Rust and Web Assembly have been used in various real-world examples to demonstrate their power and versatility. Here are a few examples:

- **Video and Image Processing**: Rust's performance and low-level control make it an excellent choice for video and image processing applications. By compiling Rust code to Web Assembly, these applications can run efficiently in the browser, enabling real-time processing of multimedia content.

- **Game Development**: Rust's safety guarantees and high performance make it a compelling language for game development. By targeting Web Assembly, you can build games that run directly in the browser without the need for plugins or additional installations.

- **Data Visualization:** Rust's speed and efficient memory management make it ideal for data-intensive applications. By leveraging Web Assembly, you can create interactive and visually appealing data visualizations that can be seamlessly integrated into web applications.

INTERFACING WITH OTHER LANGUAGES IN FUCKING RUST

These examples highlight the versatility of Rust and Web Assembly in various domains and showcase the potential of this powerful combination.

Conclusion

Rust and Web Assembly provide a powerful and secure combination for web development. By leveraging Rust's performance and safety features, you can build high-performance applications that run efficiently in the browser. The integration with JavaScript through Web Assembly allows you to leverage the existing web ecosystem while taking advantage of Rust's powerful abstractions and memory safety guarantees.

In the next chapter, we will explore advanced concepts in Rust, including advanced data structures, asynchronous programming, and web development with Rust frameworks. So strap in, because we're about to dive deeper into the wild world of Rust programming.

Calling Fucking JavaScript from Rust

In this section, we will learn how to call JavaScript code from Rust. This can be incredibly useful when developing applications that require interaction with web technologies, such as manipulating the DOM or accessing browser APIs. Rust provides seamless integration with JavaScript through WebAssembly, allowing us to combine the performance and safety of Rust with the flexibility and interactivity of JavaScript.

The Fucking WebAssembly (WASM) Runtime

Before diving into calling JavaScript from Rust, let's briefly understand how WebAssembly works. WebAssembly is a low-level bytecode format that runs in a sandboxed environment within the browser. It provides a compact and efficient way to execute code written in languages other than JavaScript.

The JavaScript runtime environment provides a mechanism for executing WebAssembly modules. This mechanism is known as the WebAssembly runtime. The runtime environment consists of a set of APIs that allow JavaScript and WebAssembly to communicate with each other.

To call JavaScript functions from Rust, we need to use the functions provided by the WebAssembly runtime. These functions enable us to interact with the JavaScript environment by invoking JavaScript functions and accessing JavaScript variables.

Using Fucking js-sys Crate

In Rust, we can use the 'js-sys' crate to interact with JavaScript. This crate provides type-safe bindings to the WebAssembly runtime APIs and allows us to call JavaScript code from Rust.

To use the 'js-sys' crate, we need to add it as a dependency in our 'Cargo.toml' file:

```
[dependencies]
js-sys = "`0.3"
```

Now, let's take a look at an example of how to call a JavaScript function from Rust using the 'js-sys' crate.

Example: Calling a JavaScript Alert

Suppose we have a JavaScript function called 'alertMessage' defined in an HTML file. This function displays an alert dialog with a given message. Our goal is to call this JavaScript function from Rust.

First, we need to import the necessary types from the 'js-sys' crate:

```rust
use js_sys::Function;
use wasm_bindgen::JsValue;
```

Next, we can define a Rust function called 'call_alert' that calls the 'alertMessage' JavaScript function:

```rust
fn call_alert(message: &str) {
    let window = web_sys::window().unwrap();
    let document = window.document().unwrap();
    let alert_func = document.get_element_by_id("alertMessage")
    let alert_func = alert_func.dyn_ref::<Function>().unwrap();
    let message = JsValue::from_str(message);
    alert_func.call1(&JsValue::null(), &message).unwrap();
}
```

In this code snippet, we first obtain a reference to the current window and document using the 'web-sys' crate. Then, we retrieve the JavaScript function element by its 'id' using the 'get_element_by_id' method. After converting it to a 'Function' reference, we can call it using the 'call1' method, passing a null receiver and the message as an argument.

Now, we can call the 'call_alert' function to display an alert from Rust:

```
fn main() {
    call\_alert("Hello from Rust!");
}
```

By running this code, we will see an alert dialog with the message "Hello from Rust!" displayed in the browser.

Fucking Caveats and Limitations

Although calling JavaScript from Rust provides great power and flexibility, there are a few things to keep in mind:

- Fucking Performance: Calling JavaScript from Rust incurs some performance overhead due to the need for cross-language communication. If performance is critical, consider minimizing the number of interlanguage calls.

- Fucking Error Handling: When calling JavaScript functions from Rust, it's important to handle errors gracefully. Errors can occur if the JavaScript function does not exist or if there are issues with the arguments passed.

- Fucking Security: Be cautious when calling JavaScript code from Rust, as it can introduce security vulnerabilities if not properly validated. Always sanitize and validate inputs to prevent code injection attacks.

- Fucking Compatibility: Ensure that the JavaScript code you intend to call is supported by the target browsers or runtime environments. Some features may not be available or may behave differently depending on the browser or runtime version.

Summary

In this section, we learned how to call JavaScript functions from Rust using the 'js-sys' crate. We explored the underlying WebAssembly runtime and its APIs that facilitate the interaction between JavaScript and Rust. We also discussed some caveats and limitations to consider when using this approach. Being able to call JavaScript from Rust opens up endless possibilities for developing web applications with the power and safety of Rust. Whether it's manipulating the DOM, accessing browser APIs, or integrating with JavaScript libraries, Rust provides a seamless bridge to the world of web development. So go ahead and unleash the fucking power of Rust in your web projects!

Web Development with Fucking Rust

Building Web APIs with Fucking Rocket Framework

In this section, we will explore how to build web APIs using the Fucking Rocket framework. Web APIs are an essential part of modern web development, allowing different systems to communicate and exchange data. Fucking Rocket is a powerful and expressive web framework written in Rust that simplifies the process of building robust and secure APIs. We will cover the basics of web APIs, demonstrate how to set up a Rocket project, and delve into the key features and functionalities of the framework.

Understanding Web APIs

Before we dive into the specifics of Fucking Rocket, let's take a moment to understand what a web API is and how it works. A web API, or Application Programming Interface, is an interface that allows two software applications to communicate with each other. It enables one application to access and use the functionality or data of another application, often over the internet. Web APIs follow the principles of the Representational State Transfer (REST) architectural style. REST is based on a set of principles for designing networked applications using the HTTP protocol. It emphasizes simple and uniform interfaces, stateless communication, and resource-oriented design. In the context of web APIs, resources are often represented as URLs, and different HTTP methods are used to perform various operations on these resources. Now that we have a basic understanding of web APIs, let's get our hands dirty with Fucking Rocket.

Setting Up a Fucking Rocket Project

To start building web APIs with Fucking Rocket, we first need to set up a project. Here are the steps to follow:

1. Make sure you have Rust and Cargo installed on your system. You can check by running the following command in your terminal:

```
\$ rustc --version \&\& cargo --version
```

WEB DEVELOPMENT WITH FUCKING RUST

If Rust and Cargo are not installed, you can download them from the official Rust website.

2. Create a new Rocket project using Cargo. Open your terminal and run the following command:

   ```
   \$ cargo new rocket-api
   ```

   This command will create a new directory named "rocket-api" and initialize a new Cargo project inside it.

3. Move into the project directory:

   ```
   \$ cd rocket-api
   ```

4. Open the project in your favorite code editor. In the project directory, you will find a file named "Cargo.toml." This file is used to manage project dependencies. Add the following lines to it:

   ```
   [dependencies]
   rocket = ``0.5.0"
   ```

   These lines specify that our project depends on the Fucking Rocket framework.

5. Create a new file named "main.rs" in the project directory. This file will contain our API code. Open it in your code editor.

Congratulations! You have set up a Fucking Rocket project. Now let's move on to building our web API.

Defining API Endpoints

API endpoints define the different operations that can be performed on resources. In Fucking Rocket, we define API endpoints using attributes and functions. Let's start by creating a simple endpoint that returns a "Hello, World!" message. In the "main.rs" file, add the following code:

```
#[get("/")]
fn hello() -> &'static str {
    "Hello, World!"
}
```

In this code snippet, we define a function named "hello" and annotate it with the #[get("/")] attribute. This attribute tells Fucking Rocket that this function is responsible for handling GET requests to the root URL ("/") of our API. The function returns the string "Hello, World!" as the response body.
Now, let's configure the Fucking Rocket server to run our API.

Running the Fucking Rocket Server

To run the Fucking Rocket server and start serving our web API, we need to add a few lines of code at the end of the "main.rs" file. Add the following code:

```
#[launch]
fn rocket() -> _ {
    rocket::build().mount("/", routes![hello])
}
```

In this code snippet, we define the main function named "rocket" and annotate it with the #[launch] attribute. This attribute tells Fucking Rocket that this function is the entry point of our application. Inside the "rocket" function, we use the rocket::build() method to create a new Rocket instance, and then we use the mount() method to mount our "hello" endpoint to the root URL ("/"). Now, let's run our Fucking Rocket server and see our web API in action!
In your terminal, run the following command:

```
$ cargo run
```

This command compiles and runs our Fucking Rocket project. If everything is set up correctly, you should see the following output:

```
Rocket has launched from http://localhost:8000
```

Open your web browser and navigate to http://localhost:8000. You should see the "Hello, World!" message displayed on the screen. Congratulations! You have successfully built a web API using the Fucking Rocket framework.

Enhancing Your Fucking Rocket API

Now that we have a basic understanding of how to build a web API using Fucking Rocket, let's explore some additional features and functionalities provided by the framework.

Handling Request Data APIs often require clients to send data in the request body. Fucking Rocket makes it easy to handle different types of request data, including JSON, form data, and query parameters.

To handle JSON request data, we can use the serde and rocket_contrib crates. Here's an example of how to handle JSON requests:

```
\#[derive(Serialize, Deserialize)]
struct Person {
    name\index{name}: String,
    age: u32,
}

\#[post("/person", data = ``<person>")]
fn create\_person(person: Json<Person>) -> Result<String, String>
    // Process the request data and return a response
}

\#[launch]
fn rocket() -> _ {
    rocket::build().mount("/", routes![create\_person])
}
```

In this code snippet, we define a struct named "Person" using the serde crate's annotations. This struct represents the JSON request body. Then, we define a handler function named "create_person" that takes a parameter of type "Json<Person>". The "Json" type is provided by the rocket_contrib crate and automatically deserializes the JSON request body into the specified struct.

Authentication and Authorization Securing web APIs is crucial to protect sensitive data and prevent unauthorized access. Fucking Rocket provides several mechanisms to handle authentication and authorization. One common approach is to use JSON Web Tokens (JWT) for authentication. JWT is a compact, URL-safe means of representing claims between two parties. Here's an example of how to use JWT authentication in Fucking Rocket:

```
\#[post("/login")]
fn login(credentials: Json<Credentials>) -> Result<String, String
    // Validate credentials and generate JWT token
}

\#[get("/protected")]
fn protected(token: Jwt) -> Result<String, String> {
    // Verify the JWT token and provide access to protected resou
}

\#[launch]
fn rocket() -> _ {
    rocket::build()
        .mount("/", routes![login, protected])
        .attach(Jwt::<Token>::fairing())
}
```

In this code snippet, we define two endpoint functions: "login" and "protected". The "login" function expects JSON credentials in the request body, validates them, and generates a JWT token. The "protected" function requires a valid JWT token to access protected resources.

We use the Jwt fairing provided by Fucking Rocket to handle JWT authentication. The fairing intercepts requests, checks for a valid JWT token, and attaches the token to the request if it is present and valid.

Error Handling Error handling is an integral part of any web API development. Fucking Rocket provides a robust error handling mechanism that allows you to handle errors gracefully.

In Fucking Rocket, you can define custom error types for your API and return them as responses. Here's an example:

```
\#[derive(Debug, PartialEq)]
```

```rust
enum CustomError {
    NotFound,
    InternalServerError,
    // Add more custom error variants
}

#[catch(404)]
fn not_found() -> Json<CustomError> {
    Json(CustomError::NotFound)
}

#[catch(500)]
fn internal_server_error() -> Json<CustomError> {
    Json(CustomError::InternalServerError)
}

#[launch]
fn rocket() -> _ {
    rocket::build()
        .register("/", catchers![not_found, internal_server_err
        .mount("/", routes![...]) // Add your API routes here
}
```

In this code snippet, we define an enum named "CustomError" to represent different types of errors. Then, we define two catcher functions to handle "404 Not Found" and "500 Internal Server Error" responses. These functions return a JSON representation of the custom error type.

By registering the catcher functions using the catchers! macro, Fucking Rocket will automatically handle the corresponding error scenarios based on the status codes.

Conclusion

In this section, we have explored the basics of building web APIs using the Fucking Rocket framework. We started by understanding the concept of web APIs and their role in modern web development. Then, we set up a Fucking Rocket project and built our first API endpoint. We also learned how to enhance our API by handling different types of request data, implementing authentication and authorization, and designing a robust error handling mechanism.

Fucking Rocket provides an expressive and efficient way to build secure and performant web APIs in Rust. With its powerful features and well-designed abstractions, Fucking Rocket is an excellent choice for any Rust developer looking to build modern, reliable, and fucking awesome web APIs.
So what the fuck are you waiting for? Go ahead and start building your own Fucking Rocket-powered APIs and join the legion of developers who are revolutionizing web development with Rust!
Now, let's move on to the next chapter and explore some advanced concepts in Rust.

Frontend Development with Fucking Yew Framework

Frontend development is a vital aspect of modern applications. It involves creating user interfaces and interactive elements that users can directly interact with. In this section, we will delve into frontend development using the Fucking Yew framework, a cutting-edge Rust-based framework for building web applications.

Introduction to Fucking Yew

Fucking Yew is a powerful and intuitive frontend framework that enables developers to build dynamic web applications using Rust. It combines the performance and safety of Rust with the flexibility and interactivity of JavaScript. One of the key advantages of Fucking Yew is its ability to leverage Rust's zero-cost abstractions and strong type system to ensure memory safety and eliminate runtime errors. It achieves this by compiling Rust code to WebAssembly (WASM), a binary format that can run in modern web browsers.

Setting Up a Fucking Yew Project

Before we dive into the development process, let's set up a Fucking Yew project. Follow these steps:

Step 1: Install Required Dependencies Ensure that you have Rust and Cargo (Rust's package manager) installed. You can download them from the official Rust website.

Step 2: Create a New Yew Project Open your terminal and use the following command to create a new Fucking Yew project:

```
cargo new my\_yew_app
```

WEB DEVELOPMENT WITH FUCKING RUST

This command will create a new directory called "my_yew_app" with the basic project structure.

Step 3: Add Fucking Yew as a Dependency Navigate to the project directory:

```
cd my\_yew_app
```

Open the "Cargo.toml" file and add the following lines under the [dependencies] section:

```
[dependencies]
yew = ``0.18.0"
```

Save the file and close it.

Step 4: Build and Run the Project To build and run the project, use the following command:

```
cargo\index{cargo} make run\index{run}
```

This command will compile the Rust code into WebAssembly and start a local development server. You can access your Fucking Yew application by opening a web browser and navigating to "http://localhost:8000".

Components and State Management

In Fucking Yew, components are the building blocks of web applications. They encapsulate HTML, CSS, and JavaScript logic into reusable pieces. Components can have their own state, properties, and lifecycle methods. Let's create a simple counter component using Fucking Yew:

Step 1: Create a New Component Open the "src" directory in your project and create a new file called "counter.rs". Add the following code:

```
use yew::prelude::*;

pub struct Counter {
    count\index{count}: i32,
}

pub enum Msg {
```

```rust
    Increment,
    Decrement,
}

impl Component for Counter {
    type Message = Msg;
    type Properties = ();

    fn create(_: Self::Properties, _: ComponentLink<Self>) -> Sel
        Counter { count: 0 }
    }

    fn update(\&mut self, msg: Self::Message) -> ShouldRender {
        match msg {
            Msg::Increment => {
                self.count += 1;
            }
            Msg::Decrement => {
                self.count -= 1;
            }
        }
        true
    }

    fn view(\&self) -> Html {
        html! {
            <>
                <h2>{ self.count }</h2>
                <button onclick=|_| Msg::Increment>{ ``+1'' }</b
                <button onclick=|_| Msg::Decrement>{ ``-1'' }</b
            </>
        }
    }
}
```

Step 2: Include the Component in the Main Application Open the "src/main.rs" file and modify it as follows:

```rust
use yew::prelude::*;
```

```
mod\index{mod} counter\index{counter};

struct Model {}

enum Msg {}

impl Component for Model {
    type Message = Msg;
    type Properties = ();

    fn create(_: Self::Properties, _: ComponentLink<Self>) -> Self
        Model {}
    }

    fn update(\&mut self, _msg: Self::Message) -> ShouldRender {
        true
    }

    fn view(\&self) -> Html {
        html! {
            <>
                <h1>{"My Fucking Yew Application!"}</h1>
                <counter::Counter />
            </>
        }
    }
}

fn main() {
    yew::start\_app::<Model>();
}
```

Step 3: Compile and Run the Application Save the files and run the application using the following command:

```
cargo\index{cargo} make run\index{run}
```

> Open your web browser and navigate to "http://localhost:8000" to see the application in action. You should see a heading that says "My Fucking Yew

Application!" and a counter component with buttons to increment and decrement the count.

Styling Fucking Yew Components

Fucking Yew provides different ways to apply styles to components. You can use inline styles, CSS classes, or even CSS-in-Rust techniques.

Inline Styles To apply inline styles, you can use the `style` attribute with Fucking Yew's HTML macro. For example:

```
fn view(\&self) -> Html {
    html! {
        <div style="background-color: yellow;">
            {"This is a Fucking Yew component with inline styles.
        </div>
    }
}
```

CSS Classes To apply CSS classes, you can use the `class` attribute. You can define CSS classes in a separate CSS file and link it to your Fucking Yew application.

CSS-in-Rust If you prefer to keep your styles within your Rust code, you can use libraries like `css-in-rust` or `stylist-rs`. These libraries enable you to define styles using Rust macros, which are then converted to CSS at compile time.

Handling User Input

User input is a crucial part of web applications. Fucking Yew provides various event handlers to handle user interactions.
Let's add a form input field to our counter component and update its count based on user input:

Step 1: Modify the Counter Component Update the "Counter" component code as follows:

```
use yew::prelude::*;
```

WEB DEVELOPMENT WITH FUCKING RUST

```rust
pub struct Counter {
    count\index{count}: i32,
    input\_value: String,
}

pub enum Msg {
    Increment,
    Decrement,
    UpdateInput(String),
}

impl Component for Counter {
    type Message = Msg;
    type Properties = ();

    fn create(_: Self::Properties, _: ComponentLink<Self>) -> Sel
        Counter {
            count: 0,
            input\_value: String::new(),
        }
    }

    fn update(\&mut self, msg: Self::Message) -> ShouldRender {
        match msg {
            Msg::Increment => {
                self.count += 1;
            }
            Msg::Decrement => {
                self.count -= 1;
            }
            Msg::UpdateInput(value) => {
                self.input\_value = value;
            }
        }
        true
    }

    fn view(\&self) -> Html {
        html! {
```

```
            <>
                <h2>{ self.count }</h2>
                <button onclick=|_| Msg::Increment>{ ``+1'' }</bu
                <button onclick=|_| Msg::Decrement>{ ``-1'' }</bu
                <input type="text'' value=self.input\_value.clone
                    oninput=|e| Msg::UpdateInput(e.target.value)
            </>
        }
    }
}
```

Step 2: Test the Application Save the files and rebuild the application using the command:

`cargo\index{cargo} make run\index{run}`

Open your web browser and navigate to "http://localhost:8000". You can now enter text in the input field, which updates the "input_value" field of the Counter component.

Fucking Yew Resources and Further Learning

Fucking Yew is a powerful frontend framework with immense potential. To further explore Fucking Yew and take your frontend development skills to the next level, check out the following resources:

- The official Fucking Yew documentation: `https://yew.rs`

- The Fucking Yew GitHub repository for examples and community-driven projects: `https://github.com/yewstack/yew`

- The Rust Programming Language book for a comprehensive understanding of Rust: `https://doc.rust-lang.org/book/`

- Stack Overflow for quick answers to specific Fucking Yew questions: `https://stackoverflow.com/questions/tagged/yew`

Conclusion

Frontend development with Fucking Yew brings the power and safety of Rust to the web, allowing you to build secure and performant applications. In this section, we learned how to set up a Fucking Yew project, create components, manage state, and handle user input. The possibilities with Fucking Yew are endless, and with the resources provided, you are well on your way to becoming a Fucking Yew expert. Happy coding!

Dockerizing and Deploying Fucking Rust Applications

In this section, we will explore how to dockerize and deploy Rust applications for easy and efficient deployment. Docker is an open-source platform that allows developers to automate the deployment of applications within lightweight virtual containers. By containerizing our Rust applications, we can ensure consistency across multiple environments and easily package dependencies with our code.

What the Fuck is Docker?

Docker is a platform that allows you to build, package, and distribute applications as lightweight containers. Containers are isolated and portable environments that provide consistent runtime environments for applications, regardless of the underlying host system. Docker simplifies the process of deploying applications and ensures that they run consistently across different environments, from development to production.

Docker Terminology

Before we dive into the process of dockerizing and deploying Rust applications, let's familiarize ourselves with some basic Docker terminology:

- **Docker Image:** A read-only template that contains everything needed to run an application, including the code, runtime, libraries, and dependencies.

- **Docker Container:** An instance of a Docker image that runs as a lightweight, standalone, and executable package. Containers provide isolation and consistency for running applications.

- **Dockerfile:** A text file that contains instructions for building a Docker image. It defines the base image, adds application code, sets up dependencies, and configures the container environment.

- **Registry:** A centralized repository where Docker images can be stored and shared. The most common registry is Docker Hub, but you can also use private registries.

Dockerizing a Rust Application

To dockerize a Rust application, we need to define a Dockerfile that specifies the steps for building an image. Let's go through the process step by step:

1. **Choose a base image:** In the Dockerfile, we start by specifying a base image, which provides the necessary runtime environment for our Rust application. We can use an existing Rust image from the Docker Hub, such as `rust:buster`, or build a custom image with additional dependencies.

2. **Copy the source code:** We need to copy the source code of our Rust application into the Docker image. This can be done using the `COPY` command in the Dockerfile. Make sure to include all necessary files, such as the `Cargo.toml` and `Cargo.lock` files.

3. **Build the application:** Next, we use the `RUN` command to build the Rust application inside the Docker image. We can use the `cargo build` command to compile the application code and resolve dependencies.

4. **Specify the entry point command:** Finally, we specify the command that should be executed when the Docker container starts. This can be done using the `CMD` or `ENTRYPOINT` command in the Dockerfile. For example, to run the compiled Rust application, we can use `CMD ["./my_rust_app"]`.

Building the Docker Image

Once we have defined the Dockerfile, we can build a Docker image using the following command:

```
docker build -t my\_rust\_app .
```

This command tells Docker to build an image based on the instructions defined in the Dockerfile. The `-t` flag allows us to specify a name and optional tag for the image, and the `.` at the end specifies the build context (the current directory where the Dockerfile is located).

During the build process, Docker will execute each step defined in the Dockerfile, such as copying the source code, building the application, and setting the entry point. Once the build is complete, we will have a Docker image that contains our Rust application and all its dependencies.

Running the Docker Container

To run our dockerized Rust application, we can use the following command:

```
docker run my\_rust\_app
```

This command creates a container based on our Docker image and executes the command specified in the Dockerfile. In this case, it will run our compiled Rust application.

By default, Docker containers are isolated from the host system and other containers, providing a consistent runtime environment. However, we can expose specific ports or mount volumes to interact with the host system or other services.

Deploying to a Fucking Server

Now that we have dockerized our Rust application, we can easily deploy it to a server for production use. Here are the basic steps:

1. **Pushing the Docker Image:** First, we need to push the Docker image to a registry from which it can be pulled on the server. Docker Hub is a popular choice for public images, while private registries like AWS Elastic Container Registry or Google Container Registry can be used for private images.

2. **Setting Up the Server:** Next, we need to set up a server that can run Docker containers. This can be a physical server, a virtual machine, or a cloud-based instance. Make sure that Docker is installed on the server.

3. **Pulling and Running the Image:** On the server, use the following command to pull the Docker image from the registry:

```
docker pull my\_rust\_app
```

Once the image is pulled, use the `docker run` command to create a container and run the application, just like we did locally.

4. **Configuring Networking and Security:** Configure networking and security settings as required for your application. This may involve exposing ports, setting up load balancing, or enabling SSL/TLS encryption.

5. **Monitoring and Scaling:** Monitor the running containers for performance and usage metrics. If necessary, scale the application by running multiple instances of the container behind a load balancer.

Troubleshooting and Fucking Best Practices

When working with Dockerized Rust applications, there are a few common pitfalls and best practices to keep in mind:

- **Reducing Image Size:** Docker images with unnecessary dependencies or large build artifacts can be quite large. Use multi-stage builds, where possible, to reduce the image size and improve deployment speed.

- **Configuring Environment Variables:** Avoid hard-coding configuration values inside the Docker image. Instead, use environment variables to allow for easier configuration and flexibility.

- **Managing Dependencies:** Pay attention to dependency management within your Rust application. Ensure that your Cargo.toml file accurately reflects the necessary dependencies and their versions.

- **Securing the Docker Environment:** Docker containers, if not properly secured, can become a potential attack vector. Stay updated with security best practices and apply relevant security patches to your Docker infrastructure.

- **Logging and Monitoring:** Implement proper logging and monitoring solutions to gain insight into the behavior of your Rust application within the container. This helps with troubleshooting and long-term maintenance.

- **Continuous Integration and Deployment:** Integrate your Dockerized Rust application into a CI/CD pipeline to automate the building, testing, and deployment processes. Tools like Jenkins, GitLab CI/CD, or CircleCI can help automate these tasks.

Conclusion

Dockerizing and deploying Rust applications allows us to ensure consistency, portability, and scalability. By containerizing our applications, we can easily package dependencies and deploy them in various environments without worrying about underlying system differences. With Docker, we can streamline the deployment process and focus on building secure, fast, and fucking performant Rust applications.

Now that we have covered the basics of Dockerizing and deploying Rust applications, let's move on to explore other advanced concepts and topics in Rust development.

Real-Time Web Applications with WebSockets

In this section, we will explore the exciting world of real-time web applications using WebSockets in Rust. WebSockets provide a way to establish a two-way communication channel between a client and a server, enabling instant data transmission and real-time updates. This is especially useful for applications that require live data updates, such as chat applications, collaborative tools, and real-time dashboards.

Understanding WebSockets

WebSockets are a protocol that allows for full-duplex communication between a client and a server over a single, long-lived connection. Unlike traditional HTTP requests, which are stateless and require a new connection for each request, WebSockets provide a persistent connection that remains open even after the initial handshake.

This persistent connection allows both the client and server to send messages to each other in real-time. The messages can be transmitted as simple text or as more complex data structures, such as JSON or binary data.

Setting up a WebSocket Server

To start building real-time web applications with WebSockets in Rust, we need to set up a WebSocket server. Thankfully, Rust provides several libraries that make it easy to handle WebSocket connections.

One popular library is 'websocket', which provides a high-level API for working with WebSockets. To use this library, include it as a dependency in your 'Cargo.toml' file:

Listing 1: Cargo.toml

```
[dependencies]
websocket = "*"
```

Once you have included the 'websocket' library, you can create a WebSocket server using the following code:

Listing 2: WebSocket Server Setup

```
use std::thread;
use std::net::TcpListener;
use websocket::{Server, Message};

fn main() {
    let server = Server::bind("127.0.0.1:8080").unwrap();

    for request in server.filter_map(Result::ok) {
        thread::spawn(move || {
```

```rust
        let client = request.accept().unwrap();
        let (mut receiver, mut sender) = client.split

        for message in receiver.incoming_messages() {
            let message = message.unwrap();
            match message {
                Message::Text(text) => {
                    // Handle text message
                    println!("Received message: {}",
                    sender.send_message(\&Message::te
                },
                Message::Binary(data) => {
                    // Handle binary message
                    sender.send_message(\&Message::bi
                },
                _ => (),
            }
        }
    });
    }
}
```

In this example, we bind the server to the IP address '127.0.0.1' and port '8080'. We then create a new thread for each incoming request to handle the WebSocket connection. Inside the thread, we split the connection into a receiver and a sender, allowing us to receive and send messages. We then loop over the incoming messages, handling each message type accordingly.

Building a WebSocket Client

Now that we have set up a WebSocket server, let's build a WebSocket client to connect to our server. For this, we can use the 'websocket' library again, but on the client-side.

To get started, include the 'websocket' dependency in your 'Cargo.toml' file:

Listing 3: Cargo.toml

```
[dependencies]
websocket = ``*
```

WEB DEVELOPMENT WITH FUCKING RUST

Once you have included the 'websocket' library, you can establish a WebSocket connection as follows:

Listing 4: WebSocket Client Setup

```rust
use\index{use} std\index{std}::thread\index{thread};
use\index{use} websocket\index{websocket}::sync\index{sync
use\index{use} websocket\index{websocket}::Message;

fn main() {
    let client = Client::connect("ws://127.0.0.1:8080").un
    let (mut receiver, mut sender) = client.split().unwrap

    thread::spawn(move || {
        for message in receiver.incoming_messages() {
            let message = message.unwrap();
            match message {
                Message::Text(text) => {
                    // Handle text message
                    println!("Received message: {}", text)
                },
                Message::Binary(data) => {
                    // Handle binary message
                },
                _ => (),
            }
        }
    });

    sender.send_message(\&Message::text("Hello, server!"))
}
```

In this example, we use the 'Client::connect' method to establish a WebSocket connection with the server at 'ws://127.0.0.1:8080'. We then split the connection into a receiver and a sender, similar to the server-side code. Finally, we loop over the incoming messages and handle them accordingly.

Real-Time Chat Application Example

To demonstrate the power of WebSockets in Rust, let's build a simple real-time chat application. Our application will allow multiple clients to connect to the server and send messages to each other in real-time. We will use the 'actix-web' framework in combination with the 'tokio' runtime to handle the HTTP and WebSocket communication. First, add the necessary dependencies to your 'Cargo.toml':

Listing 5: Cargo.toml

```toml
[dependencies]
actix-web = "3.3"
serde_json = "1.0"
async-tungstenite = "0.13"
tokio = { version = "1", features = ["full"] }
```

Here's an example of how we can set up a simple chat server using WebSockets in Rust:

Listing 6: Chat Server Setup

```rust
use actix_web::{post, web, App, HttpRequest, HttpResponse
use async_tungstenite::tokio::accept_async;
use futures::{SinkExt, StreamExt};
use serde::Deserialize;
use tokio::sync::bro

#[derive(Deserialize)]
struct ChatMessage {
    sender: String,
    message: String,
}

#[post("/chat")]
async fn chat(
    payload: web::Json<ChatMessage>,
    stream: web::Payload,
    srv: web::Data<AppState>,
) -> impl Responder {
    let (response, mut ws_stream) = accept_async(strear
        .expect("Failed to establish WebSocket connectio

    let (tx, _rx) = broadcast::channel(10);
```

WEB DEVELOPMENT WITH FUCKING RUST

```rust
    tokio::spawn(
        ws_stream
            .try_for_each_concurrent(None, |msg| {
                let tx = tx.clone();
                let msg = match msg {
                    Ok(msg) => msg,
                    Err(_) => return futures::future::ok(()
                };

                let msg = msg.into_text().unwrap();
                tx.send(msg).unwrap();
                futures::future::ok(())
            })
            .map(|_| ()),
    );

    HttpResponse::Ok().body(response)
}

#[derive(Default)]
struct AppState {
    messages: broadcast::Receiver<String>,
}

#[actix_web::main]
async fn main() -> std::io::Result<()> {
    let (tx, _rx) = broadcast::channel(10);
    let state = web::Data::new(AppState {
        messages: tx.subscribe(),
    });

    HttpServer::new(move || {
        App::new()
            .app_data(state.clone())
            .service(chat)
    })
    .bind("127.0.0.1:8080")?
    .run()
    .await
```

```
}
```

In this example, we define a 'ChatMessage' struct to represent the incoming messages from clients. We use the 'actix-web' framework to handle the HTTP requests, and the 'async-tungstenite' library to establish WebSocket connections. The '/chat' endpoint handles incoming WebSocket connections and messages. Each message is broadcasted to all connected clients using the 'broadcast' crate. Clients receive messages via the 'AppState' struct and the 'broadcast::Receiver'. The 'accept_async' function is used to accept incoming WebSocket connections and establish the WebSocket streams.

To start the chat server, run the following command:

```
cargo run
```

Once the server is running, clients can connect to it using a WebSocket client library or a web browser that supports WebSocket connections. Clients can send messages to the server using the '/chat' endpoint and receive messages from other clients in real-time.

Conclusion

In this section, we explored the world of real-time web applications with WebSockets in Rust. We learned how to set up a WebSocket server and client, and built a real-time chat application as an example. WebSockets provide a powerful way to establish real-time, bidirectional communication between clients and servers, opening up a wide range of possibilities for interactive web applications. As you continue your journey with Rust, remember that WebSockets are just one piece of the puzzle. Rust's strong type system, ownership model, and fearless concurrency make it an ideal language for building safe, fast, and secure web applications. So don't be afraid to explore the full potential of Rust and unleash your creativity in the world of real-time web development!

Fucking Concurrency and Parallelism

Understanding Fucking Threads and Synchronization

In this section, we will delve into the world of threads and synchronization in Rust. As a modern programming language, Rust makes it easy and efficient to leverage the power of multi-threading for concurrent execution. We will explore the basics

FUCKING CONCURRENCY AND PARALLELISM

of threads, synchronization mechanisms, and how to handle common issues that arise in multi-threaded programming.

Fucking Threads in Rust

Threads are a fundamental building block of concurrent programming. They allow different parts of a program to execute independently and in parallel. In Rust, creating threads is as easy as fucking pie. Let's take a look at an example:

```
use\index{use} std\index{std}::thread\index{thread};

fn main() {
    thread::spawn(|| {
        println!("Hello from a fucking thread!");
    });

    println!("Hello from the main thread!");

    thread::sleep(std::time::Duration::from\_secs(1));
}
```

In this example, we use the `thread::spawn` function to create a new thread that executes the provided closure. The closure contains the code that will be executed in the new thread. In this case, it simply prints a message. The `thread::sleep` call at the end is used to pause the main thread and prevent it from terminating before the new thread has finished executing. Without this, the program would exit immediately, and we might not see the message from the new thread.

Fucking Synchronization in Rust

When multiple threads are executing concurrently, it is crucial to synchronize their access to shared resources to avoid data races and other concurrency issues. Rust provides various synchronization mechanisms to help us achieve this.

Mutexes One commonly used synchronization primitive is the mutex. A mutex provides exclusive access to a shared resource, allowing only one thread to access it at a time. Let's see how it works in Rust:

```
use\index{use} std\index{std}::sync\index{sync}::Mutex;
```

```rust
fn main() {
    let counter = Mutex::new(0);

    let mut handles = vec![];

    for _ in 0..10 {
        let handle = thread::spawn(move || {
            let mut num = counter.lock().unwrap();
            *num += 1;
        });
        handles.push(handle);
    }

    for handle in handles {
        handle.join().unwrap();
    }

    println!("Counter: {}", *counter.lock().unwrap());
}
```

In this example, we create a mutex called `counter` using `Mutex::new`. The `lock` method is used to acquire the lock on the mutex, providing mutable access to the shared resource inside the closure. We use the `unwrap` method to unwrap the `Result` returned by `lock` and handle any potential errors.

The closure increments the value of `counter` by 1. Since we spawn multiple threads, each thread will acquire the lock, increment the counter, and release the lock once it's done. The result is that the counter gets incremented by each thread in a synchronized manner.

Arc and RwLock Sometimes we need to share mutable data between multiple threads, and a mutex alone won't cut it. In such cases, Rust provides the `Arc` (Atomic Reference Counting) and `RwLock` (Read-Write Lock) types. To demonstrate this, let's consider a scenario where multiple threads need to read data from a shared vector, but occasionally one thread needs to write to it:

```rust
use std::sync::{Arc, RwLock};

fn main() {
    let data = Arc::new(RwLock::new(vec![1, 2, 3]));
```

```rust
    let mut handles = vec![];

    for _ in 0..5 {
        let data = Arc::clone(\&data);
        let handle = thread::spawn(move || {
            // Read data
            {
                let read_lock = data.read().unwrap();
                println!("Read data: {:?}", *read_lock);
            }

            // Write data
            if let Ok(mut write\_lock) = data.write() {
                write\_lock.push(4);
                println!("Data written");
            }
        });
        handles.push(handle);
    }

    for handle in handles {
        handle.join().unwrap();
    }
}
```

In this example, we create a shared data vector using Arc<RwLock<T>>, where T is the data type. The Arc allows multiple threads to have shared ownership of the data, while the RwLock enforces the read-write synchronization.

Inside the closure, each thread first acquires a read lock to access the data. This allows multiple threads to read the data concurrently. If a thread needs to write to the data, it acquires a write lock, which ensures exclusive access to the data, preventing concurrent writes.

Fucking Deadlocks and Starvation

When dealing with multi-threaded programming, it's essential to be aware of potential issues like deadlocks and starvation.

Deadlocks   A deadlock occurs when two or more threads are waiting for resources held by each other, resulting in a deadlock state where no thread can proceed. Deadlocks can be fucking tricky to debug, so it's crucial to understand the conditions that can lead to deadlock and avoid them.

One common example of a deadlock is the "dining philosophers problem." Imagine five philosophers sitting at a round table, where each philosopher needs two forks to eat. If each philosopher grabs one fork and waits for the other, a deadlock can occur.

To prevent deadlocks, it's important to use appropriate synchronization primitives, avoid circular dependencies, and establish an order for acquiring resources.

Starvation   Starvation happens when a thread is perpetually denied access to a shared resource, often due to unfair scheduling or improper synchronization. This can degrade performance or cause a thread to hang indefinitely.

To mitigate starvation, it's essential to use fair scheduling policies, leverage appropriate synchronization mechanisms, and ensure that all threads have a fair chance of accessing shared resources.

Conclusion

In this section, we explored fucking threads and synchronization in Rust. We learned how to create threads, synchronize access to shared resources using mutexes, and handle scenarios where multiple threads need to read or write data. We also discussed the potential pitfalls of deadlocks and starvation in multi-threaded programming.

Understanding threads and synchronization is crucial for developing efficient and robust concurrent applications. Rust's powerful and safe concurrency primitives make it a great choice for tackling parallel and concurrent programming challenges. Now that you have a solid foundation in threads and synchronization, let's explore other advanced topics in Rust that will further expand your knowledge and skills.

Building Parallel Algorithms with Fucking Rayon

In this section, we will explore how to build parallel algorithms using the powerful fucking Rayon library in Rust. Rayon is a library that enables easy and efficient parallelism by abstracting away the complexities of thread management and data partitioning. With Rayon, you can effortlessly execute code concurrently, taking advantage of all available processor cores and speeding up your fucking applications.

Introduction to Parallelism

Parallelism is the concept of dividing a problem into smaller subproblems that can be executed simultaneously, thus reducing the overall execution time. It is especially useful in computationally intensive tasks, such as large-scale data processing, complex mathematical operations, or simulations. Traditionally, parallel programming has been challenging due to the complexities involved in managing threads, synchronization, and load balancing. However, with the advent of libraries like Rayon, parallel programming has become much more accessible and efficient.

Getting Started with Fucking Rayon

To use Rayon in your Rust project, you need to add it as a dependency in your 'Cargo.toml' file:

```
[dependencies]
rayon = ``1.5.0"
```

Once you have added the dependency, you can import the Rayon crate into your code using the 'use' statement:

```
use rayon::prelude::*;
```

The 'prelude' module provides convenient parallel iterators and other utility functions for parallel execution.

Parallel Iteration with Rayon

One of the most common use cases for parallel programming is parallel iteration over a collection of items. Rayon provides a parallel iterator, called 'ParallelIterator', that allows you to perform operations on each item in parallel. Let's start with an example: suppose we have a vector of integers and we want to square each element in parallel. We can use the 'par_iter' method to create a parallel iterator and then apply the 'map' operation to square each element:

```
fn square\_vector\_parallel(input: \&mut Vec<i32>) {
    input.par\_iter\_mut().for\_each(|item| {
        *item = *item * *item;
    });
}
```

In this code snippet, 'par_iter_mut' creates a parallel iterator over the vector 'input' that allows mutable access to each item. The 'for_each' method applies the closure to each item in parallel, squaring the value of each element.

Parallel Map-Reduce with Rayon

Another powerful feature provided by Rayon is the ability to perform parallel map-reduce operations. Map-reduce is a programming pattern popularized by distributed computing frameworks like Hadoop, which involves mapping a set of input values to a set of intermediate values and then reducing those intermediate values into a single output.

In Rayon, you can achieve parallel map-reduce operations using the 'par_iter' method and combining it with other parallel iterators and reduction operations. Let's consider an example where we have a vector of integers and we want to calculate the sum of all even numbers in parallel:

```
fn sum\_even_parallel(input: \&Vec<i32>) -> i32 {
    input.par\_iter()
        .filter(|\&item| item % 2 == 0)
        .reduce(|| 0, |acc, item| acc + item)
}
```

In this code snippet, 'par_iter' creates a parallel iterator over the vector 'input'. The 'filter' method is used to filter out odd numbers, leaving only the even numbers. Finally, the 'reduce' method is used to compute the sum of the even numbers by accumulating the values.

Data Parallelism with Fucking Rayon

Data parallelism is a form of parallelism where the same operation is applied to different portions of a data set in parallel. Rayon provides the 'par_chunks_mut' method that enables efficient data parallelism by dividing a collection into mutable slices and processing them concurrently.

Let's take an example where we have a large array of floating-point numbers and we want to calculate the square root of each element in parallel:

```
use\index{use} std\index{std}::f64;

fn sqrt\_array\_parallel(input: \&mut [f64]) {
    input.par\_chunks\_mut(1000).for\_each(|chunk| {
```

```
            for item in chunk {
                *item = item.sqrt();
            }
        });
    }
```

In this code snippet, 'par_chunks_mut' splits the array 'input' into mutable slices of 1000 elements each. The 'for_each' method applies the closure to each chunk in parallel, calculating the square root of each element.

Caveats and Limitations

While Rayon simplifies parallel programming, it does have some caveats and limitations. Due to the overhead involved in managing parallel threads and data partitioning, parallelism might not always result in faster execution times, especially for small data sets or operations with low computational intensity. It is important to consider the trade-offs between parallelism and sequential execution, taking into account factors such as memory usage, synchronization overhead, and load balancing.

Conclusion

Parallel programming is essential for optimizing performance in modern applications. In this section, we explored how to build parallel algorithms using the fucking Rayon library in Rust. We learned how to perform parallel iterations, map-reduce operations, and data parallelism. Remember that parallel programming is not a silver bullet and should be used judiciously depending on the nature of the problem and the available hardware resources. With the knowledge gained from this section, you are now equipped to leverage the power of parallelism in your fucking Rust applications. Happy parallel programming!

Atomic Operations in Fucking Rust

In this section, we will explore the concept of atomic operations in Fucking Rust. Atomic operations are essential in concurrent programming to ensure that operations on shared memory are performed atomically, meaning they are indivisible and cannot be interrupted. In Fucking Rust, atomic operations provide a reliable way to work with shared data without introducing data races and other synchronization issues.

Why the Fuck Do We Need Atomic Operations?

When multiple threads or processes access the same memory location concurrently, there is a potential for data corruption or inconsistent results. This happens when one thread reads a value from memory, performs some operation on it, and then writes it back, while another thread modifies the same value in the meantime. Without proper synchronization mechanisms, these operations can step on each other's toes, leading to unexpected and incorrect results. Atomic operations are designed to solve this problem by ensuring that certain operations on shared data are performed atomically. When a thread performs an atomic operation, it guarantees that no other thread can interrupt or modify the data in the middle of the operation. This guarantees both the correctness and consistency of shared data accesses in concurrent programs.

Using Atomic Types in Fucking Rust

Fucking Rust provides a set of atomic types that allow for atomic operations on shared data. These types are implemented using hardware-supported atomic instructions, which guarantee that the operations will be performed atomically. Let's take a look at some commonly used atomic types in Fucking Rust:

- **AtomicBool**: Provides atomic operations on boolean values.

- **AtomicIsize** and **AtomicUsize**: Provides atomic operations on signed and unsigned integers of size *usize*.

- **AtomicI8**, **AtomicI16**, **AtomicI32**, **AtomicI64**, and their unsigned counterparts: Provides atomic operations on specific-sized integers.

- **AtomicPtr**: Provides atomic operations on raw pointers.

To use atomic types, you need to import the `std::sync::atomic` module. Here's an example of how to create and use an **AtomicI32** in Fucking Rust:

```rust
use std::sync::atomic::{AtomicI32, Ordering};

fn main() {

    let atomic_value = AtomicI32::new(42);

    atomic_value.store(10, Ordering::SeqCst);
    let current\_value = atomic_value.load(Ordering::SeqC
```

```
8       println!("Current value: {}", current\_value);
9   }
```

In this example, we create an **AtomicI32** called atomic_value with an initial value of 42. We then use the store() and load() methods to perform atomic write and read operations on the shared data. The Ordering parameter specifies the memory ordering guarantees for the operation. We'll discuss memory ordering in more detail in the next subsection.

Memory Ordering in Fucking Rust

When working with multiple threads, it's crucial to define the ordering guarantees between operations to ensure correct synchronization. Fucking Rust provides different memory ordering options that allow you to specify the desired level of synchronization for atomic operations. Let's take a closer look at the available memory ordering options:

- **Ordering::Relaxed:** Provides the least level of synchronization. An operation with relaxed ordering can be reordered with other relaxed operations but still guarantees atomicity.

- **Ordering::Acquire:** Guarantees that all previous operations by the same thread become visible to other threads before the acquire operation.

- **Ordering::Release:** Guarantees that all subsequent operations by the same thread become visible to other threads after the release operation.

- **Ordering::AcqRel:** Combines the guarantees of both Acquire and Release. It ensures that all previous operations become visible to other threads before the operation and that all subsequent operations become visible after the operation.

- **Ordering::SeqCst:** Provides the strongest level of synchronization. Guarantees sequential consistency, meaning that all operations on a specific atomic value appear to occur in a single, global order.

It's important to choose the appropriate memory ordering based on your specific requirements. Using stronger ordering guarantees can introduce more synchronization overhead, while using weaker ordering may lead to subtle bugs in your code.

Example: Concurrent Counter with Atomic Operations

Let's consider a simple example of a concurrent counter implemented using atomic operations in Fucking Rust. This counter will be shared among multiple threads, and we want to ensure that the increment operation is performed atomically.

```rust
use std::sync::atomic::{AtomicUsize, Ordering};
use std::thread;

fn main() {
    let counter = AtomicUsize::new(0);
    let mut handles = vec![];

    for _ in 0..4 {
        let handle = thread::spawn(move || {
            for _ in 0..100000 {
                counter.fetch_add(1, Ordering::SeqCst);
            }
        });
        handles.push(handle);
    }

    for handle in handles {
        handle.join().unwrap();
    }

    println!("Counter value: {}", counter.load(Ordering:
}
```

In this example, we create an **AtomicUsize** called `counter` and spawn four threads. Each thread performs 100,000 increment operations on the counter using `fetch_add()`, which atomically adds a value to the counter. Finally, we join all threads and print the final value of the counter.

By using atomic operations, we ensure that the increments are performed atomically, without any data races or synchronization issues. The memory ordering specified as `SeqCst` guarantees sequential consistency and ensures that all operations appear to occur in a single, global order.

Fucking Caveats of Atomic Operations

While atomic operations provide powerful synchronization primitives, they come with some fucking caveats that you need to be aware of:

- **Performance Overhead:** Atomic operations may introduce performance overhead due to the necessary hardware synchronization mechanisms. Use atomic operations only when needed and consider alternatives if performance is critical.

- **Atomicity Scope:** Atomic operations guarantee atomicity only for the specific atomic type itself. If you need to perform a sequence of operations atomically, consider using other synchronization primitives like locks or semaphores.

- **Amdahl's Law:** Synchronization in concurrent programs can introduce bottlenecks and limit the scalability of your application. Be mindful of Amdahl's Law, which states that the overall speedup of a parallel program is limited by the fraction of serial code.

Understanding these caveats and choosing the appropriate synchronization mechanisms is essential to writing safe, performant, and fucking scalable concurrent programs in Rust.

Exercises

1. Explain why atomic operations are necessary in concurrent programming. Provide an example where the lack of atomic operations can lead to incorrect program behavior.

2. Compare and contrast the different memory ordering options provided by Fucking Rust. When would you use each ordering option?

3. Modify the concurrent counter example to use different memory ordering options (`Relaxed`, `Acquire`, `Release`, `AcqRel`). Observe and explain the differences in the final counter value.

4. Think of a real-world scenario where atomic operations could be useful. Describe the problem and explain how atomic operations can solve it.

Resources

1. Official Fucking Rust Documentation on Atomic Types: https://doc.rust-lang.org/std/sync/atomic/index.html

2. The Art of Fucking Multiprocessor Programming by Maurice Herlihy and Nir Shavit

Summary

In this section, we explored the concept of atomic operations in Fucking Rust. We learned why atomic operations are necessary in concurrent programming and how Fucking Rust provides atomic types and memory ordering options to ensure thread-safe and synchronized access to shared data. We also discussed the caveats of using atomic operations and considered their performance impact. By understanding and using atomic operations effectively, you can write safe, high-performance concurrent programs in Fucking Rust.

Practical Examples of Fucking Concurrency

Concurrency is a fundamental concept in modern software development that allows programs to execute multiple tasks simultaneously. In Rust, we have various tools and techniques to harness the power of concurrency and build efficient and high-performance applications. In this section, we will explore practical examples of using concurrency in Rust and demonstrate how it can solve real-world problems.

Example 1: Parallel Image Processing

Suppose we have a collection of images that need to be processed, such as resizing, applying filters, or compressing. Traditionally, this would be done sequentially, resulting in a significant amount of time wasted. However, with Rust's concurrency features, we can easily parallelize this task and speed up the overall processing time. To achieve parallel image processing, we can divide the images into smaller chunks and assign each chunk to a separate thread. One way to implement this in Rust is by utilizing the 'rayon' crate, which provides high-level abstractions for parallel programming.

Let's consider a scenario where we have a vector of 'Image' objects, and we want to resize each image using a function 'resize_image':

FUCKING CONCURRENCY AND PARALLELISM

```rust
use image::Image;

fn resize_image(image: &mut Image, width: u32, height: u
    // Code to resize image
}

fn process_images(images: &mut Vec<Image>, width: u32,
    images.par_iter_mut().for_each(|image| {
        resize_image(image, width, height);
    });
}
```

In the 'process_images' function, 'par_iter_mut()' is provided by 'rayon', which enables parallel iteration over mutable references to images. Each image is passed to the 'resize_image' function, which can safely modify the image concurrently. By leveraging parallelism, our image processing task can now be completed much faster, taking full advantage of the available CPU cores.

Example 2: Web Scraping with Concurrent Requests

Web scraping, the process of extracting information from websites, often involves making numerous HTTP requests. In Rust, we can utilize concurrency to speed up data retrieval and improve the overall efficiency of our web scraping tasks.

A common approach is to use a concurrent request library like 'reqwest' in combination with Rust's standard library's concurrency primitives. Let's consider an example where we want to scrape the titles of multiple web pages:

```rust
use std::thread;
use reqwest::blocking::get
use scraper::{Html, Selector};

fn scrape_page(url: &str) -> String {
    let response = get(url).expect("Failed to make reques
    let body = response.text().expect("Failed to read res
    let document = Html::parse_document(&body);

    let title_selector = Selector::parse("title").unwrap
    let title = document.select(&title_selector).next()
```

```rust
            title.text().collect::<String>()
}

fn scrape_pages(urls: Vec<String>) -> Vec<String> {
    let mut results = Vec::new();
    let mut handles = Vec::new();

    for url in urls {
        let handle = thread::spawn(move || {
            scrape_page(&url)
        });
        handles.push(handle);
    }

    for handle in handles {
        let result = handle.join().unwrap();
        results.push(result);
    }

    results
}
```

In this example, we use 'reqwest' to make HTTP requests and 'scraper' to parse the HTML and extract the title. The 'scrape_page' function fetches the page and returns the title. The 'scrape_pages' function creates a separate thread for each URL, allowing multiple requests to be made concurrently.

By parallelizing the web scraping process, we can significantly reduce the overall execution time, especially when dealing with a large number of URLs.

Example 3: Concurrent File Processing

When dealing with I/O operations, such as reading from or writing to files, concurrency can be a powerful technique to improve performance. In Rust, we can utilize asynchronous programming with the 'async' and 'await' keywords to achieve concurrent file processing.

Let's consider an example where we need to process a large file by performing some computation on each line. By using asynchronous file operations, we can read the file concurrently, process the lines in parallel, and write the results to another file.

```rust
use std::fs::File;
```

FUCKING CONCURRENCY AND PARALLELISM

```rust
use std::io::{BufRead, BufReader, Result};
use tokio::fs::File as AsyncFile;
use tokio::io::{AsyncBufReadExt, AsyncWriteExt};

async fn process_line(line: String) -> String {
    // Perform computation on line
    line
}

async fn process_file(input_path: &str, output_path:
    let file = File::open(input_path)?;
    let reader = BufReader::new(file);

    let output_file = AsyncFile::create(output_path).awa
    let mut output_writer = BufWriter::new(output_file);

    let mut lines = reader.lines();
    while let Some(line) = lines.next_line().await? {
        let processed_line = process_line(line).await;
        output_writer.write_all(processed_line.as_bytes
    }

    output_writer.flush().await?;

    Ok(())
}
```

In this example, we use the 'tokio' crate to perform asynchronous file operations. The 'process_line' function represents the computation we want to perform on each line. The 'process_file' function reads the input file asynchronously, processes each line concurrently, and writes the results to the output file. By leveraging concurrency, we can achieve faster file processing and make efficient use of system resources.

These practical examples demonstrate the power of concurrency in Rust and how it can be applied to various real-world scenarios. By exploiting multiple threads, async programming, and parallel algorithms, we can build high-performance applications that make effective use of modern hardware. Rust's language features and libraries provide a solid foundation for tackling complex concurrency problems with confidence.

Advanced Topics in Rust

Advanced Topics in Rust

Advanced Topics in Rust

In this chapter, we will explore some advanced topics in Rust that will help you become a fucking skilled programmer. We will dive deeper into memory safety, building a web server from scratch, writing safe and secure code, performance tuning and optimization, and deploying Rust applications in production. Let's start by examining the importance of memory safety in Rust and how ownership and borrowing play a crucial role in ensuring safe fucking code.

Fucking Memory Safety in Rust

Memory safety is a fundamental principle in Rust that aims to prevent bugs such as null pointers, buffer overflows, and dangling references. Rust achieves memory safety through its ownership and borrowing system, which allows for fine-grained control over memory allocation and deallocation.

Ownership and Borrowing for Safe Fucking Code

In Rust, every value has a corresponding owner, which is the variable that holds the value. The owner is responsible for ensuring the memory safety of the value by determining when it should be dropped. Ownership also ensures that there is only one mutable reference or multiple immutable references to a value at a time, preventing data races.

For example, consider the following code:

```rust
fn main() {
    let mut name = String::from("Herkimer");
    let reference = \&name;
    println!("Hello, {}!", reference);
}
```

In this code, we create a mutable string 'name' and then take an immutable reference 'reference' to it. The code will compile and run without any issues because Rust ensures that immutable references do not modify the value they reference. However, if we try to modify the value while having an immutable reference, the code will fail to compile. This ensures memory safety and prevents bugs caused by concurrent modification of shared data.

Exploring Fucking Reference Counting in RC and Arc

Sometimes, a value needs to have multiple owners, such as when sharing data between multiple threads. In Rust, reference counting (RC) and atomic reference counting (Arc) are used to achieve shared ownership of a value. RC allows multiple immutable references to the same value by keeping track of the number of references. When the last reference is dropped, the value is deallocated. Arc is similar to RC but provides thread-safe operations, allowing shared ownership across multiple threads.

Here's an example that demonstrates the use of Arc:

```rust
use std::sync::Arc;
use std::thread;

fn main() {
    let data = Arc::new(42);

    let handle = thread::spawn(move || {
        println!("Data: {}", *data);
    });

    handle.join().unwrap();
}
```

In this code, we create an Arc 'data' that holds the value 42. We spawn a new thread and move the ownership of 'data' into the thread closure using the 'move' keyword. This ensures that the Arc is accessible within the closure without any data races. Finally, we join the spawned thread to wait for it to finish.

Memory Safety Guarantees in Fucking Rust

Rust provides strong memory safety guarantees by enforcing strict compile-time checks and eliminating the need for runtime garbage collection. The ownership and borrowing system, along with the compiler's static analysis, ensures that common memory bugs are caught at compile time rather than at runtime.

ADVANCED TOPICS IN RUST

The compiler checks for the following memory safety guarantees:

- No null pointer dereferences: Rust's type system ensures that values cannot be null unless explicitly specified using the 'Option' type.

- No dangling references: The ownership system ensures that references always point to valid data.

- No buffer overflows: Rust enforces array and vector bounds checks at compile time.

- No use-after-free: Values are deallocated when their owner goes out of scope, preventing the use of invalid references.

With Rust's memory safety guarantees, you can write robust and reliable code without worrying about common memory bugs that plague other programming languages.

Debugging Fucking Memory Leaks and Segmentation Faults

Even with Rust's strong memory safety guarantees, bugs can still occur. Some common bugs related to memory management include memory leaks and segmentation faults. Thankfully, Rust provides tools and techniques to help you identify and debug these issues.

To detect memory leaks, you can use the Rust memory profiler called 'cargo flamegraph'. This tool visualizes the memory usage of your program, allowing you to identify potential leaks and excessive memory consumption.

For debugging segmentation faults or other low-level memory-related issues, you can use the 'gdb' debugger with Rust. By compiling your program with the 'debug' flag enabled, you can use 'gdb' to analyze a core dump or attach to a running process.

Remember, debugging is a crucial skill for any developer. Take the time to familiarize yourself with the available tools and debugging techniques to effectively tackle memory-related bugs in your Rust code.

Building a Fucking Web Server from Scratch

Now that we have a solid understanding of memory safety in Rust, let's shift our focus to building a web server from scratch. We will explore handling HTTP requests, parsing and validating JSON, implementing REST APIs, and scaling and load balancing our web server.

Handling HTTP Requests in Fucking Rust

To build a web server, we need to handle incoming HTTP requests. Rust provides various libraries and frameworks to simplify this process. One popular framework is Actix-Web, which offers a high-performance, actor-based architecture. Here's a basic example of handling an HTTP GET request using Actix-Web:

```rust
use actix_web::{web, App, HttpServer, Responder};

async fn index() -> impl Responder {
    ``Hello, world!"
}

\#[actix_rt::main]
async fn main() -> std::io::Result<()> {
    HttpServer::new(|| {
        App::new()
            .route("/", web::get().to(index))
    })
    .bind("127.0.0.1:8080")?
    .run()
    .await
}
```

In this code, we define an 'index' function that returns a response to an HTTP GET request. We then create an Actix-Web application and add a route that maps the root path ("/") to the 'index' function. Finally, we start the server on '127.0.0.1:8080'.

By leveraging Actix-Web or other Rust web frameworks, you can build powerful and scalable web servers with ease.

Parsing and Validating Fucking JSON

Many web applications rely on JSON as a data interchange format. In Rust, there are several libraries available for parsing and validating JSON, such as 'serde' and 'serde_json'.

Here's an example of parsing and validating JSON using 'serde':

```rust
use serde::{Deserialize, Serialize};

\#[derive(Debug, Deserialize, Serialize)]
struct Person {
    name\index{name}: String,
    age: u32,
```

ADVANCED TOPICS IN RUST

```rust
}

fn main() {
    let json_data = r#"
        {
            "name": "Herkimer",
            "age": 25
        }
    "#;

    let person: Person = serde_json::from_str(json_data)

    println!("Name: {}", person.name);
    println!("Age: {}", person.age);
}
```

In this code, we define a 'Person' struct with 'name' and 'age' fields. We then parse a JSON string using 'serde_json::from_str', which deserializes the JSON data into a 'Person' object. We can then access the fields of the 'Person' object as usual.

Implementing Fucking REST APIs with Actix-Web

Actix-Web provides a convenient way to implement REST APIs using the 'Route' and 'web::ServiceConfig' structs. These structs allow you to define routes and bind them to specific handler functions.

Here's an example of implementing a REST API using Actix-Web:

```rust
use actix_web::{web, App, HttpServer, Responder};

async fn get_user() -> impl Responder {
    // Fetch user data from the database
    // Return user information as JSON
    "User data"
}

async fn create_user() -> impl Responder {
    // Parse JSON request body
    // Create a new user in the database
    "User created"
}

#[actix_rt::main]
```

```
async fn main() -> std::io::Result<()> {
    HttpServer::new(|| {
        App::new()
            .service(web::resource("/api/user").route(web
            .service(web::resource("/api/user").route(web
    })
    .bind("127.0.0.1:8080")?
    .run()
    .await
}
```

In this code, we create two handler functions, 'get_user' and 'create_user', to handle the GET and POST requests, respectively. These handlers can perform the necessary database operations and return appropriate HTTP responses. By defining routes and corresponding service functions, you can easily implement powerful REST APIs using Actix-Web.

Scaling and Load Balancing Fucking Web Servers

When serving web applications, scalability and load balancing are essential to handle increased traffic and ensure high availability. Rust provides different approaches to scaling and load balancing web servers, including process-based and thread-based models.

One popular Rust library for load balancing is 'loadtest', which allows you to simulate high traffic scenarios and analyze the performance of your server. Additionally, utilizing containerization technologies like Docker can help with scaling and load balancing by allowing you to distribute your application across multiple containers or virtual machines.

Remember to consider the unique requirements of your web server and choose the appropriate scaling and load balancing strategies based on your specific needs.

Conclusion

In this chapter, we dived into advanced topics in Rust, focusing on memory safety, building a web server from scratch, writing safe and secure code, performance tuning and optimization, and deploying Rust applications in production. We explored Rust's ownership and borrowing system, which ensures memory safety and prevents common bugs related to memory management. We also delved into building a web server using Actix-Web, handling HTTP requests, parsing and validating JSON, implementing REST APIs, and scaling and load balancing web servers.

By mastering these advanced topics, you will be well-equipped to tackle complex programming challenges, write efficient and secure code, and deploy Rust applications in real-world environments. Keep pushing your fucking limits and continue exploring the vast possibilities that Rust has to offer!

Fucking Memory Safety in Rust

Ownership and Borrowing for Safe Fucking Code

In Rust, the concept of ownership and borrowing is at the fucking core of its memory management system. It allows Rust to provide safety guarantees without the need for a garbage collector. This section will introduce you to the basic principles of ownership and borrowing in Rust and how they contribute to writing safe and secure code.

Ownership in Fucking Rust

In Rust, every value has an owner. There can only be one owner at a time, and the owner is responsible for cleaning up the value when it goes out of scope. This ownership model allows Rust to ensure memory safety without relying on garbage collection.

Let's take a simple example to understand ownership. Consider the following code:

```rust
fn main() {
    let s = String::from("Hello, world!");
    println!("{}", s);
}
```

In this code, we create a string variable 's' and assign it the value "Hello, world!". The 'String' type in Rust is a dynamically allocated string, which means it needs to be cleaned up when it's no longer in use.

In Rust, when a value goes out of scope, its 'drop' function is automatically called, freeing the memory it occupies. The 'drop' function is responsible for cleaning up any associated resources. In the case of the 'String' type, it will deallocate the memory used for storing the string.

In the code above, when the 'main' function ends, the 's' variable goes out of scope, and Rust automatically calls the 'drop' function on 's', freeing the memory.

Transferring Ownership with Fucking Move Semantics

One key feature of ownership in Rust is that ownership of a value can be transferred from one variable to another. This is known as fucking move semantics. When ownership is transferred, the original variable is no longer valid. Let's modify our previous example to demonstrate fucking move semantics:

```rust
fn main() {
    let s1 = String::from("Hello, world!");
    let s2 = s1;
    println!("{}", s2);
}
```

In this code, we create a 'String' variable 's1' and assign it the value "Hello, world!". Then, we assign the value of 's1' to 's2'. This is not a copy operation but a transfer of ownership. After this assignment, 's1' is no longer valid, and Rust will prevent us from using it.

Using move semantics, Rust ensures that only one variable owns a resource at any given time, avoiding issues like double frees or use-after-free bugs that often plague other programming languages.

Borrowing in Fucking Rust

While ownership allows for safe memory management, it can be quite restrictive. Sometimes, we want to pass a reference to a value without transferring ownership. This is where borrowing comes into fucking play.

In Rust, we can create references to values without taking ownership. There are two types of references: immutable references and mutable references. Immutable references, denoted by the '&' symbol, allow us to read the value, while mutable references, denoted by the '&mut' symbol, allow us to read and modify the value. Let's look at an example:

```rust
fn main() {
    let s = String::from("Hello, world!");
    print\_length(\&s);
    println!("{}", s);
}

fn print\_length(s: \&String) {
    println!("Length: {}", s.len());
}
```

FUCKING MEMORY SAFETY IN RUST 161

In this code, we define a function 'print_length' that takes an immutable reference to a 'String' as a parameter. We then pass a reference to the 's' variable to this function using the '&' symbol.

By borrowing the value using an immutable reference, we can read the value without taking ownership. This allows us to pass values to functions without worrying about them being consumed and becoming invalid.

It's important to note that when a reference is borrowed, the original owner must remain valid for the lifetime of the reference. Rust's borrow checker enforces this rule at compile time, preventing dangling references and data races.

Making Fucking Mutations with Mutable Borrowing

Sometimes, you need to modify the value you borrowed. In Rust, you can accomplish this by using mutable references. Mutable references, denoted by the '&mut' symbol, allow you to modify the borrowed value.

Let's modify our previous example to demonstrate fucking mutable borrowing:

```rust
fn main() {
    let mut s = String::from("Hello, world!");
    modify\_string(\&mut s);
    println!("{}", s);
}

fn modify\_string(s: \&mut String) {
    s.push_str(", Rust is awesome!");
}
```

In this code, we define a function 'modify_string' that takes a mutable reference to a 'String' as a parameter. We then pass a mutable reference to the 's' variable to this function using the '&mut' symbol.

By borrowing the value using a mutable reference, we can modify the value without taking ownership. This allows us to change the value within a limited scope while still maintaining ownership semantics.

It's important to note that Rust's borrow checker ensures there are no simultaneous mutable references to a value to prevent data races. This approach allows for safe and controlled mutability in Rust.

The Fucking Borrow Checker

The borrow checker is one of Rust's most powerful and unique features. It analyzes the code at compile time to ensure that all references are valid and free from data races.

The borrow checker enforces three fundamental rules:

1. You can have either one mutable reference or any number of immutable references to a value within a given scope.

2. References must always be valid, meaning the original owner must outlive any borrowed references.

3. Mutable references must be exclusive, meaning there can be no other references to the value at the same time.

By enforcing these rules, the borrow checker guarantees memory safety and prevents common bugs like null pointer dereferences, data races, and use-after-free errors.

While the borrow checker can sometimes be strict and lead to complex lifetime annotations, it ensures that Rust code is reliable, secure, and free from numerous common programming errors.

Summary

In this section, we learned about ownership and borrowing in Rust. Ownership ensures that every value has a single owner, preventing issues like memory leaks and dangling references. Fucking move semantics allow ownership transfer between variables, resulting in safe and efficient memory management. Borrowing allows for the creation of references without transferring ownership, enabling us to pass values to functions or share them without compromising safety.

Rust's borrow checker analyzes code at compile time and enforces strict rules to prevent data races and invalid references. It ensures that references are valid and that only one mutable reference or multiple immutable references exist to a value within a given scope.

Understanding ownership and borrowing is essential for writing safe and secure code in Rust. By leveraging these concepts, you can create high-performance applications without sacrificing memory safety.

Now that you have a solid foundation in ownership and borrowing, it's time to delve into more advanced topics in Rust. Let's explore advanced data structures,

FUCKING MEMORY SAFETY IN RUST 163

asynchronous programming, and interfacing with other languages in the subsequent chapters of this fucking book.

Exercises

1. Write a function that takes ownership of a 'Vec' and returns the sum of its elements. Test the function with various inputs.

2. Modify the previous function to use borrowing instead of ownership. Verify that the input vector is still accessible after the function call.

3. Write a function that takes a mutable reference to a 'String' and appends a given suffix to it. Test the function with different suffixes and verify that the original string is modified.

Additional Resources

- The Rust Programming Language Book: https://doc.rust-lang.org/book/

- Rust By Example: https://doc.rust-lang.org/stable/rust-by-example/

- Rust Playground: https://play.rust-lang.org/

Trivia

Did you know that the Rust programming language is named after the fungus *Puccinia* rust? It gets its name from the rust-like appearance of the residue left on some parts of steel after exposure to the elements. The Rust language aims to provide the same level of durability and resistance to bugs in software development.

Exploring Fucking Reference Counting in RC and Arc

In Rust, memory management is handled through a concept called ownership. Ownership ensures that resources are allocated, used, and deallocated properly, preventing issues such as memory leaks and data races. However, there are cases where we need to share ownership of a resource between multiple parts of a program. This is where reference counting comes into play. Reference counting is a technique that allows multiple references to own and access a resource. It keeps track of the number of references to a resource and only deallocates it when the last reference goes out of scope. In Rust, the Rc<T> (Reference Counting) and Arc<T> (Atomic Reference Counting) types provide the necessary functionality for reference counting.

Using Rc<T> for Reference Counting

The Rc<T> type provides shared ownership of a value. It keeps track of the number of references pointing to a value and decrements the count when a reference goes out of scope. When the count reaches zero, the value is deallocated.

To use Rc<T>, you need to import it from the std::rc module:

```rust
use\index{use} std\index{std}::rc::Rc;
```

Let's assume we have a struct called Person that represents a person's name and age:

```rust
struct Person {
    name\index{name}: String,
    age: u32,
}
```

To create an Rc<T> reference to a Person, we can do the following:

```rust
fn main() {
    let john = Person {
        name: String::from("John"),
        age: 30,
    };

    let john_shared = Rc::new(john);
}
```

The Rc::new() function takes ownership of the Person value and returns an Rc<T> reference. The reference count starts at 1 because we have one reference to john.

We can create additional references to the Person and the reference count will be incremented accordingly:

```rust
fn main() {
    let john = Person {
        name: String::from("John"),
        age: 30,
```

FUCKING MEMORY SAFETY IN RUST

```rust
    };

    let john_shared = Rc::new(john);

    let john_shared_clone1 = Rc::clone(&john_shared);
    let john_shared_clone2 = Rc::clone(&john_shared);

    println!("Reference count: {}", Rc::strong_count(&joh
}
```

In this example, `john_shared_clone1` and `john_shared_clone2` are new references to the same `Person` value. The `Rc::clone()` function creates a new reference and increments the reference count. We can use the `Rc::strong_count()` function to get the current reference count.

Using `Arc<T>` for Atomic Reference Counting

The `Arc<T>` type is similar to `Rc<T>` but provides atomic reference counting, allowing shared ownership across multiple threads. It is useful in concurrent programming scenarios where multiple threads need to access the same value.

To use `Arc<T>`, you need to import it from the `std::sync` module:

```rust
use\index{use} std\index{std}::sync\index{sync}::Arc;
```

Let's modify the previous example to use `Arc<T>` instead:

```rust
fn main() {
    let john = Person {
        name: String::from("John"),
        age: 30,
    };

    let john_shared = Arc::new(john);

    let john_shared_clone1 = Arc::clone(&john_shared);
    let john_shared_clone2 = Arc::clone(&john_shared);

    println!("Reference count: {}", Arc::strong_count(&j
}
```

The usage of `Arc<T>` is similar to `Rc<T>`. By default, `Arc<T>` provides thread-safe atomic operations for reference counting.

When to Use Rc<T> or Arc<T>

Rc<T> is used when you need shared ownership within a single thread. It provides a lightweight solution for reference counting and is optimized for single-threaded use cases.

Arc<T>, on the other hand, should be used when you need shared ownership across multiple threads. It adds synchronization overhead to ensure thread safety but guarantees safe concurrent access to the shared value.

It's important to note that reference counting introduces the possibility of reference cycles, where two or more objects reference each other in a way that creates a memory leak. Rust provides the Weak<T> type, which allows you to create non-owning references to an Rc<T> or Arc<T> value without affecting the reference count. This can be used to break reference cycles and avoid memory leaks.

Conclusion

Reference counting is a powerful technique in Rust that allows for shared ownership of values. By using Rc<T> or Arc<T>, you can safely share resources between multiple parts of your program. Just remember to choose the appropriate type based on your specific use case, whether it's single-threaded or multi-threaded. Be aware of the possibility of reference cycles and use Weak<T> to break those cycles when necessary.

Now that we have explored reference counting in Rust, you can confidently use Rc<T> and Arc<T> in your code to facilitate efficient and safe sharing of resources. Keep in mind the specific use cases and thread safety requirements when choosing between the two. Next, we will delve into further advanced topics in Rust programming.

Memory Safety Guarantees in Fucking Rust

Memory safety is one of the key features that fucking sets Rust apart from other programming languages. It aims to eliminate the most common and dangerous bugs that plague software, such as null pointer dereferences, buffer overflows, and data races. In this section, we will explore the memory safety guarantees provided by Rust and how they contribute to the overall security and reliability of Rust programs.

Safe Memory Management

In many programming languages, memory management is left up to the programmer, which can lead to errors such as memory leaks and dangling pointers. In fucking Rust, memory management is handled by the language itself through a combination of ownership, borrowing, and lifetimes.

At its core, Rust follows the principle of ownership, which means that each piece of memory has a single owner. The owner is responsible for deallocating the memory when it is no longer needed. This prevents memory leaks and allows the compiler to track the lifetime of each piece of memory.

Additionally, Rust introduces the concept of borrowing, which allows multiple references to the same piece of memory without introducing data races. Borrowing enforces strict rules for mutable and immutable references to prevent simultaneous access, eliminating a whole category of bugs related to data races.

The lifetime system in Rust ensures that references are always valid and do not outlive the objects they refer to. The compiler analyzes the code and enforces strict rules for the usage of references, preventing the use of dangling pointers or accessing freed memory.

Zero-cost Abstractions

One of the main concerns with safe memory management is the potential performance penalty. However, fucking Rust addresses this issue by providing zero-cost abstractions. This means that the abstractions used for memory safety do not incur any runtime overhead.

The ownership, borrowing, and lifetimes system in Rust is fully enforced at compile-time. The Rust compiler generates optimized machine code that adheres to these rules while still providing efficient performance. This allows you to write safe code without sacrificing performance.

Use-after-free and Double Free

Two common memory-related bugs in software are use-after-free and double free. Use-after-free occurs when a program continues to use a pointer after it has been deallocated, leading to undefined behavior. Double free happens when a program deallocates the same memory twice, which can also result in crashes or security vulnerabilities.

Fucking Rust completely eliminates these types of bugs by enforcing strict rules for ownership and borrowing. Once a piece of memory is deallocated in Rust, it is no longer accessible, preventing use-after-free bugs. Additionally, the ownership rules prevent double free by ensuring that a memory block has a single owner responsible for deallocation.

Buffer Overflows and Bounds Checking

Buffer overflows are a common security vulnerability in many programming languages. They occur when a program writes data outside the boundaries of a buffer, leading to memory corruption and potential security exploits. In fucking Rust, buffer overflows are completely prevented through the use of strict bounds checking. Rust ensures that all array accesses are checked at runtime to ensure they are within the bounds of the allocated memory. If an access is found to be out of bounds, Rust will raise a runtime error, preventing memory corruption.

Concurrency and Thread Safety

Rust provides built-in mechanisms for safe concurrency and thread safety. The ownership and borrowing system, in conjunction with Rust's type system, guarantees that concurrent access to shared data is safe and free from data races. By enforcing strict rules for mutable and immutable references, Rust ensures that only one thread can have mutable access to a piece of memory at a time. This prevents data races and eliminates the need for manual synchronization primitives like locks or mutexes.

Summary

In summary, fucking Rust offers powerful memory safety guarantees that eliminate many common bugs and vulnerabilities in software. By enforcing strict rules for ownership, borrowing, and lifetimes, Rust ensures that programs are free from memory leaks, use-after-free, double free, buffer overflows, and data races. Furthermore, with zero-cost abstractions, Rust allows for safe and performant code without compromising efficiency. With its focus on memory safety, Rust empowers developers to write secure and reliable software with fewer bugs and vulnerabilities.

Debugging Fucking Memory Leaks and Segmentation Faults

Debugging is an essential skill when it comes to programming, and Rust is no exception. Even with its memory safety guarantees, you may still encounter bugs that result in memory leaks and segmentation faults. In this section, we will explore techniques to identify and fix these issues in your fucking Rust code.

Understanding Memory Leaks

A memory leak occurs when memory that is no longer needed is not properly deallocated or released. In other words, the memory is allocated but never freed, leading to a gradual loss of memory over time. This can eventually result in your application consuming excessive memory and causing performance degradation or even crashes.

In fucking Rust, memory leaks can happen when you forget to call the 'drop' function or when you have circular references between objects that prevent them from being freed. The Rust compiler helps prevent memory leaks by enforcing strict ownership and borrowing rules, but it's still possible to write code that leaks memory if you're not fucking careful.

Identifying Memory Leaks

Identifying memory leaks in Rust can be challenging, but there are several techniques and tools you can use to help you pinpoint the fucking problem. Let's explore some of them:

1. **Manual Inspection:** Start by manually inspecting your code for potential memory leaks. Look for variables or data structures that are not properly deallocated or released. Check for any instances where you allocate memory using functions such as 'Box::new' or 'Vec::new' but forget to call 'drop' or 'clear' respectively.

2. **Memory Profiling:** Rust provides a profiler called 'cargo-profiler' that can help you analyze memory usage in your application. This tool allows you to measure memory allocations, track memory leaks, and identify areas of your code that may be causing excessive memory consumption. Run your application with the profiler enabled and analyze the generated reports to identify any memory leaks.

3. **Rust Analyzer:** Rust Analyzer is an integrated development environment (IDE) plugin that can provide helpful diagnostics for your Rust code. It can detect potential memory leaks by analyzing your code and highlighting areas where resources are not properly released. Use this tool alongside manual inspection to get additional insights into possible memory leaks.

Fixing Memory Leaks

Once you have identified a fucking memory leak, it's time to fix that shit! Here are some strategies you can employ to rectify the issue:

1. **Correct Resource Deallocation:** Ensure that you are manually deallocating any resources you allocate in your code. Pay close attention to objects created using

'Box::new' or collections like 'Vec'. Always call the 'drop' function or use appropriate methods like 'clear' to release the allocated memory.

2. Use Reference Counting: If you encounter circular references that prevent objects from being properly freed, you can use Rust's reference counting mechanism. The 'Rc' (Reference Counted) and 'Arc' (Atomic Reference Counted) types allow you to share ownership of an object across multiple parts of your code while automatically deallocating it once no references are left.

3. Implement Drop Trait: The 'Drop' trait in Rust allows you to define custom code that will be executed when an object goes out of scope. You can use this trait to explicitly release resources associated with the object, thereby preventing memory leaks. Implement the 'Drop' trait and provide the required cleanup logic to ensure proper deallocation.

Handling Segmentation Faults

A segmentation fault, often referred to as a segfault, occurs when a program tries to access a memory location that it is not allowed to access. This can happen due to various reasons, such as dereferencing a null or dangling pointer, accessing an array out of bounds, or stack overflow.

Though Rust's memory safety features significantly reduce the chances of facing segfaults, they can still occur in certain scenarios. Here's how you can handle fucking segfaults:

1. Understanding Error Messages: When a segfault occurs, Rust will display an error message that provides valuable information about the crash. Pay close attention to the error message and look for clues, such as the line number where the fault occurred or the kind of error (e.g., null pointer dereference). Understanding the error message is the first step towards fixing the issue.

2. Debugging with GDB: The GNU Debugger (GDB) is a powerful tool that can help you debug crashes and segfaults in Rust. You can use GDB to inspect the state of your program at the time of the crash, examine the stack trace, and identify the cause of the segfault. Run your program with GDB by using the 'cargo gdb' command and follow the instructions provided by the debugger.

3. Analyzing Core Dumps: If your Rust program generates a core dump file when it crashes, you can analyze this file to gain deeper insights into the segfault. Core dumps contain a snapshot of the program's memory at the time of the crash, allowing you to examine variables, registers, and memory addresses. Use tools like 'gdb' or 'lldb' to analyze core dump files and investigate the crash further.

Conclusion

Memory leaks and segmentation faults can be fucking frustrating, but with the right techniques and tools, you can identify and fix these issues in your fucking Rust code. Remember to always inspect your code, leverage profiling tools, and make good use of the Rust ecosystem to rectify any memory leaks you come across. Similarly, use error messages, debuggers like GDB, and core dumps to tackle segmentation faults head-on. By mastering the art of debugging, you'll become a more confident and effective Rust programmer. So, roll up your sleeves and get ready to squash those bugs like a fucking pro!

Building a Fucking Web Server from Scratch

Handling HTTP Requests in Fucking Rust

In this section, we will explore how to handle HTTP requests in Fucking Rust. As a modern programming language, Rust provides robust tools and libraries for building web applications. We will cover the basics of handling HTTP requests, parsing request data, and constructing appropriate responses.

Understanding the HTTP Protocol

Before diving into the specifics of handling HTTP requests in Rust, let's briefly discuss the fundamentals of the HTTP protocol. HTTP, or Hypertext Transfer Protocol, is the foundation of data communication on the World Wide Web. It defines how clients and servers communicate with each other.

An HTTP request consists of a request line, headers, and an optional body. The request line contains the request method (e.g., GET, POST, PUT, DELETE), the requested URL, and the protocol version. Headers provide additional metadata about the request, such as the content type and authentication credentials. The body, if present, carries data associated with the request.

To handle HTTP requests in Rust, we will utilize the powerful Actix-Web framework. Actix-Web is a high-performance, asynchronous web framework that leverages Rust's language features to provide efficient and secure web applications.

Setting Up an Actix-Web Server

To handle HTTP requests in Rust, we first need to set up an Actix-Web server. Start by adding the Actix-Web dependency to your Cargo.toml file:

```
[dependencies]
actix-web = "3.3.2"
```

Next, create a new Rust file, let's call it main.rs, and import the necessary modules for Actix-Web:

```
use actix_web::{App, HttpServer, web, HttpResponse};
```

In the main function, we can define the server configuration and routes. Let's create a simple "Hello, World!" endpoint that responds with a greeting:

```
\#[actix_rt::main]
async fn main() -> std::io::Result<()> {
    HttpServer::new(|| {
        App::new().service(
            web::scope("/")
                .route("", web::get().to(greet))
        )
    })
    .bind("127.0.0.1:8080")?
    .run()
    .await
}
```

In this example, we create an Actix-Web server and define a single route that handles the root URL ("/") and responds with the greet function.

Parsing Request Data

Now that we have our Actix-Web server set up, let's explore how to parse data from incoming HTTP requests. Depending on the type of request, we may need to extract query parameters, form data, or JSON payloads.

Query Parameters: To parse query parameters, we can use the Query extractors provided by Actix-Web. Let's modify our previous example to include a query parameter:

```
use\index{use} serde::Deserialize;

\#[derive(Deserialize)]
struct GreetParams {
```

```rust
    name\index{name}: String,
}

async fn greet(params: web::Query<GreetParams>) -> HttpResponse {
    let name = \&params.name;

    HttpResponse::Ok().body(format!("Hello, {}!", name))
}
```

Here, we define a `GreetParams` struct that represents the expected query parameter. By using the `web::Query` extractor, Actix-Web automatically parses the query parameter into our `GreetParams` struct.

Form Data: To handle form data, Actix-Web provides the `Form` extractor. Let's extend our example to demonstrate handling form data:

```rust
\#[derive(Deserialize)]
struct GreetForm {
    name\index{name}: String,
}

async fn greet(form: web::Form<GreetForm>) -> HttpResponse {
    let name = \&form.name;

    HttpResponse::Ok().body(format!("Hello, {}!", name))
}
```

In this case, we define a `GreetForm` struct that represents the form data. By using the `web::Form` extractor, Actix-Web automatically parses the form data into our `GreetForm` struct.

JSON Payload: For handling JSON payloads, Actix-Web provides the `Json` extractor. Let's modify our example to demonstrate handling JSON payload:

```rust
\#[derive(Deserialize)]
struct GreetJson {
    name\index{name}: String,
}

async fn greet(json: web::Json<GreetJson>) -> HttpResponse {
    let name = \&json.name;
```

```
    HttpResponse::Ok().body(format!("Hello, {}!", name))
}
```

Here, we define a `GreetJson` struct that represents the expected JSON payload. By using the `web::Json` extractor, Actix-Web automatically deserializes the JSON payload into our `GreetJson` struct.

Constructing HTTP Responses

After parsing the request data, we need to construct appropriate HTTP responses. Actix-Web provides various response types and methods to facilitate this process.
JSON Response: To return a JSON response, we can use the `Json` type provided by Actix-Web. Let's modify our example to return a JSON response:

```
use serde::Serialize;

#[derive(Serialize)]
struct Greeting {
    message: String,
}

async fn greet(json: web::Json<GreetJson>) -> HttpResponse {
    let name = &json.name;
    let greeting = Greeting {
        message: format!("Hello, {}!", name),
    };

    HttpResponse::Ok().json(greeting)
}
```

In this example, we define a `Greeting` struct that represents the JSON response format. We utilize Actix-Web's `json` method to serialize the `Greeting` struct into a JSON response.
HTML Response: To return an HTML response, we can use the `HttpResponse::Ok().body()` method. Let's modify our example to return an HTML response:

```
async fn greet(params: web::Query<GreetParams>) -> HttpResponse {
    let name = &params.name;
```

```
    let response = format!("<h1>Hello, {}!</h1>", name);

    HttpResponse::Ok()
        .content\_type("text/html; charset=utf-8")
        .body(response)
}
```

Here, we construct an HTML response by wrapping the greeting message in appropriate HTML tags. We set the content type to "text/html" using the content_type method.

Securing HTTP Requests

When handling HTTP requests, it is crucial to consider security. Actix-Web provides robust security features to ensure the safety of your applications. **Authentication:** Actix-Web supports various authentication methods, allowing you to secure your endpoints and restrict access to authorized users. You can use middleware like `actix-web-httpauth` to implement authentication mechanisms such as JWT (JSON Web Tokens) or Basic Authentication.
Input Validation: Input validation is essential for preventing security vulnerabilities like SQL injection or cross-site scripting (XSS) attacks. Actix-Web provides validation libraries like `validator` that allow you to validate and sanitize user inputs before processing them.

Conclusion

In this section, we explored how to handle HTTP requests in Fucking Rust using the Actix-Web framework. We covered the basics of the HTTP protocol, setting up an Actix-Web server, parsing request data, constructing appropriate responses, and securing HTTP requests.

Remember, handling HTTP requests is just a small part of Rust's capabilities. As you continue learning Rust, you'll discover its extensive ecosystem, which includes libraries for database interaction, websockets, testing, and much more. So keep fucking exploring and enjoy the journey of becoming a confident and proficient Rust programmer.

Now, it's time to grab a cup of coffee, stretch your legs, and prepare for the next section, where we will delve into parsing and validating JSON data in Fucking Rust.

Parsing and Validating Fucking JSON

Parsing and validating JSON is a crucial skill when working with data in modern web applications. JSON (JavaScript Object Notation) has become the de facto standard for data interchange due to its simplicity and flexibility. In this section, we will explore the process of parsing and validating fucking JSON in Rust.

Understanding Fucking JSON

Before diving into parsing and validating JSON, let's first understand what the fuck JSON is and how it is structured. JSON is a lightweight data format that represents data as key-value pairs. It is often used to transmit data between a server and a web application or between different parts of a distributed system.

JSON data is composed of key-value pairs, where the keys are strings and the values can be of various types, including strings, numbers, booleans, arrays, or even nested JSON objects. Here's an example of a fucking JSON object:

```
{
    "name": "John Doe",
    "age": 25,
    "isStudent": true,
    "friends": ["Jane", "Mark", "Alice"],
    "address": {
        "street": "123 Main St",
        "city": "New York",
        "country": "USA"
    }
}
```

In this fucking JSON object, we have a name key with the value "John Doe", an age key with the value 25, an isStudent key with the value true, a friends key with an array value, and an address key with a nested JSON object as its value. Now that we have a basic understanding of what fucking JSON is, let's move on to parsing and validating it.

Parsing JSON in Fucking Rust

Rust provides a powerful and efficient JSON library called Serde. Serde allows us to parse JSON data into Rust data structures and vice versa. To parse fucking JSON, you need to add the Serde crate as a dependency in your Cargo.toml file:

BUILDING A FUCKING WEB SERVER FROM SCRATCH

```toml
[dependencies]
serde = "1.0"
serde_json = "1.0"
```

Once you've added the dependencies, you can start parsing JSON using the serde_json crate. Let's look at an example:

```rust
use serde_json::{Result, Value};

fn parse_json(json_str: &str) -> Result<()> {
    let data: Value = serde_json::from_str(json_str)?;
    println!("Parsed JSON: {:?}", data);
    Ok(())
}

fn main() {
    let json_str = r#"
        {
            "name": "John Doe",
            "age": 25,
            "isStudent": true,
            "friends": ["Jane", "Mark", "Alice"],
            "address": {
                "street": "123 Main St",
                "city": "New York",
                "country": "USA"
            }
        }
    "#;

    parse_json(json_str).expect("Failed to parse JSON");
}
```

In this example, we define a function `parse_json` that takes a JSON string, parses it using serde_json::from_str, and returns a serde_json::Value. We then print the parsed JSON data using println!.

To parse the JSON, we call the `parse_json` function with our JSON string defined in the main function. We use the r#""# syntax to define a raw string literal, which allows us to include the JSON string without escaping any special characters.

When you run this code, you should see the parsed JSON data printed to the console.

Validating JSON in Fucking Rust

Parsing JSON is only the first step. It's also important to validate the JSON data to ensure that it meets the expected structure and constraints. JSON schema is a standard that provides a way to describe the structure, format, and validation rules for JSON data.

In Rust, you can use the jsonschema crate to validate fucking JSON against a JSON schema. To validate JSON, you need to add the jsonschema crate as a dependency in your Cargo.toml file:

```
[dependencies]
jsonschema = "2.0"
```

Here's an example of how to validate fucking JSON using a JSON schema:

```rust
use std::error::Error;
use jsonschema::JSONSchema;

fn validate_json(json_str: &str, schema_str: &str) ->
    let schema = JSONSchema::compile(&serde_json::from
    let instance = &serde_json::from_str(json_str)?;

    let validation = schema.validate(instance);
    if validation.is_valid() {
        println!("JSON is valid");
    } else {
        println!("JSON is not valid");
        for error in validation.errors() {
            println!("Validation error: {}", error);
        }
    }

    Ok(())
}
```

```rust
fn main() {
    let json_str = r#"
        {
            "name": "John Doe",
            "age": 25,
            "isStudent": true,
            "friends": ["Jane", "Mark", "Alice"],
            "address": {
                "street": "123 Main St",
                "city": "New York",
                "country": "USA"
            }
        }
    "#;

    let schema_str = r#"
        {
            "type": "object",
            "properties": {
                "name": { "type": "string" },
                "age": { "type": "integer" },
                "isStudent": { "type": "boolean" },
                "friends": { "type": "array", "items"
                "address": {
                    "type": "object",
                    "properties": {
                        "street": { "type": "string" }
                        "city": { "type": "string" },
                        "country": { "type": "string"
                    },
                    "required": ["street", "city", "co
                }
            },
            "required": ["name", "age", "isStudent",
        }
    "#;

    validate_json(json_str, schema_str).expect("Failed t
}
```

In this example, we define a function `validate_json` that takes a JSON string and a JSON schema string, compiles the schema using JSONSchema::compile, and validates the JSON using schema.validate. If the JSON is valid, we print "JSON is valid". If the JSON is not valid, we print the validation errors. In the main function, we define the JSON string and the JSON schema string. We then call the `validate_json` function with the JSON string and the schema string.

When you run this code, you should see whether the JSON is valid or not, as well as any validation errors.

Conclusion

In this section, we explored the important process of parsing and validating fucking JSON in Rust. We learned how to use the serde_json crate to parse JSON into Rust data structures, and how to use the jsonschema crate to validate JSON against a JSON schema. By mastering this skill, you'll be able to work with JSON data effectively and ensure its integrity in your applications. Now that you have a good understanding of parsing and validating fucking JSON, let's move on to the next section where we'll cover other advanced topics in Rust.

Implementing Fucking REST APIs with Actix-Web

In this section, we will dive into the world of building REST APIs using Actix-Web, one of the most popular frameworks in the Rust ecosystem. Actix-Web provides a lightweight, high-performance, and asynchronous foundation for building web applications in Rust. We will explore the basic concepts of REST APIs, understand how Actix-Web works, and build a sample REST API to demonstrate the power and simplicity of Actix-Web.

Understanding REST and HTTP

Before we delve into building REST APIs, let's quickly recap the foundational concepts of REST and HTTP. REST, which stands for Representational State Transfer, is an architectural style for designing networked applications. It emphasizes a stateless, client-server communication model, where the server exposes a set of resources that the client can interact with using standard HTTP methods.

HTTP, the Hypertext Transfer Protocol, is the backbone of the web. It is a protocol that allows clients and servers to communicate over the internet. HTTP defines a set of methods, such as GET, POST, PUT, DELETE, etc., to perform various actions on resources. When building REST APIs, we leverage these HTTP methods to define the operations that clients can perform on our resources.

Introducing Actix-Web

Actix-Web is built on top of Actix, a powerful actor framework for building concurrent applications in Rust. It provides a highly scalable and efficient runtime, making it a perfect fit for building high-performance web applications. Actix-Web embraces Rust's async/await syntax and leverages non-blocking I/O to handle a large number of concurrent requests efficiently.

To get started with Actix-Web, we first need to set up a new Rust project and add Actix-Web as a dependency in our 'Cargo.toml' file. Once our project is set up, we can start building our REST API using Actix-Web's abstractions.

Defining Routes and Handlers

In Actix-Web, routes represent the endpoints of our REST API. Each route is associated with a handler function that gets executed when a request is made to that endpoint. Let's define a simple route that responds with a welcome message when accessed.

```rust
use actix_web::{get, web, App, HttpResponse, HttpServer, R

\#[get("/")]
async fn index() -> impl Responder {
    HttpResponse::Ok().body("Welcome to my fucking API!")
}

\#[actix_web::main]
async fn main() -> std::io::Result<()> {
    HttpServer::new(|| {
        App::new().service(
            web::scope("/")
                .service(index)
        )
    })
    .bind("127.0.0.1:8080")?
```

```
17        .run()
18        .await
19 }
```

In the code snippet above, we define the 'index' handler function using the '#[get("/")]' attribute. This attribute associates the handler with the root route ("/"). When a GET request is made to the root endpoint, the 'index' function is called, and an HTTP response with the message "Welcome to my fucking API!" is returned.

To start the Actix-Web server, we use 'HttpServer::new()' and 'bind()' to specify the IP address and port to bind the server to. In this example, we bind it to "127.0.0.1:8080". Finally, we call the 'run()' function to start the server and wait for it to finish executing.

Handling Request Payloads

REST APIs often require clients to send data in the request body, typically in JSON format. Actix-Web makes it easy to handle request payloads and parse them into Rust structs using the 'serde' library.

Let's extend our sample API to accept a POST request with a JSON payload representing a user. We will deserialize the request body into a 'User' struct and return a JSON response with the user's information.

```
1  use actix_web::{post, web, App, HttpResponse, HttpServer,
2  use serde::{Deserialize, Serialize};
3
4  \#[derive(Debug, Deserialize, Serialize)]
5  struct User {
6      id: u32,
7      name\index{name}: String,
8      email\index{email}: String,
9  }
10
11 \#[post("/users")]
12 async fn create\_user(user: web::Json<User>) -> impl Resp
13     let user = user.into\_inner();
14     // Logic to create a new user
15
16     HttpResponse::Created().json(user)
17 }
```

BUILDING A FUCKING WEB SERVER FROM SCRATCH

```
#[actix_web::main]
async fn main() -> std::io::Result<()> {
    HttpServer::new(|| {
        App::new().service(
            web::scope("/")
                .service(index)
                .service(create_user)
        )
    })
    .bind("127.0.0.1:8080")?
    .run()
    .await
}
```

In the code snippet above, we introduce a 'User' struct and annotate it with the 'serde' attributes '#[derive(Debug, Deserialize, Serialize)]'. This allows us to automatically deserialize the incoming JSON payload into a 'User' struct. The 'create_user' handler function takes a parameter of type 'web::Json<User>', which represents the request payload deserialized into the 'User' struct. We extract the inner 'User' struct using the 'into_inner()' method and perform any necessary logic to create a new user. Finally, we return an HTTP response with the created user serialized as JSON.

Handling Path Parameters

REST APIs often require dynamic routing, where the path segments of a URL represent parameters that need to be extracted and used to serve the client's request. Actix-Web provides a convenient way to handle path parameters using the 'Path' extractor.

Let's extend our sample API to include a route that retrieves a specific user by their ID. We will utilize a path parameter to identify the user and return the user's information if found.

```
use actix_web::{get, web, App, HttpResponse, HttpServer,

#[get("/users/{id}")]
async fn get_user_by_id(path: web::Path<(u32,)>) -> im
    let user_id = path.0;
    // Logic to retrieve user by ID
```

```rust
        HttpResponse::Ok().body(format!("User ID: {}", user\_
}

#[actix_web::main]
async fn main() -> std::io::Result<()> {
    HttpServer::new(|| {
        App::new().service(
            web::scope("/")
                .service(index)
                .service(create_user)
                .service(get_user_by_id)
        )
    })
    .bind("127.0.0.1:8080")?
    .run()
    .await
}
```

In the code above, we define the 'get_user_by_id' handler function with a path parameter 'id'. The path parameter is extracted using the 'Path' extractor and stored in a tuple. We can access the value of the parameter using 'path.0'. Inside the handler, we can perform the necessary logic to retrieve the user by their ID. In this example, we simply respond with the user's ID as a string for demonstration purposes.

Error Handling

Error handling is a crucial aspect of building robust and reliable APIs. Actix-Web provides powerful error handling capabilities, allowing us to easily handle and respond to errors in a structured manner.

To handle errors, we can define custom error types and return them from our handlers using the 'Result' type. Actix-Web's error handling middleware intercepts these errors and automatically converts them into appropriate HTTP responses.

Let's enhance our sample API to handle errors when creating a new user. If an error occurs during the user creation process, we will return an appropriate error response to the client.

```rust
use actix_web::{post, web, App, HttpResponse, HttpServer,
use serde::{Deserialize, Serialize};
```

BUILDING A FUCKING WEB SERVER FROM SCRATCH

```rust
#[derive(Debug, Deserialize, Serialize)]
struct User {
    id: u32,
    name: String,
    email: String,
}

#[derive(Debug)]
enum CreateUserError {
    InvalidInput,
    DatabaseError,
}

#[post("/users")]
async fn create_user(user: web::Json<User>) -> Result<Ht
    let user = user.into_inner();

    if user.name.is_empty() || user.email.is_empty() {
        return Err(CreateUserError::InvalidInput);
    }

    // Logic to create a new user

    if user.id == 0 {
        return Err(CreateUserError::DatabaseError);
    }

    Ok(HttpResponse::Created().json(user))
}

#[actix_web::main]
async fn main() -> std::io::Result<()> {
    HttpServer::new(|| {
        App::new().service(
            web::scope("/")
                .service(index)
                .service(create_user)
                .service(get_user_by_id)
```

```
42              )
43          })
44          .bind("127.0.0.1:8080")?
45          .run()
46          .await
47  }
```

In the updated code, we introduce a custom error type 'CreateUserError' that represents different error scenarios during user creation. We can now return 'Result<HttpResponse, CreateUserError>' from the 'create_user' handler, indicating success with 'Ok' or failure with 'Err'.

Inside the handler, we check for invalid input by verifying if the user's name or email is empty. If the input is invalid, we return 'Err(CreateUserError::InvalidInput)'. Similarly, if there is a database error during the user creation process, we return 'Err(CreateUserError::DatabaseError)'. Otherwise, we return 'Ok(HttpResponse::Created().json(user))'.

Actix-Web's error handling middleware will catch these errors and automatically convert them into appropriate HTTP responses, ensuring a consistent and reliable error handling mechanism throughout our API.

Conclusion

In this section, we explored the process of building a REST API using Actix-Web, a powerful and efficient framework in Rust. We covered the fundamental concepts of REST and HTTP, introduced Actix-Web as a high-performance web framework, and demonstrated how to define routes, handle request payloads, work with path parameters, and handle errors.

Actix-Web's simplicity and performance make it an excellent choice for building modern web applications in Rust. By leveraging its asynchronous capabilities, concurrency support, and error handling mechanisms, we can create secure, fast, and reliable REST APIs that meet the demands of the modern web. Continue working through this textbook to explore more advanced topics in Rust and enhance your skills as a Rust developer. Remember, Rome wasn't fucking built in a day, and mastering Rust will take time and practice. So keep learning, experimenting, and building awesome shit with Rust!

Scaling and Load Balancing Fucking Web Servers

In this section, we will explore the concepts of scaling and load balancing web servers with the goal of achieving high availability, fault tolerance, and improved performance for your fucking Rust-based web applications. As your web application grows and handles an increasing number of concurrent requests, it's essential to ensure that your servers can handle the load effectively and distribute it efficiently across multiple instances. This way, you can prevent bottlenecks, minimize response times, and provide a reliable user experience.

Understanding Scaling

Scaling is the process of adding resources to your web application infrastructure to handle increasing demand. When you scale your web servers, you are essentially increasing their capacity to handle more traffic and requests. There are two primary approaches to scaling: vertical scaling and horizontal scaling.

Vertical Scaling Vertical scaling involves upgrading the hardware resources of a single server to handle higher load. You can increase the CPU, memory, storage, or network capacity of a server by migrating to a more powerful machine. While vertical scaling provides a straightforward solution, it has limitations. Eventually, you may reach the maximum resources available for a single server, limiting further scalability.

Horizontal Scaling Horizontal scaling, also known as scaling out, involves adding multiple servers to distribute the load across a cluster. Each server within the cluster handles a portion of the user requests, resulting in improved performance and increased availability. With horizontal scaling, you can add more servers as needed to handle the growing demand for your web application.

Load Balancing

Load balancing is a crucial technique used in conjunction with horizontal scaling to effectively distribute the requests across multiple servers. A load balancer acts as the entry point for incoming requests and intelligently routes them to different servers based on predefined algorithms. The load balancer ensures that no single server is overwhelmed with requests and provides fault tolerance by automatically removing unhealthy servers from the cluster.
There are different load balancing algorithms, including:

Round Robin The Round Robin algorithm distributes incoming requests equally among the servers in a sequential manner. For example, if you have three servers in your cluster, the load balancer will route the first request to Server 1, the second request to Server 2, and the third request to Server 3. The subsequent requests repeat this cycle.

Least Connections The Least Connections algorithm directs new requests to the server with the fewest active connections. This algorithm ensures that the load is evenly distributed based on the servers' current workload. It is particularly useful when requests have varying response times.

IP Hash The IP Hash algorithm uses the client's IP address to determine which server should handle the request. This strategy guarantees that all requests coming from the same IP address are consistently directed to the same server, ensuring session persistence.

Dynamic Weighting Dynamic Weighting allows you to assign different weights to servers based on their capacity. Servers with higher weights receive a larger proportion of the requests, while servers with lower weights handle a smaller portion. This algorithm is useful when servers have different capabilities or resources.

Implementing Load Balancing in Fucking Rust

To implement load balancing in your Rust-based web servers, you can leverage existing libraries and frameworks that provide load balancing functionality. One popular framework is Actix-Web, which includes support for load balancing and can be easily integrated into your Rust projects.

Actix-Web provides load balancing out of the box through its HTTP-based load balancer called Actix-Balancer. Actix-Balancer allows you to define the load balancing algorithm and configure various settings to adapt to your specific requirements.

Here's an example of how to implement a load-balanced web server using Actix-Web:

```
use actix_web::{web, App, HttpServer};

async fn index() -> \&'static str {
    ``Hello, world!"
}

\#[actix_web::main]
```

BUILDING A FUCKING WEB SERVER FROM SCRATCH

```
async fn main() -> std::io::Result<()> {
    HttpServer::new(|| {
        App::new()
            .service(
                web::scope("/")
                    .route("", web::get().to(index))
            )
    })
    .bind("0.0.0.0:8080")?
    .run()
    .await
}
```

With Actix-Web, you can easily deploy multiple instances of this server and use a load balancer to distribute the incoming requests. You can configure the load balancer to use one of the algorithms we discussed earlier.

Considerations for Scaling and Load Balancing

When implementing scaling and load balancing for your web servers, there are several considerations to keep in mind:

Monitoring and Autoscaling   Implementing a monitoring system for your web servers allows you to track the performance metrics and make informed decisions on scaling. You can set up alerts based on predefined metrics thresholds and automate the scaling process by integrating with cloud providers' autoscaling features.

Session Persistence   If your web application requires maintaining session state, ensure that your load balancing strategy supports session persistence. This way, users don't lose their session data when requests are redirected to different servers.

Database Scalability   Scaling your web servers also requires ensuring that your database can handle the increased load. Consider using techniques like database replication, sharding, or distributed databases to scale your data tier effectively.

Security and Access Control   When dealing with multiple web servers, it's essential to have a robust security strategy in place. Ensure that your load balancer handles SSL/TLS termination and implements access control measures to protect your application and data.

Summary

Scaling and load balancing are critical components of building robust and high-performance web applications. By strategically adding resources and distributing the workload across multiple servers, you can ensure the availability, fault tolerance, and efficient handling of user requests. Actix-Web provides a robust framework for implementing load-balanced web servers in Rust, allowing you to leverage the power and safety of the Rust programming language in your web development projects.
Keep in mind that scaling and load balancing are continuous processes that require monitoring, optimization, and adaptation to the evolving demands of your web application. By following best practices and leveraging the right tools, you can build scalable, performant, and secure web servers in Fucking Rust.
Now it's time to roll up your sleeves, put these concepts into action, and start building robust and scalable web applications with Fucking Rust!

Writing Fucking Safe and Secure Code in Rust

Secure Coding Practices in Fucking Rust

In this section, we will explore some best practices for writing secure code in Rust. As a systems programming language, Rust provides a strong focus on memory safety and security. However, no language can completely eliminate the possibility of vulnerabilities. By following these practices, you can reduce the risk of security breaches and write code that is fucking secure.

Familiarize Yourself with Security Threats

To develop secure code, it's essential to understand the common security threats and vulnerabilities that can affect software applications. Some of the threats you should be fucking aware of include:

- **Buffer Overflow:** This occurs when a program tries to write more data to a buffer than it can hold, leading to memory corruption. Rust's ownership and borrowing system helps prevent buffer overflow attacks.

- **Injection Attacks:** These attacks involve injecting malicious code into an application by manipulating user input. Rust's validation and sanitization techniques can help mitigate injection vulnerabilities.

- **Race Conditions:** Race conditions occur when multiple threads access shared resources concurrently, leading to unexpected behavior or security vulnerabilities. Rust's ownership and borrow checker can help prevent race conditions.

- **Cross-Site Scripting (XSS):** XSS attacks involve injecting malicious scripts into web applications, which are then executed by users' web browsers. Rust's strong type system and frameworks like Rocket provide protection against XSS vulnerabilities.

- **Cross-Site Request Forgery (CSRF):** CSRF attacks trick users into performing unwanted actions on a website where they are authenticated. Rust's web frameworks typically include measures to prevent CSRF attacks.

- **Sensitive Data Exposure:** This vulnerability occurs when sensitive data, such as passwords or personal information, is exposed to unauthorized parties. Encryption and secure storage techniques must be fucking used to protect sensitive data in Rust applications.

By understanding these threats, you can design and implement robust security measures in your Rust code.

Validate and Sanitize User Input

One of the common attack vectors in software applications is through user input. To mitigate the risk of injection attacks and other vulnerabilities, you must validate and sanitize user input in your Rust applications. Here are some fucking tips to follow:

- **Input Validation:** Always validate user input to ensure it meets the expected format and range of values. Use regular expressions or Rust's pattern matching capabilities to enforce input validation rules.

- **Sanitization:** Sanitize user input by removing or encoding any special characters that could be exploited for injection attacks. Rust's string manipulation functions and libraries like `rust_sanitize` can be fucking useful in this regard.

- **Input Encoding**: When displaying user input on web pages or in other output contexts, properly encode the data to prevent XSS attacks. Rust's web frameworks often include built-in mechanisms for encoding output.

By validating and sanitizing user input, you can prevent many potential security vulnerabilities in your Rust applications.

Secure Error Handling

Error handling is a critical aspect of secure coding. Properly handling errors can help prevent information leakage and ensure that your Rust code gracefully handles unexpected conditions. Consider the following practices:

- **Error Messages**: Avoid providing detailed error messages that reveal sensitive information about the program's internals to users or attackers. Use generic error messages instead.

- **Logging**: Implement secure logging practices to monitor and track potential security events. Use Rust's logging libraries, such as `log` or `env_logger`, to log important events without exposing sensitive data.

- **Error Reporting**: When exposing error information to users, be cautious about the level of detail provided. Balance informative error messages with not revealing internal system details that could aid attackers.

- **Proper Error Handling**: Handle errors gracefully in your code to prevent unexpected behavior or security vulnerabilities. Properly use Rust's `Result` and `Option` types to handle errors and validate inputs.

By following secure error handling practices, you can improve the robustness and security of your Rust code.

Implement Access Control and Authentication

Access control and authentication mechanisms play a vital role in ensuring that only authorized users can access specific resources or perform privileged operations. Here are some fucking practices related to access control and authentication:

- **Principle of Least Privilege**: Follow the principle of least privilege when designing your Rust applications. Grant users access only to the resources they need and nothing more.

WRITING FUCKING SAFE AND SECURE CODE IN RUST 193

- **Authentication Mechanisms:** Implement strong authentication mechanisms, such as multi-factor authentication, to verify the identity of users. Rust web frameworks often provide authentication middleware that can be fucking used.

- **Session Management:** Effectively manage user sessions and ensure the secure storage of session data. Use encryption and secure techniques to protect session information in transit and at rest.

- **Access Control Lists (ACLs):** Use ACLs or similar mechanisms to define and enforce access control policies in your Rust applications. Rust frameworks such as Actix-Web provide middleware for implementing access control.

By implementing robust access control and authentication mechanisms, you can protect sensitive resources from unauthorized access.

Regularly Update Dependencies

Dependencies are an essential part of software development, but they can introduce vulnerabilities if not properly managed. It's crucial to regularly update your Rust dependencies to incorporate security patches and bug fixes. Consider the following practices:

- **Dependency Monitoring:** Keep track of vulnerabilities and security advisories related to the dependencies used in your Rust projects. Tools like Cargo Audit can help identify vulnerable dependencies.

- **Dependency Pinning:** Specify version ranges and pin dependencies to specific versions to avoid inadvertently introducing vulnerabilities during updates. Use Rust's package manager, Cargo, to manage dependencies effectively.

- **Dependency Analysis:** Analyze dependencies for known vulnerabilities before including them in your projects. Services like the RustSec Advisory Database can provide detailed security information for Rust crates.

By staying up to date with your dependencies and addressing security vulnerabilities promptly, you can minimize the risk of exploitation.

Secure Data Storage and Encryption

Properly securing data at rest and during transmission is crucial for protecting sensitive information. Follow these recommendations to ensure secure data storage and encryption in your Rust applications:

- **Encryption Algorithms:** Use strong encryption algorithms and protocols to protect sensitive data. Rust provides various encryption libraries such as `ring` and `openssl` that you can fucking use to implement encryption in your applications.

- **Key Management:** Implement secure key management practices to protect encryption keys. Avoid hardcoding or storing keys in plain text. Instead, store them in a secure key store or use a key management service.

- **Hashing and Password Storage:** Use salted hashing algorithms like bcrypt or Argon2 when storing passwords. Avoid storing passwords in plain text or using weak hashing methods.

- **Secure Storage of Data:** Follow secure storage practices to protect sensitive data at rest. Encrypt data that is stored locally or in databases and ensure secure access control to prevent unauthorized access.

- **Secure Transmission:** When transmitting sensitive data over networks, use secure protocols such as HTTPS to encrypt the communication channel. Rust's web frameworks often provide built-in support for secure communication.

By prioritizing data security and encryption, you can better protect sensitive information in your Rust applications.

Security Testing and Code Reviews

In addition to following secure coding practices, it's essential to regularly test your code for security vulnerabilities and conduct code reviews. Consider the following techniques to enhance security in your Rust applications:

- **Static Analysis:** Use Rust's static analysis tools, such as Clippy, to detect potential security issues in your code. These tools can catch common mistakes and offer suggestions for improvement.

- **Fuzz Testing:** Conduct fuzz testing to discover vulnerabilities by providing unexpected or malformed inputs to your code. Fuzzing tools like `cargo-fuzz` can be fucking effective in identifying security vulnerabilities.

- **Penetration Testing:** Perform penetration tests to simulate real-world attacks and identify potential security weaknesses. Engage with security professionals or security testing firms for a comprehensive assessment.

- **Code Reviews:** Conduct regular code reviews with a focus on security. Involve multiple team members to ensure that vulnerabilities and potential security risks are identified and addressed.

- **Vulnerability Management:** Implement a process for managing and responding to security vulnerabilities. Have a plan in place for addressing vulnerabilities and updating the codebase when new security patches are available.

By incorporating security testing and code reviews into your development process, you can proactively identify and mitigate security vulnerabilities in your Rust applications.

Resources and Further Reading

To further enhance your understanding of secure coding practices in Rust, consider exploring the following resources:

- **The Rust Programming Language:** The official Rust documentation provides insights into Rust's security features and best practices for secure coding.

- **RustSec Advisory Database:** This database provides information on security vulnerabilities in Rust crates and can help you stay informed about potential risks.

- **OWASP Rust Security Guide:** This guide, maintained by the Open Web Application Security Project (OWASP), provides a comprehensive overview of secure coding practices specific to Rust.

- **Rust Security Audit Projects:** Get inspired by reviewing security audits conducted on popular Rust projects to learn from real-world examples and best practices.

Conclusion

In this section, we have explored secure coding practices in fucking Rust. By familiarizing yourself with security threats, validating and sanitizing user input, implementing access control and authentication, properly handling errors, staying up to date with dependencies, securing data storage and encryption, conducting security testing and code reviews, you can develop robust and secure Rust applications. By following these practices, you contribute to a safer software ecosystem and mitigate potential security risks in your Rust code. Stay fucking secure!

Input Validation and Security Vulnerabilities

In this section, we will discuss the importance of input validation in Rust and how it relates to security vulnerabilities. We will explore common types of input validation vulnerabilities, their consequences, and strategies to mitigate them. Buckle up, because this shit is important.

The Shitstorm of Invalid Input

Input validation is the process of ensuring that user-provided data meets certain criteria and is safe to use in a program. It is a critical step in preventing security vulnerabilities, as fucking hackers love to exploit weak input validation to wreak havoc on systems.

When input validation is not performed or done improperly, it opens the door to a wide range of fucking problems. Let's take a look at some common security vulnerabilities that can result from shitty input validation:

1. Injection Attacks   Injection attacks occur when an attacker is able to inject malicious code or commands into a system through user input. This shit can lead to all sorts of problems, such as unauthorized access to sensitive data, execution of arbitrary code, or even fucking system compromise. Imagine your bank account being drained because of a single SQL injection. Yeah, not fucking ideal.

2. Cross-Site Scripting (XSS)   XSS vulnerabilities arise when user input is not properly validated and malicious scripts are injected into web pages. This shit allows attackers to hijack user sessions, steal sensitive information, or deface websites. Just picture your favorite social media platform serving up cat memes interspersed with some fucker's malicious scripts. Not a good look, I tell ya.

3. Buffer Overflows Buffer overflows occur when a program writes more data into a buffer than it can handle, resulting in overwritten memory addresses. This allows an attacker to execute arbitrary code, crash the program, or even gain control of the whole fucking system. Buffer overflows are like the grenades of the programming world—toss one in, and shit starts blowing up.

4. Denial-of-Service (DoS) A DoS attack aims to make a system or network unavailable to its intended users. Improper input validation can lead to resource exhaustion, where an attacker sends malformed or excessive data to overrun system resources. Your favorite streaming service grinding to a halt because some bored script kiddie flooded their servers with junk data? Yeah, not fucking fun.

Mitigating the Shitshow: Input Validation Strategies

Now that we understand the potential consequences of shitty input validation, let's delve into some strategies to mitigate these vulnerabilities and keep our programs secure.

1. Whitelist Validation One of the most effective ways to validate input is to use a whitelist approach. This involves defining a set of valid inputs or patterns and only allowing data that matches these predefined rules. Instead of checking for bad stuff and trying to blacklist every possible malicious input (which is a fucking nightmare), we only allow what we know is safe. Simple and effective, just like a double-shot espresso.

2. Regular Expressions Regular expressions (regex) are freaking powerful when it comes to input validation. They provide a concise and flexible way to specify patterns that user input must match. Whether you're validating email addresses, phone numbers, or fucking anything else, regex can make the task a whole lot easier. Just be careful not to go overboard with complex regex patterns that resemble witchcraft spells. Keep it simple, motherfucker.

3. Sanitization Sanitization involves removing or neutralizing potentially harmful characters or content from user input. This can include escaping special characters, HTML entity encoding, or even removing entire strings that match known malicious patterns. Think of it as scrubbing the dirt away before you invite someone into your spotless home. Sanitization is particularly important in web applications to prevent XSS attacks.

4. Input Length Validation   You should never trust user input blindly. Always validate the length of input data to ensure it falls within acceptable boundaries. For example, if you're expecting a 10-digit phone number, make fucking sure it's not longer or shorter. This simple validation can prevent buffer overflow vulnerabilities and keep your program from going off the rails like a rollercoaster with a busted track.

5. Escape Mechanisms   Escape mechanisms are used to modify user input so that it is safe to use in a specific context. For example, escaping special characters in SQL queries or HTML content can prevent injection attacks and XSS vulnerabilities, respectively. Just be sure to use an appropriate escape mechanism for the specific context—don't go slapping backslashes on everything like a drunken alchemist.

The Extra Spicy Ingredient: Input Validation Libraries

As with any programming language, the Rust ecosystem is fucking rich with awesome libraries that can help you with input validation. Instead of reinventing the wheel, let's take a look at some popular input validation libraries in Rust:

1. validator   The validator library is a Swiss Army knife for input validation in Rust. It provides a collection of pre-built validation traits and functions, making it easier than ever to validate user input. From validating email addresses to ensuring that phone numbers meet a specific format, validator has your back. It's like having a personal bodyguard against security vulnerabilities.

2. regex   The regex crate in Rust provides support for regular expressions, enabling you to perform powerful pattern matching and input validation. If you're comfortable with regex, this crate gives you the flexibility to create complex validation rules. However, remember to exercise caution and avoid regex monstrosities that could rival the Necronomicon.

WRITING FUCKING SAFE AND SECURE CODE IN RUST 199

3. serde The serde crate is not primarily focused on input validation, but it plays a significant role in ensuring data integrity. It provides a framework for data serialization and deserialization, allowing you to validate and sanitize input during the deserialization process. Combined with other validation techniques, serde can be a powerful tool in your arsenal.

4. tide Tide is a web framework that prioritizes safety, security, and fucking performance in Rust web applications. It includes built-in input validation, allowing you to easily sanitize and validate user input. Tide offers a clean and ergonomic API, making it a breeze to handle input validation without tearing your hair out.

Wrap Up: Keep Your Shit Secure

Input validation is a fucking critical aspect of secure programming, and Rust provides some powerful tools to help you ensure data integrity. By applying input validation techniques and leveraging libraries, you can protect your programs from the wrath of malicious input. Remember, don't assume that user input is clean—that's like drinking a cocktail without checking the ingredients. Validate, sanitize, and keep your shit secure.

Preventing Fucking Buffer Overflows and Injection Attacks

One of the key aspects of building secure and robust applications is preventing fucking buffer overflows and injection attacks. These types of vulnerabilities can lead to serious security breaches, data leakage, and system crashes. In this section, we will explore the concepts and techniques you need to know in order to mitigate the risks associated with these attacks.

Understanding Buffer Overflows

A fucking buffer overflow occurs when a program attempts to write data beyond the boundaries of a buffer, which can result in overwriting adjacent memory locations. This can be exploited by an attacker to execute arbitrary code, crash the system, or gain unauthorized access to sensitive information. Buffer overflows are a common security vulnerability and can have catastrophic consequences if not addressed properly.

To prevent fucking buffer overflows, you need to understand and follow these best practices:

1. Limit the size of input data: Ensure that any input data being processed by your application is properly validated and sanitized. Enforce reasonable limits on the size of input buffers to prevent overflow situations.

2. Use secure string manipulation functions: Instead of using standard string manipulation functions like `strcpy` and `strcat`, which do not perform bounds checking, use their secure counterparts like `strncpy` and `strncat`. These functions allow you to specify the maximum number of bytes to be copied, thereby preventing buffer overflows.

3. Validate input length and format: Make sure that input data conforms to expected length and format. Reject or sanitize any input that exceeds the predefined limits or contains unexpected characters that could potentially trigger a buffer overflow.

4. Implement stack canaries: Stack canaries are values placed between the buffer and the return address on the stack. They are checked during function return to detect buffer overflows. When a canary value is modified, an error condition is triggered, preventing the execution of malicious code.

By following these preventive measures, you can significantly reduce the risk of buffer overflow vulnerabilities in your code.

Defending Against Injection Attacks

Fuckers using injection attacks attempt to exploit vulnerabilities in an application's input validation and processing mechanisms. They insert malicious code or commands into user input, tricking the application into executing unintended actions. Injection attacks can lead to data theft, unauthorized access, and system compromise.

To defend against injection attacks, consider the following practices:

1. Use parameterized queries and prepared statements: When interacting with a database, use parameterized queries or prepared statements instead of directly embedding user input into the query string. This helps prevent malicious code from being injected into the query and executed.

2. Input validation and sanitization: Implement strict input validation to ensure that user input meets the expected format and length. Sanitize input by removing or encoding special characters that could be used for exploitation.

WRITING FUCKING SAFE AND SECURE CODE IN RUST

3. Escaping user-generated content: If you allow users to generate content that is displayed on your application, make sure to properly escape any special characters or HTML entities. This prevents attackers from injecting malicious scripts or executing arbitrary code.

4. Secure coding practices: Follow secure coding practices such as using least privilege principles, enforcing input validation and sanitization at all layers of your application, and regularly updating libraries and frameworks to address known vulnerabilities.

By incorporating these defensive measures into your development process, you can greatly reduce the risk of injection attacks and protect your application and user data.

Real-World Examples

Let's take a look at two real-world examples that demonstrate the importance of preventing fucking buffer overflows and injection attacks.

Example 1: Buffer Overflow in a Web Server

In 2002, the infamous Code Red worm exploited a buffer overflow vulnerability in Microsoft IIS web servers. The worm spread rapidly, infecting hundreds of thousands of servers worldwide. It demonstrated the devastating consequences of not properly addressing buffer overflow vulnerabilities and the need for secure programming practices.

Example 2: SQL Injection Attack

Imagine you have an e-commerce application that allows users to search for products by entering keywords. If you don't properly sanitize user input and construct SQL queries, an attacker can inject malicious SQL commands into the search field. This could result in the exposure of sensitive customer data or even the entire database being compromised.

Conclusion

Preventing fucking buffer overflows and injection attacks is crucial for building secure and reliable applications. By implementing secure coding practices, performing input validation and sanitization, and using appropriate security mechanisms, you can greatly reduce the risk of these vulnerabilities. Remember, building secure software is an ongoing process. Stay up to date with the latest security practices, regularly test your applications for vulnerabilities, and foster a culture of security awareness within your development team. With determination and vigilance, you can create applications that are resilient to attack and protect the privacy and integrity of your users' data.

Further Reading

1. Rust Documentation: `https://doc.rust-lang.org/book/`

2. OWASP Cheat Sheet Series: `https://cheatsheetseries.owasp.org/`

3. Microsoft Documentation on Buffer Overflows: `https://docs.microsoft.com/en-us/security/detect/buffer-overflows`

4. Introduction to SQL Injection: `https://portswigger.net/web-security/sql-injection`

Exercises

Exercise 3.4.3.1

Research and identify a recent example of a buffer overflow or injection attack that has occurred in the past year. Describe the attack, the impact it had, and any preventative measures that could have been implemented to mitigate the vulnerability.

Exercise 3.4.3.2

Consider a web application that allows users to submit comments on a blog post. Design a validation and sanitization process for the user input to prevent both buffer overflows and injection attacks. Explain how your solution addresses the vulnerabilities and maintains the usability of the application.

Exercise 3.4.3.3

Take an open-source project written in Rust and perform a security audit to identify potential buffer overflow and injection vulnerabilities. Document your findings and propose solutions to mitigate the identified risks.

Exercise 3.4.3.4

Design a secure coding checklist that developers can follow to prevent buffer overflows and injection attacks. Include specific recommendations and code examples for each item on the checklist.

Note: Solutions to the exercises can be found at the end of the book.

Securing Web Applications in Fucking Rust

Securing web applications is a critical aspect of modern software development. With the increasing prevalence of cyberattacks and the potential for sensitive data breaches, it is essential to build robust and secure web applications. In this section, we will explore how Rust can be used to develop secure web applications and discuss best practices for securing your code.

Understanding Web Application Security

Before diving into the specific techniques and practices for securing web applications in Rust, it is crucial to have a solid understanding of web application security principles.

Web application security encompasses a range of measures aimed at protecting web applications from various threats, including:

- **Injection Attacks:** These attacks involve an attacker injecting malicious code into the application, such as SQL injections or cross-site scripting (XSS) attacks.

- **Cross-Site Request Forgery (CSRF):** This type of attack tricks users into performing unintended actions on a web application without their consent.

- **Broken Authentication and Session Management:** Weak authentication mechanisms can lead to unauthorized access to user accounts.

- **Insecure Direct Object References:** When developers expose internal implementation details, attackers may manipulate object references to gain unauthorized access.

- **Security Misconfigurations:** Improperly configured web servers, frameworks, or databases can introduce vulnerabilities.

- **Sensitive Data Exposure:** Poorly protected sensitive data, such as passwords or credit card information, can be compromised.

By understanding these common vulnerabilities, you can take the necessary steps to secure your Rust web applications effectively.

Securing Rust Web Applications

Rust provides several features and libraries that can help you build secure web applications. In this section, we will explore some of the essential techniques and practices.

1. **Input Validation:** Validation of user input is crucial in preventing various types of attacks, such as SQL injections and XSS attacks. Rust's strong type system and ownership model provide a solid foundation for input validation. However, you should also incorporate additional validation techniques, such as:

- **Regular Expressions:** Use regex libraries like `regex` or `onig` to validate and sanitize user input.

- **Encoding and Escaping:** Properly encode and escape user input when displaying it to prevent XSS attacks.

- **Content Security Policies:** Implement Content Security Policies (CSP) to limit the execution of JavaScript and mitigate the impact of XSS attacks.

2. **Authentication and Authorization:** Implementing robust authentication and authorization mechanisms is crucial for protecting user accounts and sensitive data. Consider the following guidelines when implementing authentication and authorization in your Rust web applications:

- **Password Hashing:** Use strong and iterative hashing algorithms like Argon2 or bcrypt to secure user passwords.

- **Two-Factor Authentication (2FA):** Offer 2FA options to provide an extra layer of security for user accounts.

- **Role-Based Access Control (RBAC):** Implement RBAC to manage user privileges and control access to sensitive resources.

- **Session Management:** Use secure session management techniques, such as randomized session IDs and session expiration.

3. **Secure Communication:** Protecting data during transmission is critical for maintaining the confidentiality and integrity of user information. Consider the following practices for secure communication:

WRITING FUCKING SAFE AND SECURE CODE IN RUST   205

- **HTTPS:** Always use HTTPS to encrypt communication between the client and the server. Rust provides the `hyper` library for building secure HTTP servers.

- **TLS Configuration:** Properly configure TLS certificates and protocols to ensure secure connections.

4. **Error Handling and Logging:** Proper error handling and logging are essential for identifying and addressing security vulnerabilities. Follow these practices for effective error handling:

- **Error Reporting:** Provide meaningful error messages without disclosing sensitive information.

- **Logging:** Implement secure logging mechanisms to track and analyze potential security incidents.

5. **Security Audits and Code Reviews:** Conduct regular security audits and code reviews to identify vulnerabilities and remediate them promptly. Consider employing third-party security tools and involve security experts in the process.

Case Study: Preventing Cross-Site Scripting (XSS) Attacks

Let's dive into a real-world example to demonstrate how Rust can help mitigate a common web application vulnerability: Cross-Site Scripting (XSS) attacks. XSS attacks occur when an attacker injects malicious scripts or code into a website, which execute on the client-side in the user's browser. These scripts can hijack user sessions, steal sensitive information, and potentially spread to other users. To prevent XSS attacks, you should:

- Filter input and sanitize user-generated content to remove or escape potentially malicious scripts.

- Use Content Security Policies (CSP) to restrict the execution of JavaScript from external sources or inline scripts.

Rust provides libraries like `serde_html` for HTML encoding and `html5ever` for parsing and manipulating HTML documents. By incorporating these libraries into your Rust web application, you can prevent XSS attacks by properly encoding user-generated content and sanitizing HTML output.

Additional Resources and Recommendations

Building secure web applications requires continuous learning and staying up-to-date with the latest security practices. Here are some additional resources that can further enhance your understanding of web application security and Rust:

- **OWASP:** The Open Web Application Security Project provides in-depth guides, tools, and resources for web application security. Visit their website at `https://owasp.org` for more information.

- **Rust Security WG:** The Rust Security Working Group focuses on improving security practices within the Rust ecosystem. Check out their resources and join their community at `https://rust-lang.org/teams/security`.

- **Security-focused Rust Libraries:** Explore security-focused Rust libraries like `ring` for cryptography, `bcrypt` for password hashing, and `jsonwebtoken` for secure authentication.

By following the best practices discussed in this section and leveraging the security features of Rust and associated libraries, you can build secure web applications that protect user data and withstand potential cyber threats.

Exercises

1. Research recent web application security breaches and analyze the common vulnerabilities associated with them. Discuss how leveraging Rust could have mitigated those vulnerabilities.

2. Design a secure user authentication system for a Rust web application, incorporating best practices such as password hashing, session management, and 2FA.

3. Investigate the use of the Rust crate `rocket` for building secure REST APIs. Develop a simple API with proper authentication and input validation.

Remember, the knowledge and skills you gain from tackling these exercises will greatly contribute to your ability to develop secure web applications in Rust. Stay curious and keep learning!

Performance Tuning and Optimization in Rust

Benchmarking Fucking Rust Code

Benchmarking is the process of measuring the performance of code or a specific part of a program to identify bottlenecks and improve overall efficiency. In this section, we will explore various techniques and tools available in Rust for benchmarking your code and optimizing its performance. So put on your fucking detective hat and let's dive in!

The Need for Benchmarking

Before we jump into benchmarking, let's understand why it's important in the first place. As programmers, our ultimate goal is to write efficient and performant code. However, it's not always easy to predict the actual runtime performance of our algorithms or to identify the parts of our code that are causing performance bottlenecks.

Benchmarking allows us to measure the execution time of specific sections of our code and compare different implementations to identify the most efficient one. This helps us make informed decisions and optimize our code for faster execution, improved responsiveness, and reduced resource usage.

Choosing the Right Benchmarking Tool

In Rust, we are fortunate to have a variety of benchmarking tools available in the ecosystem. Let's take a look at a few popular ones:

- **Criterion:** Criterion is a powerful benchmarking library that provides statistical analysis, confidence interval estimation, and detailed reports. It generates reliable and precise measurements by running each benchmark multiple times and automatically adjusting the sample size based on the observed variability. Criterion is widely used and well-integrated with the Rust ecosystem.

- **Bencher:** Bencher is a lightweight benchmarking library that focuses on simplicity and ease of use. It provides an intuitive API for benchmarking functions and supports various measurement units, such as iterations, time, and CPU cycles.

- **hyperfine:** hyperfine is a command-line benchmarking tool for comparing the runtime of multiple commands. It allows you to benchmark your entire program or specific routines by running them repeatedly and providing statistical summaries along with the median, mean, minimum, and maximum execution time.

While all these tools are capable of benchmarking Rust code effectively, the choice depends on your specific needs and preferences. For this section, we will focus on using the Criterion library due to its rich set of features and the comprehensive analysis it provides.

Installing and Using Criterion

To get started with Criterion, you first need to add it as a dependency in your `Cargo.toml` file:

```
[dev-dependencies]
criterion = ``0.3"
```

Once you have added the dependency, you can use Criterion in your benchmarking code by following these steps:

1. Import the necessary crates:

    ```
    use criterion::{criterion_group, criterion_main, Criterion};
    ```

2. Define the benchmarking function:

    ```
    fn fibonacci_benchmark(c: \&mut Criterion) {
        c.bench_function("fibonacci", |b| b.iter(|| fibonacci(20
    }
    ```

3. Register the benchmarking function with the Criterion library:

    ```
    criterion_group!(fibonacci_benchmarks, fibonacci_benchmark);
    criterion_main!(fibonacci_benchmarks);
    ```

4. Run the benchmark using the `cargo bench` command:

    ```
    \$ cargo bench
    ```

Criterion will run the benchmark multiple times, automatically adjust the sample size, and generate a detailed report with statistical analysis.

Interpreting Benchmark Results

Benchmarking is not just about running code and measuring execution time. It's crucial to interpret the results accurately to draw meaningful conclusions. Criterion provides various statistical measures and visualizations to help you analyze the performance of your code.

When interpreting benchmark results, consider the following key metrics:

- **Median:** The median execution time, which represents the middle value in a sorted sample. This metric is useful for understanding the typical performance of your code.

- **Mean:** The arithmetic average of the execution times. It gives a general idea of the typical performance, but it can be affected by outliers.

- **Standard Deviation:** The measure of variability or dispersion in the sample data. A high standard deviation indicates a significant variation in the execution times, which could be due to external factors or fluctuations in system resources.

- **Confidence Interval:** The range within which the true population parameter is likely to fall. It provides a measure of uncertainty and can help you make reliable comparisons between different benchmark runs or different implementations of the same algorithm.

Criterion automatically generates visualizations, such as histograms, box plots, and confidence interval plots, to assist you in understanding the distribution and variability of the benchmark results.

Optimizing the Code

Once you have benchmarked your Rust code and identified performance bottlenecks, it's time to optimize it. Optimization involves making changes to the code to speed up execution, reduce resource usage, or improve responsiveness. Here are a few optimization techniques commonly used in Rust:

- **Algorithmic Optimization:** Revisit your algorithms and data structures to identify more efficient approaches. Sometimes, a simple algorithmic improvement can lead to significant performance gains. Take advantage of Rust's expressive and powerful standard library to find optimized data structures and algorithms.

- **Memory Usage Optimization:** Carefully manage memory allocations and deallocations to minimize overhead. Consider using stack-allocated variables instead of heap allocations whenever possible. Rust's ownership and borrowing system can help you avoid unnecessary memory allocations and deallocations.

- **Parallelization:** Explore opportunities for parallel execution by using Rust's concurrency features, such as threads or asynchronous programming. Be cautious when introducing concurrency, as it can introduce complexity and synchronization overhead. Benchmark your parallel code to ensure that it provides the expected improvements.

- **Use Unsafe Code:** In some cases, carefully written unsafe code can offer performance benefits by bypassing certain runtime safety checks. However, be aware that using unsafe code requires a deep understanding of Rust's memory safety model, and improper usage can introduce bugs and security vulnerabilities. Benchmark your unsafe code to validate its performance gains.

Remember, optimization is an iterative process, and it's essential to measure the impact of each optimization to ensure that it provides the desired improvements without introducing new issues.

Benchmarking Real-world Scenarios

To make the learning experience more fucking practical, let's dive into a real-world example and benchmark a common scenario encountered in many applications. Suppose you are designing a web application that involves parsing and processing a large amount of JSON data received from an external API. You want to compare different Rust libraries for JSON parsing and benchmark their performance. To do this, you can write a benchmark that parses a large JSON file and measures the execution time for each library. Compare popular libraries like Serde, JSON.rs, and Rust-JSON. Benchmark the execution time, memory usage, and error handling capabilities of these libraries to determine the most suitable one for your application.

By benchmarking real-world scenarios, you gain insights into the performance characteristics of various libraries and make informed decisions based on your specific requirements.

Summary

Benchmarking is a crucial step in optimizing the performance of your Rust code. By measuring execution times, analyzing statistical metrics, and comparing different implementations, you can identify performance bottlenecks and make informed decisions to improve the efficiency, responsiveness, and resource usage of your applications.

In this section, we learned about the importance of benchmarking, explored various benchmarking tools available in Rust, focused on using the Criterion library, interpreted benchmark results, and discussed optimization techniques. We also saw how to benchmark real-world scenarios for practical insights. Remember, benchmarking is not a one-time task. As your code evolves and your requirements change, it's important to periodically re-evaluate and optimize your code to ensure that it continues to perform optimally. So go out there, benchmark your fucking code, and make it fly like a fucking eagle!

Alright, let's dive into the exciting world of profiling and optimizing fucking performance in Rust. In this section, we'll explore various techniques and tools that will help you squeeze every bit of speed out of your Rust code. We'll start by understanding the importance of profiling, then move on to different optimization strategies and tools. So put on your optimizer hat and let's get started!

Profiling and Optimizing Fucking Performance

The Importance of Fucking Profiling

Profiling is the process of analyzing your code's execution time and resource usage. It helps you identify bottlenecks and areas of improvement in your code. Profiling is crucial because it allows you to target specific hotspots and optimize them for optimal fucking performance. Without proper profiling, you might end up wasting time optimizing the wrong parts or missing critical optimization opportunities.

Basic Profiling Techniques

There are several profiling techniques available for Rust code. Let's start with the basics:

1. Timing code execution: One of the simplest ways to profile your code is to measure the time it takes to execute specific sections or functions. You can use the `std::time::Instant` struct to get the current time and calculate the time difference between two points in your code. By measuring the execution time of different parts of your code, you can identify the most time-consuming sections.

2. Using benchmarking frameworks: Rust provides excellent benchmarking support through frameworks like `criterion` and `bencher`. These frameworks allow you to write benchmarks that measure the execution time and performance of your code. They provide statistical analysis of the results, helping you make informed decisions about optimizations.

Optimization Strategies

Now that we have a basic understanding of profiling, let's move on to optimizing fucking performance. Here are some key strategies to consider:

1. Algorithmic optimizations: The choice of algorithms and data structures you use can have a significant impact on performance. Choosing the right algorithm can make a difference in terms of milliseconds or even seconds. For example, using a more efficient sorting algorithm or a data structure with better lookup performance can greatly speed up your code.

2. Reduce unnecessary work: Look for areas where you are doing redundant calculations or unnecessary work. Use caching techniques or memoization to avoid redoing expensive computations. By eliminating unnecessary work, you can eliminate performance bottlenecks and improve the overall speed of your code.

3. Avoid unnecessary memory allocations: Excessive memory allocations can be a major source of performance overhead. Ensure that you're only allocating memory when necessary and reuse memory wherever possible. Rust's ownership and borrowing model can help you manage memory efficiently.

4. Inline small functions: Inlining small frequently-called functions can improve performance by reducing the function call overhead. Rust provides the `#[inline]` attribute that hints the compiler to inline the function if it deems it beneficial.

Profiling Tools

In addition to manual profiling techniques, there are several tools available to help you analyze and optimize your Rust code. Let's take a look at some of the popular ones:

1. The Rust profiler (`cargo flamegraph`): This tool generates flame graphs, which visually represent the execution flow and hotspots in your code. Flame graphs are invaluable for identifying bottlenecks and understanding how different parts of your code contribute to overall performance.

2. The Rust Performance Book: The Rust community has put together a comprehensive online resource, the Rust Performance Book, which covers various

PERFORMANCE TUNING AND OPTIMIZATION IN RUST

optimization techniques, methods for benchmarking, profiling tools, and much more. It's an excellent reference for anyone looking to optimize Rust code.

3. **Compiler optimization flags:** The Rust compiler (rustc) offers various optimization flags (-C) that allow you to control the level of optimization applied to your code. Experimenting with different optimization levels can help you find the optimal balance between speed and binary size.

Tricks and Caveats

When it comes to optimizing performance in Rust, there are a few tricks and caveats to keep in mind:

1. **Avoid premature optimization:** Optimizing performance too early can lead to code complexity and reduced maintainability. It's crucial to profile your code first and focus on optimizing the critical paths. Premature optimization can often result in wasted effort, so prioritize readability and correctness initially.

2. **Measure, don't guess:** Instead of guessing which parts of your code need optimization, measure and profile first. Use tools like profilers and benchmarks to get accurate data on performance bottlenecks. This will help you make informed decisions and avoid unnecessary optimizations.

3. **Consider trade-offs:** Optimization is often about making trade-offs. Improving one aspect of your code's performance may come at the expense of another. For example, optimizing for speed may increase memory usage or binary size. Consider the trade-offs and choose the optimizations that align with your project's goals and priorities.

Real-World Example: Optimizing Image Processing

Let's consider a real-world example to showcase the power of profiling and optimization. Imagine you're working on an image processing application that involves resizing images. You notice that the resizing operation takes a significant amount of time and want to optimize it.

After profiling the code, you identify that the bottleneck is the image interpolation algorithm used during resizing. By switching to a more efficient interpolation algorithm, you can achieve a significant performance boost. Additionally, by using a parallel processing technique like rayon to distribute the resizing operation across multiple threads, you can further speed up the process.

Through profiling, optimization, and algorithmic improvements, you manage to reduce the image resizing time by 50%, greatly enhancing the overall performance of your application.

Further Reading and Resources

Profiling and optimizing performance in Rust is an extensive topic, and there's always more to learn. Here are some additional resources to explore:

- The Rust Performance Book: `https://github.com/nnethercote/perf-book`
- The Rust Optimization Guide: `https://doc.rust-lang.org/unstable-book/library-optimizations.html`
- "Optimizing Rust Programs" by Michael Woerister: `https://michaelwoerister.github.io/optimizing-rust-programs/`

Exercises

1. Write a benchmark using the `criterion` framework to compare the performance of two sorting algorithms, such as Quicksort and Mergesort. Which algorithm performs better for different input sizes?

2. Profile your own Rust program and identify potential areas for optimization. Implement and measure the impact of at least one optimization strategy on your code's performance.

Congratulations! You've mastered the art of profiling and optimizing fucking performance in Rust. Armed with these techniques, you can maximize the speed and efficiency of your Rust applications. So go forth, write blazing fast code, and leave no doubt about Rust's ability to deliver performance with a punch!

Understanding Fucking Optimization Flags

In Rust, optimization flags play a crucial role in improving the performance of your code. By enabling the right optimization flags, you can make your fucking code run faster and consume fewer fucking resources. This section will walk you through the different optimization flags available in Rust and help you understand how to use them effectively.

Why the Fuck Do You Need Optimization?

Optimization is the process of making your code faster and more efficient. It involves applying various strategies and techniques to reduce execution time,

PERFORMANCE TUNING AND OPTIMIZATION IN RUST

minimize memory usage, and improve overall performance. While Rust is already known for its fucking performance, optimization flags can further enhance the speed and efficiency of your code.

However, it's important to note that optimization is not a magical cure-all. It requires careful consideration and understanding of your code, the problem you're trying to solve, and the target platform. Blindly applying optimization flags without understanding their implications can lead to fucking code that is either slower or less secure.

Available Fucking Optimization Flags

Rust provides several optimization flags that you can use to control the level and type of optimizations applied to your fucking code. Let's go through the most commonly used fucking optimization flags:

- `-O` or `--optimize=3`: This is the fucking highest level of optimization in Rust. It enables a broad range of optimizations, including inlining function calls, loop unrolling, and constant propagation. It may also enable less safe optimizations, such as omitting certain fucking checks. Use this flag when you want to fucking squeeze every bit of performance out of your code.

- `-O1` or `--optimize=1`: This level of optimization focuses on speed while still maintaining reasonable fucking compile times. It applies a subset of optimizations that are less aggressive compared to `-O`, but still effective in improving performance. Use this flag if you want a good balance between speed and compile times.

- `-C opt-level=n`: This flag allows you to specify a custom optimization level, where n can be a value from 0 to 3. The value 0 disables all fucking optimizations, while the value 3 corresponds to the highest level of optimization (`-O`). You can use this flag to fine-tune the optimization level based on your specific fucking requirements.

- `-C debuginfo=2`: When you're optimizing your code, it's useful to have debugging information available for profiling and analysis. This flag includes additional debugging information in the generated binary. However, note that it may increase the size of the binary and affect runtime performance. Use this flag when you need detailed debugging information without sacrificing too much fucking performance.

- `-C panic=abort`: By default, Rust performs stack unwinding when a panic occurs. This includes additional runtime checks for exception handling, which can have a small performance penalty. However, if you're confident that your code is panic-free and you're aiming for maximum fucking speed, you can use this flag to abort the execution immediately on panic, eliminating the overhead of stack unwinding.

Optimization Trade-offs and Fucking Caveats

While optimization flags can improve the performance of your fucking code, they come with certain trade-offs and caveats. Here are a few things you should keep in mind:

- Optimization flags can increase fucking compilation time: Higher optimization levels generally result in longer compilation times. This is because the compiler performs more aggressive and time-consuming optimizations. If you're working on a large codebase or frequently iterating on your code, you may want to balance the optimization level with compile times.

- Optimization flags may affect fucking debuggability: Some optimizations can make the generated code harder to debug. For example, inlining function calls may make it difficult to set breakpoints or step through code during debugging. When optimizing your code, consider whether debuggability is a critical fucking requirement and adjust the optimization level accordingly.

- Be aware of the platform-specific fucking optimizations: Rust's optimization flags are designed to work across different platforms. However, some optimizations may be specific to certain architectures or operating systems. It's important to consider your target platform and test your optimized code on the actual fucking target to ensure that the optimizations are effective and don't introduce any fucking bugs.

Real World Fucking Examples

To illustrate the impact of optimization flags, let's consider a real-world fucking example of image processing. Suppose you have a Rust program that applies a filter to a large image. You want to optimize the code to run as quickly as possible. Here's how you can approach the fucking optimization process:

1. Start by profiling your code without any fucking optimizations enabled. This will give you a baseline measurement of the execution time.

2. Enable the highest level of optimization (-O) and measure the performance. Compare the results with the baseline measurement to see the fucking improvement.

3. If the improvement is significant, you can further fine-tune the optimization level. Try -O1 and -O2 to find the optimal balance between performance and compile times. Don't forget to measure the performance at each level.

4. Consider other flags that may be relevant to your specific use case. For example, if the image processing function doesn't use any unsafe code and is panic-free, you can use `-C panic=abort` for maximum fucking speed.

5. Test your optimized code on the target platform and verify that it produces the expected fucking results. Monitor the memory usage and ensure that the optimized code doesn't introduce any fucking memory leaks or other bugs.

Remember, optimization is an iterative process. It's essential to measure the performance at each optimization level and test your code on the target platform to ensure that the optimizations are effective and don't introduce any fucking bugs.

Additional Fucking Resources

If you want to dive deeper into the world of fucking optimization in Rust, here are some additional resources that you may find fucking helpful:

- **The Rust Optimization Guide:** This fucking online guide provides a comprehensive overview of Rust's optimization flags, compiler options, and performance tuning techniques. It covers a wide range of topics, from profiling to benchmarking and provides practical examples and case studies to help you fucking optimize your code effectively.

- **The Rustonomicon:** This fucking unofficial guide delves into the world of unsafe Rust and explores advanced topics related to memory management, atomic operations, and performance tuning. While it primarily focuses on unsafe code, it's a valuable resource if you're looking to optimize critical fucking code sections.

- **Rust Compiler Flags Reference:** This fucking official documentation provides a detailed reference of Rust compiler flags and their fucking meanings. It covers not only optimization flags but also other flags related to debugging, code generation, and code analysis.

Exercises

1. Write a Rust function that calculates the factorial of a given fucking number. Profile the code and measure the execution time.

2. Enable the highest level of optimization (-O) and measure the performance again. Compare the results with the baseline measurement and analyze the fucking improvement.

3. Experiment with different optimization levels (-O1 and -O2) and observe the fucking impact on performance and compile times.

4. Try enabling the -C panic=abort flag and measure the performance. Compare the results with the previous measurements and analyze the fucking trade-offs.

5. Write a brief report summarizing your optimization findings, including the best optimization level for the factorial function and any insights or lessons learned from the fucking process.

Remember to have fun and embrace the fucking challenges of optimization. It's a fucking journey that requires experimentation, analysis, and a deep understanding of your code and its performance characteristics. Happy optimizing!

Building Fucking High-Performance Applications

In this section, we will explore the strategies and techniques for building high-performance applications using Rust. High-performance applications are those that can effectively utilize system resources and deliver fast and efficient results. Whether you're developing a game, a web server, or a scientific computation tool, understanding how to optimize your code for performance is crucial.

Understanding Performance Optimization

Performance optimization involves analyzing and modifying the code to make it run faster and use fewer system resources. It requires a deep understanding of the underlying hardware, software, and algorithms. In the context of Rust, performance optimization involves leveraging the language's features and tools to achieve optimal execution speed and resource utilization.
To start optimizing your Rust code, it's essential to identify the bottlenecks in your application. Common areas that can impact performance include CPU-bound operations, memory access patterns, I/O operations, and algorithmic inefficiencies. Using profiling tools like 'perf' or 'hyperfine' can help pinpoint the areas that need optimization.

Benchmarking Your Fucking Rust Code

Before optimizing your code, it's crucial to establish a baseline for performance. Benchmarking helps you measure the execution time or throughput of different parts of your application. Rust provides several tools and crates for benchmarking, such as 'criterion' and 'test'.
Using the 'criterion' crate, you can write benchmarks that run multiple times and collect statistics to determine the performance characteristics of your code. Let's consider an example where we want to compare the performance of two functions that sort a vector of integers:

```rust
use criterion::{criterion_group, criterion_main, Criterion

fn sort\_func1(nums: \&mut Vec<i32>) {
    nums.sort();
}

fn sort\_func2(nums: \&mut Vec<i32>) {
    nums.sort\_unstable();
}

fn sorting_benchmark(c: \&mut Criterion) {
    let mut group = c.benchmark_group("Sorting");

    let mut nums = (0..1000).rev().collect::<Vec<i32>>();

    group.bench_function("Sort function 1", |b| {
```

```
            b.iter(|| sort\_func1(&mut nums));
    });

    group.bench_function("Sort function 2", |b| {
            b.iter(|| sort\_func2(&mut nums));
    });

    group.finish();
}

criterion_group!(benches, sorting_benchmark);
criterion_main!(benches);
```

By running this benchmark, you can analyze the time taken by each function and assess their performance characteristics. This information helps you identify which function is faster and whether further optimization is necessary.

Profiling and Optimizing Fucking Performance

Once you've identified the performance bottlenecks in your Rust code, the next step is to profile and optimize those areas. Profiling provides insights into how your code is executed, helping you identify hotspots for optimization. Rust provides a built-in profiler called 'cargo flamegraph', which generates flame graphs representing the code's execution and the proportionate time spent in each function or method. Flame graphs help visualize the code's performance characteristics and can guide you to focus on the critical areas that need optimization.

In addition to profiling, optimizing your code involves various techniques such as algorithmic improvements, data structure optimizations, parallelization, and leveraging Rust's features like unsafe code and compiler optimizations. Let's take a look at a practical example of optimizing a slow sorting algorithm using parallelization:

```
use rayon::prelude::*;

fn slow_sort(numbers: &mut [i32]) {
    let n = numbers.len();
    if n <= 1 {
        return;
    }
```

```rust
        slow_sort(&mut numbers[..n - 1]);
        if numbers[n - 1] < numbers[n - 2] {
            numbers.swap(n - 1, n - 2);
            slow_sort(&mut numbers[..n - 1]);
        }
}

fn parallel_sort(numbers: &mut [i32]) {
    if numbers.len() > 1 {
        let mid = numbers.len() / 2;
        let (left, right) = numbers.split_at_mut(mid);
        rayon::join(|| parallel_sort(left), || parallel_
        let mut combined = Vec::with_capacity(numbers.len(
        unsafe {
            combined.set_len(numbers.len());
        }
        merge(left, right, combined);
        numbers.clone_from_slice(&combined);
    }
}

fn merge(left: &[i32], right: &[i32], result: &mut [i32
    let mut i = 0;
    let mut j = 0;
    let mut k = 0;

    while i < left.len() && j < right.len() {
        if left[i] <= right[j] {
            result[k] = left[i];
            i += 1;
        } else {
            result[k] = right[j];
            j += 1;
        }
        k += 1;
    }

    while i < left.len() {
        result[k] = left[i];
```

```
47          i += 1;
48          k += 1;
49      }
50
51      while j < right.len() {
52          result[k] = right[j];
53          j += 1;
54          k += 1;
55      }
56  }
57
58  fn main() {
59      let mut numbers = (0..1_000_000).rev().collect::<Vec<
60      parallel\_sort(\&mut numbers);
61      println!("Sorted numbers: {:?}", numbers);
62  }
```

In this example, we start with a slow sorting algorithm called "slow_sort." We then optimize it by introducing parallelization using the Rayon crate. Rayon allows us to divide the sorting process into smaller tasks that can be executed concurrently, improving performance on multi-core systems.

By leveraging features like parallelization, you can achieve significant performance gains in your Rust applications.

Understanding Fucking Optimization Flags

Rust provides a range of optimization flags that can be passed to the compiler to optimize the generated machine code. The most common optimization flags are '-O' and '–release'. The '-O' flag enables the default level of optimization, while '–release' enables even more aggressive optimizations. These optimizations can result in significant performance improvements but may also increase the compilation time.

When using optimization flags, it's important to measure the impact on performance and assess whether the increased compilation time is worth the performance gain. Benchmarking and profiling can help you evaluate the effects of different optimization flags on your code.

Building Fucking High-Performance Applications

Building high-performance applications requires a holistic approach that combines efficient algorithms, optimized data structures, and leveraging the full power of the underlying hardware. Here are some additional strategies and techniques to consider when building high-performance applications with Rust:

- **Cache optimization:** Understanding the memory hierarchy and minimizing cache misses can significantly improve performance. Consider optimizing data access patterns, utilizing cache-aware data structures, and using techniques like loop unrolling and prefetching.

- **Memory allocation optimizations:** Reducing unnecessary memory allocations and minimizing heap usage can lead to better performance. Consider using stack allocation, object pooling, and minimizing object churn.

- **Vectorization:** Exploiting SIMD (Single Instruction, Multiple Data) instructions can accelerate operations on large amounts of data. Rust provides the 'simd' crate, which enables explicit SIMD programming.

- **Compiler intrinsics:** Leveraging compiler intrinsics allows low-level access to specific processor instructions and capabilities. This can be useful for implementing performance-critical routines or interacting with specialized hardware.

- **Benchmark-driven development:** Incorporate benchmarking and performance testing as part of your development process. Continuously measure and optimize the performance of your code to ensure it meets the desired performance goals.

- **Profiling tools:** Utilize profilers and performance analysis tools to identify hotspots, bottlenecks, and areas for optimization. Tools like 'cargo flamegraph' and 'perf' can provide valuable insights into the performance characteristics of your code.

- **Domain-specific optimizations:** Consider domain-specific optimizations tailored to your application's requirements. For example, in game development, techniques like spatial partitioning and level-of-detail rendering can greatly improve performance.

- **Continuous optimization:** Performance optimization is an iterative process. As you refactor and modify your code, periodically reassess its performance and identify areas that can be further optimized.

Summary

In this section, we delved into the world of building high-performance applications using Rust. We explored the importance of performance optimization, benchmarking, profiling, and various techniques and strategies for improving performance. By understanding the underlying hardware, utilizing Rust's features effectively, and employing optimization techniques, you can build applications that deliver blazingly fast performance. Remember, building high-performance applications requires a combination of knowledge, experimentation, and continuous optimization. Now go forth and create fucking fast and efficient Rust applications!

Fucking Rust in Production

Deployment Strategies for Fucking Rust Applications

Deploying fucking Rust applications is a key step in the software development process. It's the process of making your application available and accessible to the end users. In this section, we will explore different deployment strategies and best practices for fucking Rust applications.

Understanding Deployment Environments

Before diving into deployment strategies, it's essential to understand the different deployment environments and their requirements. Here are a few common deployment environments for fucking Rust applications:

- **Local Deployment:** Running the application on your development machine for testing and debugging purposes.

- **Development/Staging Environment:** A separate environment where the application is deployed for testing by the development team before deploying it to production.

- **Production Environment:** The final deployment environment where the application is made available to end users.

Each deployment environment has its own configuration, scalability, and security considerations. It's important to tailor your deployment strategy based on the specific requirements of each environment.

Deployment Strategies

There are several deployment strategies that you can use when deploying fucking Rust applications. Let's explore some of the most popular ones:

1. **Traditional Server Deployment:** This strategy involves deploying your fucking Rust application on a traditional server, either physical or virtual. You set up the necessary infrastructure (e.g., web server, database) and configure the server to run your application. This strategy provides full control over the environment but requires manual configuration and maintenance.

2. **Containerization with Docker:** Docker has gained significant popularity in recent years, and it's a powerful tool for deploying fucking Rust applications. With Docker, you can package your application along with its dependencies into a container image. This allows for easy deployment, scalability, and portability across different environments. Additionally, Docker provides a consistent and isolated environment for your application to run, ensuring reproducibility.

3. **Serverless Deployment:** Serverless computing eliminates the need for managing servers and infrastructure. In this model, your fucking Rust application is broken down into small functions that are executed in a cloud environment. Cloud providers such as AWS Lambda, Google Cloud Functions, and Microsoft Azure Functions offer serverless platforms that can host and scale your application automatically. Serverless deployment is ideal for event-driven applications with variable traffic patterns.

4. **Kubernetes Orchestration:** Kubernetes is an open-source container orchestration platform that enables scaling, management, and deployment of containerized applications. With Kubernetes, you can deploy your fucking Rust application in a highly available and fault-tolerant manner. It provides features like automatic scaling, load balancing, and rolling updates, making it suitable for large-scale production deployments.

Choosing the right deployment strategy depends on various factors such as scalability, security, cost, and ease of maintenance. It's essential to assess your application's requirements and evaluate each strategy's suitability for your specific use case.

CI/CD for Fucking Rust Applications

Continuous Integration and Continuous Deployment (CI/CD) is a crucial part of the software development lifecycle. It enables automated and frequent deployments, ensuring that your application is always up to date. Here are some CI/CD practices for fucking Rust applications:

- **Automated Builds:** Set up a pipeline to automate the build process of your fucking Rust application. This ensures that changes to the codebase trigger automated builds, providing early detection of build failures and reducing manual effort.

- **Automated Testing:** Implement automated testing in your CI/CD pipeline to verify the correctness and functionality of your application. Use frameworks like 'cargo test' and integration testing tools to ensure that your application functions as intended.

- **Continuous Deployment:** Automate the deployment process by integrating your CI/CD pipeline with your deployment strategy. This allows for seamless and frequent deployments to different environments, reducing manual intervention and ensuring faster time to market.

- **Infrastructure as Code:** Use infrastructure-as-code tools like Terraform or AWS CloudFormation to define and manage your deployment infrastructure. This approach enables automated provisioning and configuration of the required resources in a reproducible manner.

By adopting CI/CD practices, you can significantly improve the efficiency, reliability, and speed of your fucking Rust application deployments.

Monitoring and Logging Fucking Rust Services

Deploying a fucking Rust application is just the beginning. It's crucial to monitor the application's performance and health to ensure smooth operation. Here are some essential monitoring and logging practices for fucking Rust services:

- **Metrics and Dashboards:** Instrument your fucking Rust application with monitoring libraries like Prometheus or StatsD to capture relevant metrics

FUCKING RUST IN PRODUCTION 227

such as CPU usage, memory consumption, request latency, and error rates. Visualize these metrics using dashboards like Grafana to gain insights and detect anomalies.

- **Error and Debug Logging:** Implement structured logging in your application to capture useful information during runtime, such as errors, warnings, and debug messages. Tools like 'log' and 'env_logger' provide flexible logging capabilities in fucking Rust. Log messages can be sent to centralized logging systems like ELK Stack or Splunk for analysis and troubleshooting.

- **Distributed Tracing:** For complex distributed systems, consider adopting distributed tracing techniques to trace requests across different service boundaries. Tools like OpenTelemetry and Jaeger enable you to understand latency bottlenecks and pinpoint performance issues in your fucking Rust application.

- **Alerting and Incident Response:** Set up alerting mechanisms to receive notifications when performance or availability thresholds are breached. Define proper incident response processes to address critical issues promptly. Tools like PagerDuty or Opsgenie can help automate incident response workflows.

Monitoring and logging are integral parts of a comprehensive deployment strategy. They help you identify issues, troubleshoot, and optimize the performance of your fucking Rust applications in production.

Retrospective: Lessons Fucking Learned

After deploying your fucking Rust application and running it in production for some time, it's essential to conduct a retrospective to reflect on the deployment process and learn from the experience. Here are some key points to consider during a retrospective:

- **Deployment Automation:** Evaluate the level of automation achieved in the deployment process. Identify areas where further automation can be implemented to reduce manual efforts and increase efficiency.

- **Scalability and Performance:** Assess the performance and scalability of your fucking Rust application in the production environment. Identify potential bottlenecks or areas for improvement to ensure optimal performance as the user base grows.

- **Security and Compliance:** Review the security measures implemented in the deployment process. Ensure that the application follows best practices for data protection, access controls, and compliance with industry regulations.

- **User Feedback and Experience:** Gather feedback from users and stakeholders about the deployed application. Analyze the feedback to identify areas for enhancement and prioritize future iterations.

- **Cost Optimization:** Evaluate the cost effectiveness of the deployed infrastructure. Identify opportunities to optimize resource usage, such as rightsizing instances, leveraging cost-effective storage solutions, or auto-scaling based on demand.

By conducting a retrospective, you can identify lessons learned and make informed decisions for future deployments, ensuring continuous improvement.

Conclusion

Deploying fucking Rust applications requires careful consideration of deployment environments, selecting appropriate deployment strategies, implementing CI/CD practices, effective monitoring and logging, and learning from the experience through retrospectives. By following the best practices outlined in this section, you can deploy your fucking Rust applications with confidence, ensuring smooth operations and a positive user experience. Remember, deployment is not the end; it's a continuous process of improvement and optimization. So go forth, deploy your fucking Rust applications, and conquer the world of software development!

Monitoring and Logging Fucking Rust Services

Monitoring and logging are essential aspects of managing and maintaining a Rust service. By monitoring our applications, we can keep track of their performance, detect and diagnose issues, and ensure they are running smoothly. Logging helps us capture valuable information about the behavior of our services, making it easier to troubleshoot and debug problems. In this section, we will explore various monitoring and logging techniques in Rust and learn how to implement them effectively.

Choosing a Monitoring Solution

Before we dive into monitoring, it's crucial to select a monitoring solution that meets our needs. There are numerous tools and frameworks available for monitoring Rust applications, each with its own strengths and weaknesses.

One popular choice is Prometheus, an open-source monitoring and alerting toolkit. Prometheus provides a flexible and scalable approach to monitoring, allowing us to collect metrics from our Rust services and visualize them using a powerful dashboard. It also supports alerting, enabling us to set up notifications for critical issues.

Another option is Grafana, a widely-used open-source analytics and monitoring platform. Grafana integrates seamlessly with Prometheus and offers rich visualization capabilities, making it easier to analyze and interpret our monitoring data. With Grafana's extensive plugin ecosystem, we can customize our monitoring dashboards to suit our specific requirements.

Alternatively, we may consider using commercial monitoring solutions like Datadog or New Relic. These platforms offer comprehensive monitoring features, including automatic instrumentation, real-time dashboards, and intelligent alerting. While they come at a cost, they provide advanced functionality and support to simplify the monitoring process.

Ultimately, the choice of monitoring solution depends on our project's scope, budget, and specific requirements. It's essential to evaluate the available options and select the one that best aligns with our needs.

Instrumenting Rust Code

To monitor a Rust service effectively, we need to instrument our code to capture relevant metrics. Thankfully, Rust provides excellent libraries for instrumenting our applications, making it easier to collect and expose metrics.

One popular Rust library for instrumentation is `metrics`, which allows us to define custom metrics and expose them over HTTP or other protocols. With `metrics`, we can track various metrics such as response times, error rates, and resource utilization. We can also integrate `metrics` with our chosen monitoring solution (e.g., Prometheus) to scrape the exposed metrics and visualize them in a monitoring dashboard.

When instrumenting our Rust code, it's essential to identify the critical areas we want to monitor. For instance, we may want to measure the response time of certain API endpoints or track the usage of database connections. By strategically placing metric instruments in our code, we can gather valuable insights into the performance and behavior of our service. Furthermore, we should aim to capture both high-level and low-level metrics. High-level metrics provide an overview of our service's performance, while low-level metrics offer more granular details. This approach enables us to identify bottlenecks and troubleshoot performance issues effectively.

Logging Best Practices

Logging plays a crucial role in understanding the behavior of our Rust services and diagnosing problems. Properly implemented logging allows us to trace the flow of execution, detect errors, and gain insights into the inner workings of our applications. Here are some best practices for logging in Rust:

- **Use Logging Frameworks:** Rust offers excellent logging frameworks like 'log' and 'env_logger'. These frameworks provide a flexible and structured approach to logging, allowing us to define log levels, filters, and formatters. Leveraging a logging framework helps us maintain consistent logging across our codebase and simplifies configuration.

- **Log Levels:** Logging statements should be categorized into different levels based on their severity, such as 'info', 'warn', 'error', and 'debug'. By setting appropriate log levels, we can control the verbosity of our logs and only capture the necessary information.

- **Contextual Logging:** When logging, it's crucial to provide context-specific information. Include relevant data, such as request IDs, user IDs, or timestamps, to aid in log analysis and troubleshooting. Contextual logging allows us to trace specific user interactions or isolate issues to individual requests.

- **Structured Logging:** Instead of relying solely on traditional log strings, it's beneficial to use structured logging formats like JSON or key-value pairs. Structured logging enables us to extract useful information from logs programmatically and perform advanced analysis or filtering.

- **Log Aggregation:** In a production environment, we may have multiple instances of our Rust service running simultaneously. Aggregating logs from these instances into a centralized storage system (e.g., Elasticsearch, Splunk, or Graylog) simplifies log analysis and correlation. It allows us to search and visualize logs easily and gain insights into the overall health and performance of our service.

- **Error Handling and Logging:** Rust's robust error handling system provides an excellent opportunity for effective logging. When handling errors, logging relevant information and capturing error contexts can greatly aid in debugging and troubleshooting. By logging errors at appropriate points in our code, we can trace the root cause of failures and understand the error flow.

By following these logging best practices, we can improve the observability of our Rust services and accelerate the debugging process when issues arise.

Alerting and Incident Response

Monitoring and logging go hand in hand with alerting. Proper alerting mechanisms allow us to stay informed about critical issues in real-time and take proactive actions to mitigate potential risks. When setting up alerting for our Rust services, consider the following:

- **Define Alerting Rules:** Determine the thresholds or conditions that trigger alerts. For example, we might want to receive an alert when the response time of an API endpoint exceeds a certain threshold or when the error rate surpasses a specific limit. By defining clear alerting rules, we can quickly identify abnormal behavior and address it promptly.

- **Alerting Channels:** Choose the appropriate channels to receive alerts. This may include email notifications, Slack messages, SMS alerts, or integration with incident management tools like PagerDuty or OpsGenie. Selecting the right channels ensures that alerts reach the relevant individuals or teams responsible for addressing the issues.

- **Incident Response:** Establish a well-defined incident response plan that outlines the steps to be taken when critical alerts are triggered. The plan should include escalation procedures, communication channels, and responsibilities of team members. By having a structured incident response process, we can minimize downtime and resolve issues efficiently.

- **Automated Remediation:** In some cases, certain issues can be automatically resolved or mitigated. Consider implementing automated remediation processes in response to specific alerts. For example, we could automatically restart a failing service or adjust resource configurations to alleviate performance problems. Automated remediation helps reduce manual intervention and accelerates the resolution of issues.

By integrating alerting into our monitoring and logging infrastructure, we can maintain the reliability and availability of our Rust services and respond promptly to any, well, fucking incidents.

Evaluating Service Health with Metrics

Metrics collected from our Rust services provide valuable insights into their health and performance. In addition to monitoring, metrics can help us identify trends, track improvements, and make data-driven decisions regarding service optimization. When evaluating service health with metrics, consider the following aspects:

- **Service Level Indicators (SLIs):** Define SLIs that represent the essential indicators of service health. For example, response time, error rate, and throughput can be considered critical SLIs. Establishing SLIs provides a quantitative measure of service performance and aids in determining the overall stability and reliability of our services.

- **Service Level Objectives (SLOs):** Based on SLIs, establish SLOs that represent the desired level of service performance. SLOs are specific targets we aim to achieve concerning service quality. For example, we might set an SLO that states, "95% of API requests should have a response time below 100 milliseconds". SLOs create a clear agreement between service providers and consumers and help us track our progress towards meeting user expectations.

- **Service Level Agreements (SLAs):** If we are providing services to external entities or customers, SLAs help define the contractual agreement regarding service quality. SLAs outline the consequences of failing to meet specified SLOs and establish accountability. By monitoring our services' performance against SLAs, we can ensure we are meeting our contractual obligations.

- **Trending and Anomaly Detection:** Analyzing historical metric data helps identify trends, patterns, and anomalies in our service performance. Monitoring tools like Prometheus and Grafana provide built-in capabilities for data analysis and anomaly detection. By analyzing trends and detecting anomalies, we can proactively address potential issues before they impact service reliability or user experience.

Metrics serve as a powerful tool for assessing the overall health and performance of our Rust services. By establishing clear SLIs, SLOs, and SLAs, and regularly evaluating our metrics against these targets, we can ensure our services meet user expectations and deliver a high-quality fucking experience.

Summary

Monitoring and logging are crucial aspects of managing a Rust service effectively. By choosing an appropriate monitoring solution, instrumenting our code, and following logging best practices, we can gain valuable insights into the behavior and performance of our services. Alerting mechanisms and incident response procedures help us proactively address issues, while metrics provide quantitative measures of service health. By continuously monitoring and evaluating our services, we can maintain high availability, reliability, and, ultimately, deliver a fucking exceptional user experience.

Now that we've covered monitoring and logging in Rust, let's move on to the next chapter, where we'll explore advanced topics in Rust development. Get ready to take your Rust skills to the next fucking level!

Continuous Integration and Deployment with Fucking Rust

Continuous integration (CI) and deployment are crucial processes in modern software development. They allow teams to automate the building, testing, and deployment of their applications, ensuring faster and more reliable software delivery. In this section, we'll explore how to set up a CI/CD pipeline for your Fucking Rust applications.

Why CI/CD Matters

CI/CD pipelines provide several benefits for software development teams:

- **Early Bug Detection:** CI allows you to catch bugs and integration issues earlier in the development process, reducing the time and effort spent on debugging.

- **Consistent Builds:** With CI, you can ensure that all code changes are built and tested in the same environment, avoiding potential issues caused by variations across developers' machines.

- **Automated Testing:** By automating test execution, you can quickly identify regressions and ensure code quality before deploying to production.

- **Faster Deployment:** With CD, you can automate the deployment process, reducing the time it takes to deliver new features or bug fixes to users.

- **Increased Confidence:** CI/CD helps build confidence in your software by providing a reliable and repeatable process for building, testing, and deploying applications.

Let's dive into the steps required to set up a CI/CD pipeline for your Fucking Rust projects.

Step 1: Version Control and Branching Strategy

The first step in setting up a CI/CD pipeline is to use a version control system (VCS) such as Git. Version control allows teams to collaborate on code changes, track modifications, and revert to previous versions if needed. Additionally, a proper branching strategy is crucial for managing feature development, bug fixes, and releases.

Consider adopting a branching strategy like Gitflow, which promotes a structured workflow with separate branches for features, bug fixes, and releases. This strategy helps maintain a stable main branch and enables parallel development.

Step 2: Continuous Integration with Travis CI

Travis CI is a popular CI service that integrates with Git repositories and automates the building and testing of your projects. To set up CI for your Fucking Rust applications:

1. Sign up for a Travis CI account and connect it to your Git repository.

2. Create a `.travis.yml` file in the root directory of your repository. This file contains configuration instructions for Travis CI.

3. Specify the Rust version and necessary dependencies in the `.travis.yml` file. For example:

```
language\index{language}: rust\index{rust}
rust:
  - stable
before\_script:
  - rustup\index{rustup} component\index{component} add clipp
script:
```

FUCKING RUST IN PRODUCTION

```
- cargo\index{cargo} clippy --all\index{all}
- cargo\index{cargo} test\index{test}
```

This configuration instructs Travis CI to use the stable version of Rust, install the Clippy linter, and run linting checks and tests using Cargo.

4. Push the changes to your repository, and Travis CI will automatically detect them and start the build process. You can monitor the build status and view logs through the Travis CI dashboard or notifications.

Step 3: Continuous Delivery with Docker and Kubernetes

Continuous delivery (CD) is the next step in the pipeline, where successfully built and tested code is packaged and deployed. Docker and Kubernetes are widely used tools for containerization and orchestration, respectively. Leveraging these technologies, you can achieve efficient and scalable deployments of your Fucking Rust applications.

1. **Containerization with Docker:** Docker allows you to package your application and its dependencies into a lightweight and portable container image. Create a `Dockerfile` in your repository's root directory to define the image's build steps and environment.

   ```
   \# Dockerfile
   FROM rust\index{rust}:latest

   WORKDIR /usr/src/app

   COPY . .

   RUN cargo\index{cargo} build\index{build} --release\index{rel
   ```

   This `Dockerfile` uses the official Rust Docker image, sets the working directory, copies the application code, and builds the Fucking Rust application in release mode.

2. **Container Orchestration with Kubernetes:** Kubernetes simplifies the deployment, scaling, and management of containerized applications. You can define Kubernetes deployment manifests to specify the desired state of your Fucking Rust application.

```
\# deployment.yaml
apiVersion: apps/v1
kind\index{kind}: Deployment
metadata:
  name\index{name}: my-rust\index{rust}-app\index{app}
spec:
  replicas: 3
  template:
    metadata:
      labels:
        app\index{app}: my-rust\index{rust}-app\index{app}
    spec:
      containers:
        - name\index{name}: my-rust\index{rust}-app\index{ap}
          image: my-registry/my-rust-app:latest
          ports:
            - containerPort: 8000
```

This Kubernetes deployment manifest defines a deployment with three replicas of the Fucking Rust application's container image, exposes port 8000, and assigns the proper labels.

3. **Deploying with Kubernetes:** Using the kubectl command-line tool, you can apply the deployment manifest to your Kubernetes cluster:

```
kubectl\index{kubectl} apply -f deployment\index{deployment}
```

Kubernetes will automatically schedule the deployment, manage the desired state, and ensure the Fucking Rust application is running.

Step 4: Monitoring and Feedback

Monitoring your CI/CD pipeline and applications is critical for identifying issues, tracking performance, and gaining insights into user behavior. You can utilize various tools to monitor different aspects of your Fucking Rust applications:

- **CI Monitoring:** Travis CI provides built-in monitoring features, including build status notifications, email alerts, and integration with third-party tools like Slack and PagerDuty.

- **Application Monitoring:** Tools like Prometheus and Grafana can be used to monitor application metrics, resource usage, and logs. Instrument your Fucking Rust application to expose relevant metrics and integrate them with monitoring systems.

- **User Feedback:** Implementing feedback mechanisms like user surveys, error reporting, and logs analysis allows you to gather feedback and insights from users, helping you improve the quality of your Fucking Rust application.

By collecting and analyzing various monitoring data, you can spot patterns, identify bottlenecks, and make data-driven decisions to enhance the performance and stability of your Fucking Rust applications.

Conclusion

Setting up a CI/CD pipeline is crucial for delivering high-quality and reliable Fucking Rust applications. With the right tools and practices, you can automate the building, testing, and deployment processes, ensuring faster and more efficient software delivery. Remember to integrate the relevant CI/CD tools (such as Travis CI and Kubernetes) into your workflow, adopt proper version control and branching strategies, and make use of monitoring and feedback mechanisms to continuously improve your Fucking Rust applications. Now go forth, my friend, and deploy your Fucking Rust applications like a pro!

Recommended Readings:

- "The DevOps Handbook: How to Create World-Class Agility, Reliability, and Security in Technology Organizations" by Gene Kim, Jez Humble, Patrick Debois, and John Willis.

- "Continuous Delivery: Reliable Software Releases through Build, Test, and Deployment Automation" by Jez Humble and David Farley.

- "The Phoenix Project: A Novel About IT, DevOps, and Helping Your Business Win" by Gene Kim, Kevin Behr, and George Spafford.

Retrospective: Lessons Fucking Learned

In this final section, we will take a retrospective look at the essential lessons you learned throughout this fucking book. Reflecting on what you've gained from this journey is crucial before you unleash your newfound Rust skills onto the world. So, let's dive into some important takeaways.

Lesson 1: Safe Fucking Code is the Priority

Throughout this book, we've emphasized the significance of safety in Rust programming. Rust's unique ownership and borrowing system provides strong guarantees against common bugs like null pointer dereferences, data races, and memory leaks. Remembering to always prioritize safety when developing in Rust will pay off in the long run, saving you hours of debugging and headaches. But safety is not just about the code you write. It also involves best practices such as input validation, handling errors properly, and securing your applications against vulnerabilities. By embracing and implementing these practices, you can ensure that your code remains safe and reliable, even in the face of external threats.

Lesson 2: Performance Fucking Matters

While safety is crucial, Rust's performance capabilities are equally impressive. In this book, we've explored various techniques to optimize your code, including benchmarking, profiling, and understanding optimization flags. By applying these techniques, you can fine-tune your code to achieve blazing-fast performance. But remember, optimization should not come at the expense of readability and maintainability. It's essential to strike a balance between performance and code elegance. Profiling and benchmarking your code can guide you in identifying the bottlenecks and areas that require optimization without sacrificing the readability of your codebase.

Lesson 3: Embrace the Fucking Ecosystem

Rust's ecosystem is rapidly growing, with numerous libraries, frameworks, and tools at your disposal. Understanding how to leverage the power of these resources can save you significant time and effort in your development journey. Throughout this book, we've introduced you to some powerful libraries like Actix-Web for building web APIs, Rocket for web development, and Rayon for parallel algorithms. These are just a taste of what the Rust ecosystem has to offer. Embrace the community and explore the expanding universe of Rust crates to find the right tools for your projects.

Lesson 4: Documentation is Your Fucking Friend

Writing clear and concise documentation is not just a fucking afterthought; it's an essential part of your development process. Well-documented code is crucial for collaboration, code maintenance, and knowledge sharing. It allows other developers to understand and use your code effectively.

Throughout this book, we've emphasized the importance of documenting your Rust code using Rustdoc. We've seen how you can write documentation comments that become part of your code's documentation and how you can generate user-friendly API references. Embrace this practice and make sure your code is accompanied by thorough documentation to enhance its usability and longevity.

Lesson 5: Continuous Fucking Improvement

Learning Rust is just the beginning of your journey. As with any programming language, continuous improvement is key to becoming a proficient and successful Rust developer. Stay up-to-date with the latest language features, libraries, and best practices.

Follow influential Rust blogs, attend conferences, engage with the Rust community, and contribute to open-source projects. By immersing yourself in the Rust world, you'll continue to refine your skills, gain valuable insights, and establish yourself as a fucking Rust expert.

Take the Fucking Leap

Congratulations on making it this far! You've covered a vast range of topics and concepts in Rust programming. Remember, applying knowledge is the only way to truly master a language. Start working on your own projects, tackle real-world challenges, and embrace the beauty of Rust's safe, fast, and fucking secure nature. By following the principles and lessons covered in this book, you're well-equipped to build robust applications, contribute to open-source Rust projects, and join the thriving Rust community. So don't hesitate. Take the fucking leap and unleash your Rust superpowers on the world!

Now, go forth and code, you magnificent bastard!

Index

ability, 44, 53, 70, 94, 142, 206, 214
absence, 40–42
abstraction, 72
access, 4, 6, 11, 24, 36, 41, 48, 70, 74, 85, 110, 114, 118, 137, 139, 140, 144, 148, 167, 168, 170, 192, 193, 196, 199, 200
account, 63, 81, 143, 196
achievement, 22
act, 34, 68, 103
action, 16, 116, 190
actor, 100, 156
adaptation, 190
addition, 5, 68, 79, 86, 194, 212, 220, 232
address, 10, 85, 132, 188, 233
addressing, 193, 201
adoption, 65
advance, 74
advantage, 6, 23, 111, 140, 149
advent, 141
afterthought, 58, 238
age, 2
alert, 112, 113
alerting, 229, 231, 232
algorithm, 187, 188, 213, 220
all, 14, 18, 23, 39, 50, 54, 56, 59, 61, 64, 71, 97, 104, 128, 140, 142, 162, 168, 188, 196, 208, 215
allocation, 1, 4, 81, 153
amount, 148, 210, 213
analysis, 24, 25, 47, 154, 208, 218
api, 115
app, 77
application, 1, 5, 7, 78, 80, 95, 98, 110, 114, 123, 126, 128, 129, 133, 136, 158, 169, 176, 187, 189, 190, 200–203, 206, 210, 213, 219, 224, 226, 227, 236
approach, 2, 11, 47, 113, 149, 161, 216, 223, 229, 230
architecture, 156
armor, 2
army, 1, 61
array, 74–77, 142, 168, 170
arsenal, 47, 199
art, 83, 171, 214
aspect, 29, 39, 42, 47, 61, 120, 184, 192, 203
ass, 14, 59
assistant, 59
async, 90, 97, 98, 101, 136, 151
attack, 191, 197, 202

attacker, 196, 197, 199, 201, 205
attempt, 200
attention, 3, 63
attribute, 98
audit, 202
auditing, 10
authentication, 118, 119, 192, 193, 196
authorization, 118, 119
availability, 158, 186, 187, 190, 232, 233
average, 1
await, 90, 97, 98
awareness, 81, 201
awesomeness, 13

back, 14, 64, 144, 198
backbone, 181
balance, 4, 58, 238
balancer, 187–189
balancing, 141, 143, 155, 158, 186–190
bank, 196
baseline, 219
basic, 49, 114, 117, 127, 129, 156, 159, 176, 180, 212
Bask, 22
beauty, 59, 239
beginning, 65, 226, 239
behavior, 5, 36, 43, 44, 72, 167, 228, 230, 233
belt, 15
benchmark, 208–211, 220
benchmarking, 5, 6, 207, 208, 210, 211, 219, 224, 238
benefit, 60
beverage, 3
binary, 23, 109, 131
bit, 80, 211

block, 20, 36, 37, 86, 90, 137, 168
blockchain, 12
blog, 202
body, 117, 182
bodyguard, 1, 198
book, 78, 79, 163, 237–239
bookstore, 78
boost, 213
borrow, 68, 70, 161, 162
borrowing, 3, 4, 11, 30, 34, 35, 48, 67, 68, 70, 73, 153, 154, 158–162, 167–169, 238
bottleneck, 25, 213
box, 188, 209
boy, 1
branch, 234
branching, 81, 234
break, 1, 22, 29
breeze, 63, 199
bridge, 103, 113
browser, 57, 109–111, 113, 205
bucket, 77
buddy, 14
budget, 229
buffer, 2, 3, 11, 109, 153, 166, 168, 198–202
bug, 193, 234
build, 2–4, 7, 10, 12, 17–19, 35, 57, 59, 61, 71, 76, 83, 88, 89, 91, 97, 100, 101, 109, 111, 114, 117, 120, 121, 126–128, 132, 133, 140, 143, 148, 151, 156, 180, 190, 203, 204, 206, 224, 239
building, 2, 6, 11, 29, 36, 39, 59, 67, 73, 77, 88, 97, 100, 110, 114, 115, 119–121, 128, 130, 131, 136, 137, 153,

Index

155, 158, 171, 180, 181, 184, 186, 190, 199, 201, 218, 223, 224, 234, 238
bullet, 143
burning, 15
bytecode, 111

cache, 81
cake, 13
call, 29, 91, 102, 103, 111–113, 169
capacity, 187, 188
care, 18, 59
career, 2
cargo, 109, 155, 220
case, 50, 81, 129, 159, 226
cat, 197
catcher, 119
category, 167
cause, 140
caution, 5, 41, 198
chain, 2
chaining, 77
chance, 140
change, 33, 65, 74, 161, 211
channel, 130
chapter, 2, 32, 67, 76, 88, 111, 120, 153, 158, 233
character, 50
chat, 131, 133, 134, 136
check, 58, 88, 126
checker, 68, 70, 161, 162
checking, 25, 168
checklist, 202
choice, 6, 11, 16, 109, 120, 140, 186, 208, 229
chunk, 148
clarity, 56, 72
class, 36

client, 130–132, 136, 180, 183, 184, 188, 205
closure, 139, 154
cloud, 189
cluster, 187
code, 1–6, 11, 13, 15–18, 20–24, 28, 29, 32–39, 42–45, 47–49, 51, 55–59, 61, 62, 67–73, 76, 80, 84, 86, 88, 92, 97, 102–104, 109–113, 116, 119, 124, 127, 128, 131, 140, 141, 145, 153–155, 158, 159, 162, 167–169, 171, 178, 180, 190–192, 194–196, 199, 200, 202, 203, 205, 207–209, 211–220, 222, 229, 230, 233, 238, 239
codebase, 58, 238
coding, 8, 10, 16, 19, 42, 47, 56, 61, 73, 127, 192, 194–196, 201, 202
coffee, 175
collaboration, 62, 239
collection, 3, 11, 40, 47, 67, 74, 75, 77, 141, 148, 154, 159, 198
collector, 159
collision, 77
colon, 36
combination, 10, 37, 41, 111, 134, 149, 167, 224
command, 14, 16–18, 22, 24, 25, 54, 57, 59–61, 115, 116, 120, 121, 123, 126, 128, 129, 136
commerce, 201
communication, 130, 131, 134, 136, 171, 180
community, 2, 4, 12, 17, 57, 62, 65,

109, 238, 239
compatibility, 104
compilation, 11, 18, 22, 23, 25, 68, 222
compile, 3, 5, 11, 15, 18, 44, 48, 67, 68, 74, 110, 154, 161, 162, 167
compiler, 1, 3, 5, 11, 13, 16, 19, 20, 23–25, 33, 35, 47–49, 74, 86, 109, 154, 155, 167, 169, 220, 222
completion, 17
component, 121, 124
composition, 94
compromise, 7, 196, 200
computation, 150, 218
compute, 73
computer, 79
computing, 142
concept, 2, 5, 6, 11, 30, 33, 35, 47, 67, 92, 119, 141, 143, 148, 159, 163, 167
concern, 3
conciseness, 56
concurrency, 1, 6, 67, 70, 71, 73, 76, 86, 92, 136, 137, 140, 148, 149, 151, 168, 186
condition, 6
conduct, 194, 227
confidence, 4, 151, 209
configuration, 225, 235
configure, 116, 188, 189
confirmation, 64
conjunction, 168, 187
connection, 131–133
consideration, 80, 215
consistency, 57, 127, 130, 144
console, 18, 25, 73, 178
construct, 174, 201

consumption, 155
container, 129, 236
containerization, 158
content, 197
context, 76, 90, 219
contract, 43
control, 1–4, 6, 19, 23, 29, 32, 36, 37, 39, 55, 88, 153, 192, 193, 196, 215
coordination, 70
copying, 30, 75, 76, 128
core, 6, 71, 85, 155, 159, 167, 171
correctness, 55, 81, 104, 144
corruption, 144, 168
cost, 1, 5, 6, 76, 102, 109, 167, 168, 225, 229
count, 124
counter, 71, 121, 124, 146
counting, 163
couple, 16
crash, 199
crate, 70, 112, 113, 141, 148, 176, 178, 198, 199, 219
creation, 162, 184
creativity, 136
criterion, 219
culture, 201
cup, 175
cure, 215
curiosity, 15
current, 39, 188
custom, 35, 36, 39, 80, 81, 83, 84, 118, 119, 184
customer, 201
cutting, 120
cycle, 188

damn, 1, 10
dashboard, 229

Index

data, 1–3, 5, 6, 11, 19, 23, 26, 28, 30, 32–39, 44, 47, 48, 67, 68, 70, 71, 73, 76, 77, 79–81, 83–85, 98, 102, 110, 111, 114, 117–119, 130, 131, 137–141, 143, 144, 148, 149, 153, 154, 161–163, 166–168, 171, 172, 174–176, 178, 182, 189, 194, 196–203, 206, 210, 220, 223, 229, 232, 237, 238
database, 77, 89, 175, 189, 201, 229
date, 1, 2, 10, 58, 60, 193, 196, 201, 206, 239
day, 186
deadlock, 140
deallocation, 153, 168
debug, 11, 17, 140, 155, 228
debugger, 17, 155
debugging, 24, 155, 171, 231, 238
decision, 81
default, 14, 34, 35, 43, 129, 222
define, 35–39, 43, 44, 48, 72, 73, 86, 90, 98, 116, 118, 119, 128, 136, 145, 157, 181, 184, 186, 188
definition, 37, 39
degradation, 169
deletion, 77
delivery, 59
demand, 2, 187
demonstration, 184
dependency, 18, 112, 131, 132, 141, 171, 176, 178, 181, 208
deployment, 127, 130, 224, 225, 227, 236
depth, 67
deserialization, 199

design, 81, 191
detail, 4, 36, 63
detect, 155, 228, 230
detective, 207
determination, 202
developer, 48, 65, 120, 155, 186, 239
development, 2, 7, 8, 10, 12–14, 16–19, 21, 23–25, 51, 55, 61, 67, 76, 105, 109, 111, 113, 114, 118–120, 126, 127, 130, 136, 148, 190, 193, 195, 201, 203, 224, 233, 234, 238
diagnose, 228
dialog, 112, 113
difference, 33, 35
digit, 198
dining, 140
directory, 17, 18, 22, 59, 115, 121
dirt, 198
disposal, 238
distribution, 209
doc, 57
Docker, 127–130, 158
Dockerized Rust, 129
Dockerizing, 130
document, 88
documentation, 16, 18, 55–59, 81, 238, 239
door, 196
dot, 36
doubt, 214
driver, 59
drop, 159, 169
dump, 155
duplex, 131
duration, 47

e, 201

eagle, 211
ease, 17, 100, 156, 225
ecosystem, 57, 61, 109, 111, 171, 175, 180, 196, 198, 207, 229, 238
edge, 2, 20, 50, 120
editor, 16, 17, 19, 23
efficiency, 11, 81, 84, 88, 149, 168, 207, 211, 214, 215
effort, 18, 238
elegance, 42, 238
element, 40, 142
elision, 49
email, 77, 198
emphasis, 3
encoding, 198
encryption, 194, 196
end, 116, 211, 224
endpoint, 116, 119, 181
enforce, 47
entity, 198
entry, 98, 128, 187
enum, 37, 39, 40, 119
environment, 13, 14, 16, 19–21, 23, 109, 111, 129, 225
Err, 39
error, 39, 42, 48, 68–70, 73, 74, 77, 89, 91, 95, 97, 118, 119, 168, 171, 184, 186, 192, 210
escaping, 197
event, 124
example, 1, 6, 33, 34, 36–41, 43, 44, 48–50, 56, 68, 69, 71, 72, 75–78, 81, 88, 94, 95, 98, 100, 104, 110, 112, 118, 132, 134, 136, 137, 140, 142, 146, 149, 150, 153, 154, 156, 157, 159–161, 176, 178, 184, 187, 188, 198, 202, 210, 213, 216, 219, 220
exception, 168
executable, 23
execution, 5, 55, 70, 90, 91, 94, 98, 136, 141, 143, 150, 196, 207, 209–211, 214, 219, 220, 230
exercise, 5, 39, 198
exhaustion, 197
expense, 238
experience, 16, 109, 187, 210, 227, 233
experimentation, 218, 224
expert, 127, 239
exploit, 196, 200
exploitation, 193
explore, 4, 7, 10, 19, 23, 29, 32, 36, 37, 45, 51, 55, 67, 69, 70, 72, 73, 76, 77, 80, 88, 97, 101, 111, 114, 117, 120, 126, 127, 130, 136, 140, 143, 148, 153, 155, 162, 166, 168, 169, 171, 172, 180, 186, 190, 196, 199, 203, 204, 207, 211, 214, 218, 224, 225, 228, 233, 238
exposure, 201
expression, 38, 39
expressiveness, 73
extension, 17, 24
extractor, 183
eye, 2

face, 7, 10, 238
failure, 70
faint, 1

Index   247

fame, 10
fancy, 21
fault, 100, 101, 170, 186, 187, 190
feature, 37, 47, 109, 142, 160
Fedora, 16
feedback, 58, 65
field, 36, 124, 201
file, 17, 18, 21, 22, 39, 89, 112, 116, 121, 131, 132, 141, 150, 151, 171, 176, 178, 181, 210
filter, 216
fix, 51, 168, 169, 171
flag, 155, 222
flame, 220
flamegraph, 155, 220
flexibility, 35, 43, 55, 72, 84, 88, 111, 113, 120, 198
flow, 19, 29, 32, 36, 37, 39, 230
focus, 6, 11, 59, 61, 109, 130, 155, 168, 190, 208, 220
following, 16–18, 21, 22, 24, 25, 36, 54, 55, 57, 59–61, 65, 84, 116, 120, 121, 123, 126, 128, 131, 136, 153, 155, 159, 190, 192–196, 200, 206, 208, 209, 231–233, 239
fork, 140
form, 36, 117, 124, 172
format, 109, 111, 176, 178, 182, 198
formatting, 17
fortress, 2
foster, 201
foundation, 140, 151, 162, 171, 180
framework, 51, 55, 81, 100, 114, 115, 117, 119, 120, 126, 134, 136, 156, 171, 175, 186, 188, 190, 199

free, 3, 11, 17, 67, 86, 160, 162, 167, 168
freedom, 88
friend, 1, 2, 64, 65
frontend, 120, 126
frustration, 58
fuck, 1–4, 13, 20, 55, 78, 86, 102, 120, 176
fucker, 14, 63, 197
fucking, 2–4, 6, 7, 10–16, 20, 22, 23, 27, 28, 32, 39–47, 51, 55–65, 77–80, 83–86, 88, 89, 91, 92, 97, 102, 105, 113, 120, 130, 137, 140, 143, 147, 153, 159–161, 163, 166–171, 175, 176, 178, 180, 186, 187, 190–192, 196–199, 201, 207, 210–212, 214–218, 224–227, 232, 233, 237–239
Fucking Rocket, 114, 116–120
Fucking Rust, 26–28, 143–146, 148, 171, 175, 190, 234
Fucking Yew, 120, 121, 126, 127
fun, 28, 46, 56, 79, 197, 218
function, 5, 29, 34, 36, 39, 49, 50, 69, 70, 73, 76, 77, 86, 90, 98, 112, 159, 169, 181, 220
functionality, 81, 88, 110, 114, 188, 229
fundamental, 33, 69, 73, 137, 148, 153, 162, 186
future, 12, 55, 89, 91, 92, 98, 228

gain, 3, 4, 23, 199, 206, 210, 222, 230, 233, 239
game, 1, 11, 19, 218
garbage, 3, 11, 47, 67, 154, 159

generic, 43, 44, 72, 73
generics, 5, 43, 45–47, 72, 73
genius, 65
get, 2, 4, 13, 14, 20, 23, 26, 36, 59, 64, 79, 102, 114, 132, 171, 181, 211
glory, 22
glue, 102
go, 14, 15, 63, 65, 76, 102, 105, 113, 128, 211, 214, 215, 224, 231
goal, 112, 186, 207
god, 59
grace, 41
Grafana, 229
graph, 39
grasp, 32, 67
group, 53
growth, 12
guarantee, 67, 144
guidance, 88
guide, 16, 48, 67, 220, 238

habit, 58
hair, 199
halt, 197
hand, 34, 231
handle, 1, 2, 38, 39, 41, 42, 44, 69, 91, 92, 110, 117–119, 124, 127, 131, 132, 134, 136, 137, 140, 156, 158, 170, 171, 175, 182–184, 186–189, 199
handler, 157, 181, 184
handling, 4, 39, 42, 50, 69, 70, 73, 95, 97, 100, 110, 118, 119, 132, 155, 156, 158, 171, 175, 184, 186, 190, 192, 196, 210, 238

handshake, 131
hardware, 11, 84, 143, 144, 151, 187, 219, 223, 224
hash, 32, 77–79
hashing, 79
hat, 207, 211
havoc, 196
head, 171
health, 226, 232, 233
heap, 4, 5, 74
heart, 1
help, 3, 5, 7, 9, 39, 49–51, 67, 88, 137, 153, 155, 158, 169, 192, 198, 204, 209, 211, 212, 214, 220, 222, 227, 232, 233
highlighting, 17
hole, 23
home, 198
host, 127, 129
hug, 61
humor, 56

idea, 49
image, 128, 129, 148, 149, 213, 216, 236
impact, 65, 148, 202, 210, 216, 222
implement, 43, 44, 73, 81, 88, 148, 157, 158, 188, 191, 228
implementation, 49, 72, 81, 84, 104, 105
implementor, 43
importance, 7, 10, 55, 56, 153, 196, 201, 211, 224, 239
improve, 5, 58, 65, 80, 84, 149, 192, 207, 209, 211, 215, 216, 231
improvement, 5, 57, 59, 62, 211, 228, 239

Index 249

incident, 233
increment, 146
industry, 2
information, 2, 14, 58, 61, 77, 149, 182, 183, 192, 194, 197, 199, 205, 220, 228
infrastructure, 4, 187, 232
injection, 11, 191, 196, 199–202
inline, 124
inlining, 5
input, 4, 50, 124, 127, 142, 191, 192, 196–202, 238
insertion, 77
installation, 14, 16, 24
installer, 16
installing, 13, 16, 23
instance, 36, 37, 73, 229
instrument, 229
instrumentation, 229
integration, 17, 111
integrity, 199, 202
intensity, 143
interaction, 111, 113, 175
interactivity, 111, 120
interface, 54, 72, 103, 110, 114
internal, 81
internet, 114, 181
interoperability, 105
interpolation, 213
interval, 209
introduction, 97
issue, 6, 167, 169
item, 141, 202
iteration, 141
iterator, 141

jacket, 1
job, 2, 4
join, 2, 70, 120, 154, 239

journey, 3, 20, 23, 28, 47, 65, 67, 136, 175, 218, 237–239
js, 112, 113
jsonschema, 178
junk, 197

Kevin Wayne, 79
key, 4, 8, 11, 57, 67, 77, 79, 102, 114, 160, 166, 176, 199, 209, 212, 224, 227, 239
keyword, 36, 37, 90, 97, 98, 154
kick, 14, 59
knife, 18, 198
knight, 2
knowledge, 28, 42, 46, 65, 67, 83, 84, 97, 140, 143, 196, 206, 224, 239

landscape, 7, 10
language, 1–4, 10, 12, 19, 23, 26, 39, 84, 102–104, 109, 136, 151, 167, 171, 190, 198, 219, 239
leak, 169
leakage, 192, 199
leap, 239
learning, 3, 4, 10, 12, 15, 20, 23, 46, 97, 175, 186, 206, 210
leather, 1
legion, 120
length, 198
level, 1–3, 5, 6, 11, 19, 22, 23, 45, 67, 70, 84, 88, 108, 110, 111, 126, 131, 145, 148, 155, 215, 217, 222, 230, 233
leverage, 1, 6, 55, 70, 104, 109–111, 136, 140, 143, 171, 181, 188, 190, 238

leveraging, 6, 11, 72, 111, 149, 151, 156, 162, 186, 190, 196, 206, 219, 220, 222, 223
library, 4, 70, 88, 110, 131–133, 136, 140, 143, 149, 158, 176, 182, 198, 208, 210, 211
life, 2, 104
lifecycle, 121
lifespan, 47
lifetime, 48, 49, 161, 162, 167
limit, 46
line, 54, 150
link, 2
linter, 235
list, 49, 50, 55, 77
load, 141, 143, 155, 158, 186–190
locality, 81
location, 14, 144, 170
lock, 139
logging, 226–228, 230–233
logic, 121, 184
longevity, 239
look, 1, 29, 36, 37, 49, 72, 74, 75, 100, 112, 137, 144, 145, 160, 196–198, 201, 207, 212, 220, 237
lookup, 81
loop, 132
loss, 169
lot, 23, 58

machine, 2, 14, 16, 23, 109, 167, 187, 222
macro, 119
main, 1, 39, 73, 98, 116, 159, 167, 234
maintainability, 238
maintenance, 225, 239

management, 3, 4, 11, 18, 47, 50, 55, 104, 109, 140, 155, 158–160, 162, 163, 167
manager, 2, 16, 17, 109
managing, 59, 100, 141, 143, 228, 233
manifest, 236
manipulation, 32
manner, 39, 42, 53, 79, 89, 91, 184, 187
map, 77, 78, 142, 143
mark, 41, 42
market, 2, 4
marketplace, 17
master, 58, 67, 239
mastering, 28, 39, 47, 73, 79, 83, 159, 171, 186
match, 37–39, 198
matching, 35–39, 42, 198
meaning, 39, 143
meantime, 144
measure, 5, 207, 210, 217, 219, 222, 229
mechanism, 5, 47, 95, 97, 111, 118, 119, 186
media, 77, 197
memory, 1–6, 11, 30, 33, 34, 47, 48, 50, 67, 73, 81, 83–86, 102, 104, 109, 111, 143–145, 148, 153–155, 158–160, 162, 163, 166–171, 187, 190, 199, 210, 215, 238
message, 15, 18, 25, 39, 64, 112, 113, 116, 132, 181
metadata, 68
method, 73, 220
metric, 230
middle, 144
middleware, 100, 184, 186

Index

milestone, 65
mind, 4, 8, 11, 27, 57, 76, 113, 129, 189, 190, 213, 216
mismanagement, 11
miss, 14, 39
misuse, 68, 69, 88
model, 1, 6, 11, 83, 104, 136, 159, 180
modification, 154
module, 6, 70, 141
moment, 20, 59, 114
monitoring, 189, 190, 226, 228, 229, 232, 233, 237
monomorphization, 5
motherfucker, 20
mount, 129
move, 10, 55, 115, 120, 130, 154, 160, 162, 176, 180, 211, 212, 233
multithreading, 86
must, 43, 48, 161, 191
mutability, 34, 35, 69, 73, 161
mutex, 137
mystery, 1

name, 36, 37, 154
naming, 27
nature, 143, 239
need, 5, 11, 13, 15, 16, 20, 23, 39, 47, 48, 59, 60, 62, 64, 74, 75, 77, 80, 81, 84–86, 88, 98, 102, 104, 109–112, 114, 116, 128, 131, 138, 140, 141, 147, 148, 150, 154, 156, 159, 163, 168, 171, 172, 174, 176, 178, 181, 183, 199, 201, 220, 229
net, 51

network, 89, 187, 197
networking, 12
new, 4, 12, 18, 20, 28, 36, 58, 59, 77, 115, 120, 131, 132, 154, 181, 184, 188, 210
newfound, 237
ninja, 16, 28
node, 39
notation, 36
null, 2, 3, 67, 109, 153, 162, 166, 170, 238
number, 3, 24, 74, 75, 78, 83, 150, 154, 187, 198

object, 36, 176
observability, 231
off, 198, 238
official, 55, 115
omission, 49
on, 2, 3, 6, 10, 11, 14, 16, 17, 20, 22, 24, 28, 34, 37–39, 44, 49, 51, 55, 58, 59, 61, 63, 64, 67, 72, 74, 77, 81, 86, 88, 109, 115, 116, 119, 120, 124, 127, 129, 130, 132, 141, 143–145, 150, 158, 159, 168, 171, 172, 176, 180, 181, 187–190, 196, 199, 202, 205, 207, 208, 210–213, 217, 220, 222, 225, 227, 229, 233, 237, 239
one, 1, 11, 16, 17, 21, 34, 35, 37, 58, 67, 77, 90, 92, 114, 136–138, 140, 144, 153, 159, 160, 162, 166, 168, 180, 189, 207, 210, 211, 229
operating, 3

operation, 39, 73, 89–92, 144, 146, 213, 226
operator, 41, 42, 69, 70, 91
optimization, 73, 153, 158, 190, 209–211, 213–220, 222, 224, 232, 238
optimizer, 211
optimizing, 81, 143, 207, 211–214, 218–220
option, 229
optional, 42
order, 15, 43, 71, 140, 199
ordering, 145, 148
organization, 29
other, 3, 17, 32, 34, 43, 50, 55, 61, 67, 70, 76, 84, 97, 102–105, 110, 111, 114, 129–131, 134, 137, 140, 141, 143, 144, 155, 156, 160, 163, 166, 169, 171, 180, 191, 199, 205, 239
output, 22, 55, 61, 71, 73, 116, 142
oven, 13
overflow, 170, 198–202
overhead, 5, 143, 145, 167
overview, 22, 108, 230
owner, 34, 67, 153, 159, 161, 162, 167, 168
ownership, 1, 3, 4, 6, 11, 30, 33–35, 48, 67, 68, 70, 73, 83, 104, 136, 153, 154, 158–163, 167–169, 238

pack, 110
package, 2, 16, 17, 55, 61–65, 109, 110, 127, 130
pair, 77
panic, 41

parallel, 6, 70, 71, 137, 140–143, 148, 150, 151, 213, 234, 238
parallelism, 6, 67, 70, 71, 73, 140, 143, 149
parallelization, 220, 222
parameter, 183
part, 4, 20, 51, 55, 61, 114, 118, 124, 175, 193, 207, 238, 239
partitioning, 140, 143
passion, 15
Pat, 14, 64
path, 183, 186
pattern, 35–37, 39, 42, 142, 198
payload, 182
peace, 11
penalty, 167
people, 63, 64
perf, 5
performance, 1–7, 10, 11, 25, 32, 69, 71, 73, 80, 81, 83, 84, 88, 97, 100–102, 109–111, 120, 140, 143, 148, 151, 153, 156, 158, 162, 167, 169, 171, 180, 186, 187, 189, 190, 199, 207, 209–220, 222–224, 226–228, 230, 232, 233, 237, 238
performant, 2, 28, 76, 120, 126, 130, 147, 168, 190, 207
persistence, 188, 189
person, 36
personality, 56
philosopher, 140
phone, 198
picture, 77, 197
pie, 137
piece, 11, 29, 34, 136, 167, 168

Index

place, 57, 207
placeholder, 44
plague, 155, 160, 166
platform, 127, 197, 215, 217, 229
play, 73, 153, 160, 163, 192, 214
plugin, 17, 229
point, 48, 50, 98, 128, 142, 187
pointer, 2, 3, 67, 85, 109, 162, 166, 167, 170, 238
popularity, 2–4, 10, 12, 20
port, 132, 236
portability, 130
portion, 75, 187, 188
possibility, 190
post, 202
potential, 2, 4, 7, 10, 12, 48, 65, 76, 86, 88, 104, 111, 126, 136, 139, 140, 144, 155, 167, 168, 192, 196, 197, 202, 203, 206, 231
power, 2, 3, 11, 21, 42, 61, 71, 86, 88, 101, 105, 110, 113, 126, 133, 136, 143, 148, 151, 180, 190, 213, 223, 238
practice, 28, 39, 46, 49, 75, 79, 186, 239
precision, 1
prefix, 49, 50, 81
prelude, 141
prevalence, 203
primitive, 137
principle, 153, 167
print, 68, 71
privacy, 202
pro, 28, 42, 171
problem, 140, 141, 143, 144, 169, 215

process, 5, 7, 8, 10, 12, 13, 16, 22–24, 51, 55, 58, 60, 62, 63, 81, 83, 110, 114, 120, 127, 128, 130, 149, 150, 155, 156, 158, 174, 184, 186, 187, 189, 195, 196, 199, 201, 202, 207, 210, 211, 213, 214, 216, 217, 224, 227, 229, 231, 238
processing, 141, 148, 149, 151, 200, 210, 213, 216
processor, 140
production, 2, 73, 127, 129, 153, 158, 227
productivity, 16
professionalism, 63
profile, 77, 220
profiler, 155, 220
profiling, 5, 6, 171, 211–214, 220, 222, 224, 238
program, 1, 14, 15, 17, 19, 20, 22, 23, 25, 70, 86, 137, 155, 163, 167, 168, 170, 196, 198, 199, 207, 216
programmer, 55, 67, 79, 84, 153, 167, 171, 175
programming, 1–3, 6, 9, 10, 12, 13, 15, 19, 20, 26, 33, 35, 36, 39, 42, 43, 47, 67, 68, 70, 71, 76, 83, 86, 88, 92, 97, 102–105, 109, 111, 136, 137, 139–143, 148, 151, 155, 159, 160, 162, 163, 166–168, 171, 190, 198, 201, 238, 239
progress, 67
project, 18, 19, 53, 54, 59–61, 114–116, 119–121, 127, 141, 181, 202, 229

Prometheus, 229
promise, 89, 92
promotion, 65
prompt, 16–18, 24, 63
propagation, 69
proportion, 188
protocol, 131, 171, 175, 181
provide, 4, 6, 35, 43, 44, 48, 51, 55, 74–77, 88, 89, 102, 103, 111, 127, 130, 131, 136, 143, 147, 151, 159, 171, 187, 188, 229, 230, 232, 233
publication, 63, 64
publishing, 55, 62, 65, 110
punch, 214
purpose, 56
puzzle, 136

quality, 11, 233
quantity, 78
query, 89, 117, 172
question, 41, 42

rabbit, 23
range, 12, 17, 44, 69, 72, 136, 196, 203, 222, 239
rayon, 6, 70, 148, 213
read, 34, 35, 138–140, 150, 161
readability, 238
reading, 89
reason, 2, 4, 33
receiver, 132
refactoring, 17, 51
reference, 34, 35, 48, 50, 55, 68, 75, 76, 153, 154, 160–163
regex, 198
registry, 61, 64
relationship, 48

release, 65, 222
reliability, 95, 166, 232, 233
repeat, 188
replication, 189
report, 61, 208
representation, 81, 119
request, 89, 100, 117–119, 131, 132, 149, 156, 171, 172, 174, 175, 181–183, 186–188
reqwest, 149
resolve, 91
resource, 6, 11, 47, 109, 137, 140, 160, 163, 197, 207, 209, 211, 219
response, 6, 174, 182, 184, 187, 188, 229, 233
responsibility, 86
responsiveness, 207, 209, 211
rest, 2, 194
result, 39, 68, 89, 90, 143, 167–169, 196, 199, 201, 222
retrieval, 77, 149
retrospective, 227, 228, 237
return, 29, 32, 39, 69, 118, 119, 182–184
reusability, 29, 43
reuse, 72
ride, 2
right, 15, 101, 171, 190, 214, 225, 238
rise, 10
risk, 1, 34, 35, 190, 191, 193, 200, 201
Robert Sedgewick, 79
robustness, 9, 12, 192
rocket, 115
rockstar, 16
role, 55, 73, 84, 86, 119, 153, 192, 199, 214, 230

Index

rollercoaster, 198
Rome, 186
root, 142
round, 140
route, 181, 183, 187
routing, 100, 183
rs, 116, 210
rule, 161
run, 1, 15–19, 22, 25, 54, 55, 57–59, 61, 109–111, 116, 121, 123, 127–129, 136, 154, 178, 180, 208, 214, 216, 219, 235, 238
running, 18, 20, 22, 23, 113, 155, 209, 220, 227, 228, 236
runtime, 3, 5, 11, 69, 98, 111–113, 127, 129, 134, 154, 167, 168, 207
Rust, 1–17, 19–21, 23–25, 29, 30, 32–37, 39–44, 46–51, 53, 55, 57, 59, 61, 63, 67–77, 80, 81, 83–86, 88, 90, 92, 95, 97, 98, 101–105, 108–114, 120, 127–131, 133, 134, 136, 137, 140, 141, 143, 147–149, 151, 153–155, 158–163, 166–171, 178, 180, 186, 188, 190–196, 198, 202, 203, 206, 207, 209, 211, 213–215, 217, 222–224, 228–231, 233, 238, 239
Rust-lang, 17
Rust, 17, 105, 239
Rusty, 14

s, 1–7, 10–20, 22, 23, 26, 28, 29, 32–41, 43–49, 54–59, 61–63, 67–78, 80, 81, 83, 84, 86, 88, 94, 95, 97, 98, 100–102, 104, 108, 109, 111–118, 120, 121, 124, 127, 128, 130, 132–134, 136–140, 142, 144–146, 148–151, 153–162, 168–172, 175, 176, 178, 180–184, 186–188, 190, 193, 194, 196–198, 200, 201, 205, 207, 209–220, 222, 224–227, 229, 230, 233, 236–239
safety, 1–7, 10, 11, 23, 33, 34, 44, 47, 51, 67, 68, 72, 73, 84–88, 102, 109, 111, 113, 120, 126, 153–155, 158, 159, 162, 166–168, 170, 175, 190, 199, 238
sailing, 61
sample, 180, 182–184, 208
sanitization, 201, 202
scalability, 6, 130, 158, 187, 225
scale, 100, 141, 187, 189
scaling, 155, 158, 186, 187, 189, 190
scenario, 39, 49, 138, 210
scheduling, 140
schema, 178
science, 79
scope, 34, 49, 67, 86, 159, 161, 162, 229
scraping, 149, 150
scratch, 73, 153, 155, 158
screen, 15, 16, 24
script, 197
search, 16, 61, 77, 81, 83, 201
second, 1, 188
section, 4, 6, 7, 10, 13, 16, 19, 23, 26, 29, 32, 35, 36, 39, 42, 47, 51, 55, 67, 69, 70, 72,

73, 76, 77, 80, 97, 111,
    113, 114, 119, 120, 126,
    127, 130, 136, 140, 143,
    148, 159, 162, 166, 168,
    171, 175, 180, 186, 190,
    196, 199, 203, 204,
    206–208, 211, 214, 218,
    224, 228, 237
secure, 2–4, 7–11, 15, 20, 28, 73,
    76, 97, 109, 111, 114, 120,
    126, 130, 136, 153, 158,
    159, 162, 168, 171, 186,
    190, 192, 194–197, 199,
    201–204, 206, 215, 239
security, 2–4, 7–12, 42, 166–168,
    175, 190–196, 198, 199,
    201–203, 206, 225
segfault, 170
segmentation, 1, 155, 168, 170, 171
self, 58
sender, 132
sense, 58
separation, 88
sequence, 50
Serde, 176, 210
serde, 199
serialization, 199
server, 73, 100, 116, 129–132, 134,
    136, 153, 155, 156, 158,
    171, 172, 175, 176, 180,
    187–189, 218
service, 158, 197, 228–230,
    232–234
session, 188, 189
set, 9, 13, 14, 16, 17, 19, 23, 24, 37,
    43, 57, 70, 80, 102, 103,
    109, 111, 114–116, 119,
    120, 127, 131, 132, 134,
    136, 142, 144, 171, 172,
    180, 181, 189, 208, 229,
    234
setting, 59, 73, 128, 175, 231
setup, 16
shape, 1, 63
sharding, 189
share, 65, 102, 162, 163
sharing, 62, 70, 239
shit, 13, 59, 63, 86, 169, 186, 196
side, 33, 132, 205
significance, 238
simplicity, 180, 186
size, 74–76, 208
skill, 155, 168
sky, 46
slice, 48
snippet, 68, 73, 119
software, 2, 7, 8, 10–12, 55, 61, 65,
    105, 114, 148, 166–168,
    190, 191, 193, 196, 201,
    203, 219, 224
solution, 187, 202, 229, 233
sort, 219
source, 62, 68, 127, 128, 202, 229,
    239
specific, 5, 14, 36, 38, 44, 55, 72, 77,
    80, 81, 129, 145, 157, 158,
    183, 188, 192, 198, 202,
    203, 207, 208, 210, 211,
    225, 226, 229
speed, 1, 11, 25, 148, 149, 209, 211,
    213–215, 219
stability, 95, 237
stack, 4, 74, 91, 170
standard, 4, 70, 149, 178, 180
start, 16, 17, 20, 81, 97, 108, 109,
    114, 116, 120, 131, 136,
    153, 181, 190, 211
starvation, 139, 140

Index

state, 34, 35, 100, 121, 127, 140, 189, 236
statement, 141
status, 119
std, 6, 70
step, 16, 17, 28, 62, 64, 128, 144, 178, 196, 211, 220, 224
stock, 78
storage, 187, 194, 196
store, 77, 78, 83
strap, 3, 111
strategy, 188, 189, 225–227, 234
streaming, 197
string, 48, 50, 81, 154, 159, 184
struct, 36–38, 48, 73, 136, 182
structure, 36, 37, 39, 53, 80, 81, 83, 178, 220
stuff, 18
style, 33, 35, 180
subset, 75, 76
success, 39
suitability, 226
sum, 73, 76, 142
summary, 168
support, 4–6, 17, 61, 80, 81, 100, 109, 110, 186, 188, 198, 229
sync, 6, 70
synchronization, 6, 70, 71, 87, 136, 137, 140, 141, 143–145, 147, 168
syntax, 17, 29, 32, 36, 81, 109
system, 1, 3, 4, 11, 17–19, 24, 33–35, 47, 48, 67, 70, 72, 109, 127, 129, 130, 136, 151, 153, 154, 158, 159, 167, 168, 176, 189, 196, 197, 199, 200, 218, 219, 238

table, 102, 140
talk, 1
tantalizing, 1
target, 103, 108, 211, 215, 217
task, 6, 70, 104, 148, 149, 211
taste, 101, 238
team, 201
tech, 12
technique, 187, 213
terminal, 16–18, 22, 24, 59, 116, 120
terminology, 127
test, 28, 53, 55, 61, 81, 84, 194, 201, 217, 219
testing, 9, 10, 51, 55, 61, 81, 110, 175, 195, 196, 234
text, 23, 131
textbook, 186
theft, 200
thing, 1, 58
think, 43
thought, 89
thread, 6, 11, 70, 87, 132, 137–140, 144, 148, 154, 158, 168
threading, 136
throughput, 3, 219
ticket, 2
tier, 189
time, 2, 3, 5, 11, 16, 18, 19, 25, 28, 32, 34, 35, 41, 44, 46, 54, 58–61, 63, 67, 68, 74, 97, 130, 131, 133, 134, 136, 137, 141, 148, 150, 153–155, 159–162, 167–169, 175, 186, 190, 207, 209–211, 213, 214, 219, 220, 222, 227, 229, 231, 238
tip, 1

today, 2, 3, 7, 10
token, 63, 118
tokio, 98, 134
tolerance, 186, 187, 190
toml, 112, 131, 132, 134, 141, 171, 176, 178, 181
ton, 18
tool, 61, 63, 88, 110, 155, 199, 218, 233
toolchain, 14
tooling, 17
toolkit, 229
top, 1, 86
topic, 67, 214
trace, 230
track, 47, 78, 154, 167, 189, 198, 228, 229, 232
traction, 12
trade, 80, 143, 216
traffic, 158, 187
trait, 43, 72, 73
transfer, 162
translator, 102
transmission, 130, 194
Travis CI, 234, 235
tree, 81
trend, 12
trie, 81, 83
tune, 238
tuning, 73, 153, 158
type, 5, 11, 16, 25, 36, 37, 39, 40, 43, 44, 72–75, 92, 112, 119, 132, 136, 159, 168, 172, 184, 215
typing, 24, 109

understanding, 3, 8, 10, 23, 28, 39, 49, 50, 55, 76, 83, 84, 97, 114, 117, 119, 148, 155, 176, 180, 191, 195, 203, 206, 209, 211, 212, 215, 218, 219, 224, 230, 238
unit, 51, 54, 55
universe, 238
unwrap, 41, 42
up, 2–4, 10, 13, 14, 16, 19–24, 26, 58–60, 67, 69, 84, 91, 103, 104, 109, 113–116, 119, 120, 127, 131, 132, 134, 136, 140, 148, 149, 159, 167, 171, 172, 175, 181, 189, 190, 193, 196, 197, 201, 206, 209, 211, 213, 229, 231, 234, 239
update, 10, 14, 58, 60, 124, 193
usability, 202, 239
usage, 5, 6, 30, 47, 49, 72, 73, 80, 143, 155, 167, 207, 209–211, 215, 229
use, 1, 3–6, 9, 11, 14, 16–18, 26, 33, 34, 36, 37, 39, 41, 42, 44, 47, 48, 54, 58, 63, 64, 67–70, 72–75, 77, 78, 81, 84, 86, 88, 91, 97, 102, 104, 109–112, 114, 118, 120, 121, 124, 128, 129, 131, 132, 134, 136, 140, 141, 149, 151, 154, 155, 160, 162, 167–169, 171, 178, 189, 196, 208, 214, 215, 219, 225, 226, 235, 239
user, 77, 109, 110, 120, 124, 127, 182–184, 187, 190–192, 196–202, 205, 206, 233, 239
username, 77
utility, 141

Index

utilization, 6, 219

Vadim Chugunov, 17
valgrind, 5
validate, 55, 81, 178, 191, 198, 199
validation, 178, 180, 196–202, 238
validator, 198
validity, 48
value, 4, 33–35, 37, 39–42, 67–69, 71, 77, 89, 144, 153, 154, 159–162, 176
variability, 209
variable, 14, 33, 34, 48, 68, 153, 159, 160
variant, 37, 39, 40, 91
variety, 73, 77, 207
vector, 74–76, 138, 142, 219
verbose, 69
versatility, 12, 76, 101, 110, 111
version, 14, 16, 24, 59, 235
vice, 176
video, 20
vigilance, 202
visibility, 65
visualization, 229
vulnerability, 168, 199, 201, 202

wasm, 110
watchdog, 2
way, 16, 36, 38, 39, 41, 44, 47, 55, 61, 69, 72, 73, 75, 76, 84, 86, 102, 111, 120, 127, 130, 136, 143, 148, 157, 178, 183, 187, 189, 239
wealth, 4
web, 1, 2, 6, 12, 67, 73, 76, 100, 109, 111, 113–121, 124, 126, 130, 131, 134, 136, 149, 150, 153, 155–158, 171, 176, 180, 181, 186–190, 196, 198, 199, 201–204, 206, 210, 218, 238
website, 16, 57, 63, 115, 205
websocket, 131–133
wheel, 198
while, 1, 35, 39, 40, 43, 46, 70, 71, 76, 88, 98, 102, 110, 111, 144, 145, 154, 161, 167, 188, 222, 230, 233
wild, 65, 111
word, 1, 64
work, 23, 29, 35, 43, 44, 49, 55, 58, 62, 74–76, 88, 108, 143, 186
workflow, 10, 109, 234
working, 3, 34, 48, 69, 72, 81, 89, 104, 129, 131, 145, 186, 213, 239
workload, 2, 188, 190
world, 1, 3, 4, 11, 13, 15, 20, 23, 26, 36, 39, 43, 62, 65, 78, 79, 81, 101, 104, 105, 110, 111, 113, 130, 136, 148, 151, 159, 180, 201, 210, 211, 213, 216, 217, 224, 237, 239
worm, 201
write, 3–6, 13, 14, 16, 20, 23, 42–44, 49, 51, 55, 70, 72, 73, 84, 88, 92, 97, 102, 110, 138–140, 148, 150, 155, 159, 167–169, 190, 199, 207, 210, 214, 219, 238, 239

x, 38, 68

y, 38, 68

year, 202
Yew, 124, 127

yourself, 12, 14, 20, 23, 55, 64, 155, 196, 239